MW00989098

CENTENARY STITCHES

TELLING THE STORY OF ONE WW1 FAMILY THROUGH VINTAGE KNITTING AND CROCHET

AS SEEN IN THE FILM

Tell Them of Us
DIRECTED BY NICK LOVEN

ELIZABETH LOVICK, EDITOR

GRAPHIC DESIGNER
JUDITH BRODNICKI

COSTUMIER & PHOTO STYLIST
PAULINE LOVEN

TECHNICAL EDITOR
ELLY DOYLE

This book is dedicated
to all the women,
all over the world,
who stayed at home
and knitted for their men
away at war,
both in the past and today.

You 'kept the home fires burning',
kept the country running
even as your hearts were breaking.

We salute you.

EL 2014

Published by
Northern Lace Press • Orkney, Scotland

Copyright © Northern Lace Press 2014

Contents

SHAWLS / WRAPS

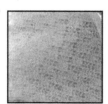

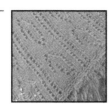
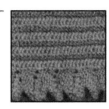
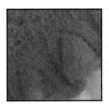

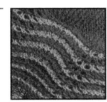
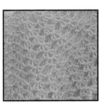

SWEATERS / CARDIGANS / WAISTCOATS

THERE'S MORE!

SWEATERS / CARDIGANS / WAISTCOATS (CONT.)

Stocking Stitch Jacket
Page 96
Sizes: 26 (30, 34, 38, 42, 46, 50, 54, 58)"
Aran weight yarn

Scarf Vest
Page 51
Sizes: XXS (XS, S, M, L, 1X, 2X, 3X, 4X)
DK weight yarn

Aran Ganseys for Children and Teens
Page 124
Sizes: 26 (28, 30, 32, 34, 36)"
Aran weight yarn

Service Cardigan
Page 127
Sizes: Men's S (M, L, 1X, 2X, 3X)
Aran weight yarn

Crossover
Page 55
One size
DK weight yarn

William's Gansey
Page 92
Sizes: 32 (36, 40, 44, 48, 52, 56, 60, 64, 68)"
5 ply/Sport weight yarn

Ann's Tuxedo Jacket
Page 98
Sizes: XXS (XS, S, M, L, 1X, 2X, 3X, 4X)
DK weight yarn

William's Waistcoat
Page 28
Sizes: XS (S, M, L, 1X, 2X, 3X)
Aran weight yarn

Sailor Sweater for Adults and Children
Page 120
Sizes: XXS (XS, S, M, L, 1X, 2X, 3X)
Aran weight yarn

Rough & Ready Cardigan
Page 116
Child Sizes: C1 (C2, C3, C4)
Adult Sizes: XXS (XS, S, M, L, 1X, 2X, 3X, 4X)
Aran weight yarn

CosyCoat
Page 13
Sizes: 28 (32, 36, 40, 44, 48, 52, 56, 60)"
Aran weight yarn

Violet's Jacket
Page 25
Sizes: 32 (40, 50, 55)"
Aran weight yarn

MISCELLANEOUS ITEMS WE COULDN'T RESIST

Cushion for a Soldier
Page 137
One size
DK weight yarn

Reins
Page 145
Sizes: 2 (4, 6, 8) years
4 ply cotton yarn

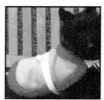

Coat & Lead for a Little Dog
Pages 149 & 151
One size
Coat: DK weight yarn
Lead: 4 ply cotton weight yarn

Socks for Servicemen
Page 130
One size
DK weight yarn

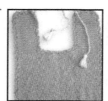

Bib for an Infant
Page 144
One size
4 ply cotton yarn

Wash Mitt & Washcloth for a Child
Page 147
One size
DK weight yarn

Sunflower Pincushion
Page 153
One size
DK weight yarn

Ball for a Child
Page 148
One size
DK weight yarn

Cloth for Polishing the Floor Iron Holder
Page 152
One size
DK weight yarn

ACCESSORIES FOR HEADS / NECKS / HANDS

Diced Bag Hat
Page 110
Sizes: Toddler (Child, Teen, Adult, Large Adult)
4 ply/fingering weight yarn

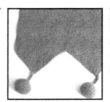

Scarf with Shaped Ends
Page 102
One size
DK weight yarn

Crocheted Tie with Fringe
Page 50
One size
4 ply yarn

Pompom Scarf & Hat
Page 143
Sizes: Toddler (Child, Teen, Adult, Plus)
DK weight yarn

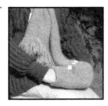

Skater Scarf & Tam
Page 101
One size
DK weight yarn

Tassel Tie
Page 49
One size
3 ply yarn

Grace's Tam & Scarf
Page 105
Sizes: Toddler (Child, Teen, Adult, Plus)
DK weight yarn

Fife Collarette & Muff
Page 64
One size
DK weight yarn

Beaded Tie
Page 58
One size
Crochet cotton No 8 yarn

Tam 'o Shanter
Page 88
One size
4 ply/fingering weight yarn

Cheerful Muff & Hat
Page 140
Sizes: Toddler (Child, Teen, Adult, Plus)
4 ply/fingering weight yarn

Straight & Striped Tie
Page 115
Sizes: Lady (Gent)
4 ply cotton yarn

Turban & Fingerless Mitts
Page 111
Sizes: Child (Teen, small Woman, Woman, Plus)
DK weight yarn

Garter Stitch Muffler & Tam
Page 138
Sizes: Toddler (Child, Teen, Woman, Man)
5 ply/Sport weight yarn

Nubia Scarf
Page 76
One size
4 ply/fingering weight yarn

Motor Cap for a Youth
Page 123
Sizes: Teen (Adult)
5 ply/Sport weight yarn

Helmet for a Serviceman
Page 135
One Size
DK weight yarn

Riflemen's Gloves
Page 132
One size
DK weight yarn

William's Muffler & Fingerless Mittens
Page 136
Sizes: Child (Teen, Woman, Man, Large Man)
4 ply/fingering weight yarn

Service Gloves
Page 133
One size
DK weight yarn

PREFACE

I am often asked how I came to be involved with the film, and I am ashamed to say, I can't remember! I think it was on Ravelry (a sort of Facebook for knitters), and I do know it was November 2013. At the time Pauline Loven, the Costumier for the film, was wondering whether anyone might be able to re-create a knitted jacket shown in an old photo. As much of my work involves re-creating knitted pieces I volunteered and it all grew from there.

That first jacket was for Grace Crowder, one of the main characters. The photo was of the 'real' Grace sitting on the sea wall at Bridlington, and wearing a jacket typical of the WW1 period. It was relatively straight forward to get the stitch pattern and most of the other details needed. As Pauline had found out that all the Crowders were redheads, she chose the lovely light teal for the jacket.

Pauline had also found out that Grace herself was a knitter, so once Grace had her jacket, she needed accessories to match. The scarf and tam followed, and then various other items - William's gansey, Ann's 'cloud'. I also designed things for others to make.

People started asking whether these patterns were available, so in the Spring of 2014 Pauline asked me to edit a book of patterns from the film and this is the result.

More than a hundred knitters from the UK and USA became involved. Some of them are mentioned in the pattern page for an item they knitted, and all are listed on page 158. It has been a learning curve for all of us. What does 'narrow' mean, and what size is a 'steel needle'? Was the crochet terminology UK or US? I think we also became more aware of what life would have been like for the women who stayed at home while their men-folk were away at war.

I could not have produced this book without the help of Judith Brodnicki and her graphic design skills, and Elly Doyle and her technical editing skills. Both have been towers of strength as we were up against tight deadlines. The wonderful photos taken by Pauline Loven and screen grabs by Nick Loven greatly enhance the book, and I am indebted to their kindness in allowing me access to their work.

We hope you enjoy the fruits of our labours!

Elizabeth Lovick
September 2014

Knitting in WW1

ELIZABETH LOVICK

There is not one art
practised by ladies which is
more deservedly popular
than Knitting. It is so easy,
requires so little eyesight,
and is susceptible of so much
ornament, that it merits the
attention of every lady; and
in giving instructions for
acquiring it, we add, also,
such admirable diagrams of
the various processes, we are
sure no difficulty will be felt in
executing any pattern.

The Lady's Workbook
John Cassell, London; date unknown

Greetings cards sent to The Front, along with a tract. Photo is my grandmother, Rene Pagden, a St John's Ambulance nurse.

We live in an age where it is cheaper to buy clothes than to knit them, and so when people knit, it is purely for pleasure. A hundred years ago things were very different. For most of the population, if you needed a knitted garment someone in the family made it for you; it was only the better off who could afford to have their sweaters knitted for them by contract knitters.

It was in the Victorian Era when the fashion of 'knitted everything' started! Hand knitting had been around for a long time, but it was in the mid 19th Century, with more people living above the bread line and with time on their hands, that the passion for knitting and crochet took hold. Pattern leaflets began to be printed and the emerging Middle Class started to fill their houses with knitted knickknacks and embellish their furniture with crocheted covers. At this time the Labouring Classes (as they were known) were knitting essentials - underclothes and socks, sweaters and shawls - whereas the better off were knitting and crocheting decorative items for the home and lace shawls for themselves.

With the turn of the century, followed by the death of Queen Victoria and the start of the Edwardian Era, attitudes to what was acceptable changed. In particular, women began to participate in sports such as bicycling, tennis and golf. Some women had done this before, but it had been considered eccentric; now it was acceptable behaviour. Knitted fabric stretches more easily than woven, and young women quickly realised that knitted sweaters were ideal wear for their sporting activities. Patterns for garments designed for exercise abounded. Sports clothing became fashionable and better off women turned their needles away from knickknacks to sweaters for themselves and their menfolk.

But the outbreak of war changed everything. Suddenly utilitarian knitwear was needed for both the troops on the front line and those living at home. In a few short months the position of women in Middle and Upper Class society changed from being purely decorative to being the managers of the house and estate while their men were in France.

The change is noticeable in the knitting patterns of the time. Every publication now had garments

A selection of knitting tools from the period. Top left is a skein winder!

which could be knitted for soldiers, sailors and airmen. The Red Cross in both the UK and the USA published books of approved patterns for socks, mittens, scarves, balaclavas etc all aimed at keeping the men warm in the trenches, on the high seas and in the air. They also published patterns for items for hospitals - bandage covers, bed socks, knee caps, body belts, bed jackets etc. The Red Cross provided wool, and needles if required, and asked that any left over wool would be returned. The knitting of hats proved so popular in the USA in the winter of 1914/15 that the American Red Cross begged knitters not to make any more, but to make socks and gloves instead.

At this time every girl was taught to knit in school, or by their governess if they did not go to school. By the age of 6 or 7 girls were expected to be able to knit dish cloths and scarves, and were starting to be taught how to turn the heel of a sock. Once socks had been mastered, gloves were taught, then 'fancy' or lace work. As today, some girls had an aptitude for knitting and some did not. But all except the very richest were expected to knit their own socks, underwear and shawls.

Knitting yarns and needles were available in the general stores in the villages, and in special departments of the bigger city stores. As today there were many brands of yarn, some sold in the shops and others by post. In particular the 'Shetland' wools, coming mainly from Shetland and Scotland, had shade cards and postal order forms as today. The price of yarn varied depending on the type of fibre which went into its manufacture. Coarser wool yarns were the cheapest, while the angora yarns were expensive. (Having an angora trim on your muff or hat was a status symbol for girls for most of the 20th Century!)

By the outbreak of war in 1914, sweaters were almost universal day wear for boys, rich and poor alike. Rich boys had new ones; poor boys had their older brothers' cast offs, or their father's old sweaters cut down. These sweaters were styled on fishermen's sweaters, or ganseys, and were perfect for playing (and working) in. They were much more comfortable and flexible than shirts and jackets, and were easier to mend and adapt to growing lads. The cuffs on sleeves could be ripped back and extra inches could be knitted on as the boy grew, and any holes could easily be darned. The poorest girls also wore these ganseys, while their wealthy peers where encased in tight dresses and pinafores.

During the Victorian era everyone wore shawls, the fancier the better: lacy, frilled, large, small, black or coloured, no woman would leave the house without one. Although the fashion for shawls was waning in the Edwardian era, most villagers wore them for warmth, not looks. Thick or fine, shawls were (and are) endlessly versatile, easy to throw on and take off, and could be used by any female in the household. As the privations of the great War took hold, and fuel for fires became more difficult to obtain, shawls and wraps became worn universally again. And for the women who enjoyed knitting, making themselves a pretty shawl was a nice change from churning out the necessary socks, drawers and mufflers.

As well as the practical value of knitting, the emotional value of knitting was high as the War dragged on. The repetitive nature of making the stitches is known to be soothing, and making 'comforts' for absent husbands, sons and brothers gave women a sense of connection to their men. Many women spent days, weeks or months not knowing whether their loved ones were alive or dead, and knitting kept their hands busy and minds away from the dark thoughts which accompany worry. When bad news came, doing something as everyday as knitting helped many to cope with their grief.

A hundred years on, the many knitters working on this project have felt a connection to the women left at home with their men away at war. Many of us have thought of our forebears who would have been knitting the same patterns, having the same problems with making mistakes and such like! We, too, have had to decide, as they did, what colour yarn to use, which buttons or ribbon to choose. We have looked in our cupboards to see whether we have enough yarn for a particular project, or whether a friend might have the extra ball we need.

The patterns in this book are all either direct 'translations' of patterns which would have been used during the great War, or are new designs based on illustrations of clothing at the time. They have been chosen from the many other garments knitted for the film to represent the work done by the hundred strong band of knitters from the UK, France and the USA who have, like those women of 100 years ago, worked every stitch with care.

— Elizabeth Lovick, 2014

GLORY OF WOMEN
SIEGFRIED SASSOON

You love us when we're heroes,
  home on leave,
Or wounded in a mentionable place.
You worship decorations; you believe
That chivalry redeems the war's
  disgrace.
You make us shells. You listen with
  delight,
By tales of dirt and danger fondly
  thrilled.
You crown our distant ardours
  while we fight,
And mourn our laurelled memories
  when we're killed.

You can't believe that British troops
  'retire'
When hell's last horror breaks
  them, and they run,
Trampling the terrible corpses–
  blind with blood.
O German mother dreaming by the
  fire,
While you are knitting socks to send
  your son
His face is trodden deeper in the
  mud.

THE RETURNING WARRIOR

Here is peace.
Wearily I go through the streets.
I can't avoid the view
Of St. Stephan's Cathedral.
Here is peace.
Such a beautiful word.
And when I think of the place
Where so many lay.
Poor comrades,
You no longer see my beautiful Vi-
enna.
For you, everything is over.
Poor comrades.

Written by an 11 year old girl from Vienna
Translated from the German by Hilary Detmers

WAG Screen

PAULINE LOVEN

WAG Screen is a community filmmaking group who make films about Lincolnshire's history and heritage. We comprise media professionals and historians working alongside graduates, undergraduates, actors (most of us working for very little or nothing), as well as volunteers and those who join in for the experience. We try to offer each contributor as much in return as they put in, from practical experience to references to show-reels and just plain fun. We have neither office nor overheads, but manage our projects virtually. With each project we gather an ever widening band of wonderful and talented people and there is a real family atmosphere at each of our shoots.

A constant in all of WAG Screen's films has been the director/cameraman/editor Nick Loven, Pauline Loven producer/period-costumier/casting/fundraiser and Chris Roberts, producer/sound/lighting. Nick is a sensitive director, drawing the best out of the actors, while also being a technically sophisticated director of photography and a master storyteller through his editing.

Pauline's drive and unwillingness to accept second best, even when resources might otherwise suggest accepting it, help raise the production values to a high level.

WAG Screen is not constantly active though, as most members have to return to their careers at the end of a production, but now and again we feel that there is a story that must be told. With the anniversary of the First World War approaching we felt strongly that we should do something to mark it. After much deliberation we decided to tell the story of one small Lincolnshire war memorial, but we should choose it without any knowledge of the stories it might tell. We had in mind a twenty-minute drama-documentary.

We chose the small village of Thimbleby in Lincolnshire because of its remarkable range of vernacular houses, Victorian village school and working water pump, all surrounding the village church. Only then did we begin to research the war memorial. Many WW1 military records are lost, so we held our breath as we researched, fearing that we may find nothing of the five men listed. We were right too - we found little more than name, rank and number for three of the men on the memorial and only a little more on the fourth.

Nick Loven on camera. © Jazz Hayer

Pauline Loven

However, we found that the family of one, Robert Crowder, had held his memory dear and had kept a remarkable archive of unpublished material. The family had erected a stained glass window in his memory and kept all his letters written home from the front line. His brother wrote his memoirs and sister-in-law had kept an autograph album through her years as a VAD nurse in the local hospital. Combined with photographs, family memories and artefacts, we found we had enough material for a full length film. We had too just the story we wanted to tell, one that represented so many of that generation who were torn from their ordinary lives and thrown into the hell of war. Robert Crowder was not famous; he was neither an officer nor a decorated hero, though he was undoubtedly incredibly brave. He was just a gardener and a country boy who played the organ in his village church and loved, and was loved by, his family.

Costuming a Period Film

PAULINE LOVEN

As WAG Screen's costumier I spent a year researching and gathering vintage resources to begin creating the costume for the film which would be set on the home front in WW1. One thing worried me though – I was aware just how much clothing was knitted during the period and I cannot knit. Knitting also takes a long time to create, but to only include sewn clothing would have been a distortion. So, one Sunday morning, I speculatively tweeted for a volunteer knitter — confident that my words would disappear into the ether. But I didn't know then the character of knitters. Within an hour I had one hundred volunteers and quickly created a Facebook group to gather them in. In no time at all there were three hundred volunteers and a Ravelry group had been created too. Knitters, as I quickly discovered, are gregarious, generous and efficient, and a management system immediately evolved led by Liz Lovick, managed by Jane Lawrence and augmented by Judith Brodnicki. Out of the group we had over one hundred active knitters, designers, crocheters and researchers, and Centenary Stitches was born.

Pauline at Work researching VAD nurses costumes in a museum collection.

To explain a little of my thought process behind the costume design: knitting clothing is more easily within the reach of lower income families than sewing clothing and we were telling the story of a small Lincolnshire village including many classes of people. Fabric had to be purchased by the yard, usually requiring three of four yards at a time. Wool can be bought by the ball, or spun from fleece, and the cost can be spread. Knitting doesn't require expensive machinery either, just a few pairs of needles. It

Lydia Staniaszek © Nick Loven

can also be done almost anywhere, and at any time. An experienced knitter doesn't need much light either (most of the time).

During the war, knitting became a vital part of the home-front war effort, with millions of pairs of socks being knitted by women and children and sent to the front line via the Red Cross. Balaclavas, hats, mufflers, mitts, gloves, chest warmers, cholera belts (a knitted band to comfort the abdomen) and even bandages were knitted and sent to the front as well.

Knitted clothing also shows the changing fashions of the time, something I was keen to reflect, with a distinct move from shawls to cardigans, waistcoats and jumpers. Driven by the need to become active members of society, women had begun to abandon the wearing of corsets. This trend was accelerated by a scarcity of corsetry due to shortage of metal for their spiral wires and steel busks. However, corsets kept the body core insulated and warm, needing only a shawl to cover the shoulders to keep the chill off. Once corsets are no longer worn, cardigans, waistcoats and jumpers become vital for warmth. They are also liberating; shawls restrict the movement of the arms as they are needed to keep the shawl in place, sweaters now permit the playing of sports as well as active involvement in the workplace and factory.

So many times people have said of the wonderful clothes created for 'Tell Them of Us', 'I would wear that'. Women's clothing in this period becomes recognisably modern. It is part of the story I wanted to tell, so a huge thank you to the amazing team of knitters who helped create such a believable and accurate wardrobe for the film.

The Village of Thimbleby

PAULINE LOVEN

Thimbleby is a small rural village situated on the edge of the Lincolnshire Wolds close to the market town of Horncastle in Lincolnshire, England. Its charming small greenstone church, dedicated to Saint Margaret, is medieval in appearance, but has had a chequered history. Rebuilt in 1744 and again in 1879 it has had to have its lovely tower removed for safety and there is currently (2014) a campaign for its restoration.

Thimbleby's Victorian village school still stands. It was built in 1856 and is now used as a village hall. Nearby is the working village water pump dating from 1857. Most impressive though, is the range of wonderful Lincolnshire vernacular houses – mud and stud cottages. With their white-washed mud walls, simple timber frames, smoke hoods and thatched roofs, these are rare and precious survivals of Lincolnshire's traditional building style. They date from around 1600 to 1700, but some may have earlier origins.

The 1911 census return shows that Thimbleby village had a total population of 195 people. The road was rough and the gardens picket-fenced to keep the sheep out when they were driven through. There was a village shop and bakery. The 1914-18 Roll of Honour shows that thirty-two of the villag-

The thatched roof homes of Thimbleby as seen in the film.

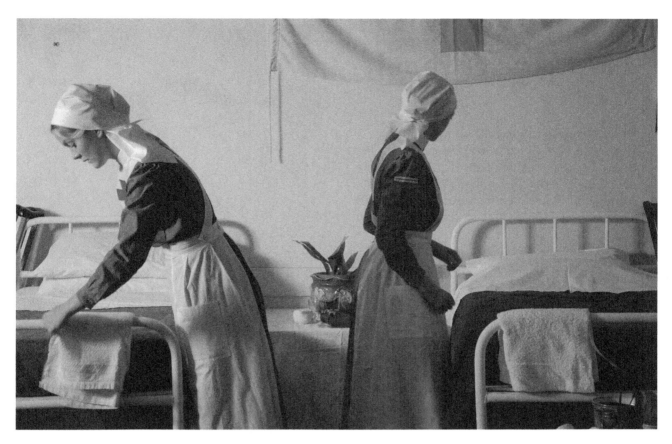

ers were involved in the war effort (probably most of the able bodied men from 18-40 years) and the war memorial shows that five of them never came home. Today the population is about 250 people.

The Crowder family nursery business and house was (and is) at the Horncastle end of Thimbleby parish and on the main road into that market town. Horncastle had at the time a railway line which led to Lincoln and thence London. During the war Horncastle's Drill Hall (now Stanhope Hall) was used by the Red Cross as a hospital, due to its proximity to the railway network. It takes about ten minutes to walk from the Crowder's home to the railway station.

We have tried so far as is possible to use the original locations for the film. Thimbleby village, church and shop were our main locations for much of the story. However, the Crowder family home has been absorbed into today's Crowders' Nursery, so we used another, similar, house nearby, Baumber Park Farm B&B. Filmmaking is rarely straightforward and a perfect exterior doesn't always mean the perfect interior for filming, so the Crowder home interiors were filmed at another location in Lincoln. We also filmed in what were the ward and corridors of the Red Cross VAD hospital in Horncastle.

Above: Recreating the Red Cross VAD hospital.

Below: Lucy White's wedding as seen in the film.

The Crowder Family

ROBERT HOLLAND

William Crowder spoke little of his war experiences until 1976, when he corresponded with Peter Liddle, an academic historian. Those letters gave many details about the family and their life together before, during and after the Great War. Here are some extracts of some of those letters.

ON THE FAMILY
"I was born on April 29 1894. It was a Sunday and I turned out to be all that people born on that day are expected to be "blyth and gay". My mother (who I adored) was thirty when I was born and already had a charming little girl "Grace" (3). My father was so often ill. [He was] left very badly off by his father but preferred to pay his debts in full rather than be made bankrupt. My mother had my brother [Robert] two years later and her health suffered. She was often in the hydro up in Matlock."

"Before the war life at home was a very leisurely affair very different from nowadays. We had our bicycles to get about on and a pony to drive a "trap" and a tub trap. When we went further afield we took the train. This was always an adventure especially coming home from school or going down to the coast for our summer holidays. How exciting it was staying in boarding houses and having our own rooms. Taking provisions with us. All great fun."

ON SCHOOLDAYS
"We went to Horncastle Grammar School as dayboys (my sister went to a school at Woodhall Spa). It was a mixed boy and girl effort and whilst there I managed to collect the form prize every year but after that I never got another prize. Whilst Bob stayed on at the school it was decided that it was high time I left home! My father didn't want me to go to a school where the Headmaster had been a parson. I don't know why that was. The school he chose was Lincoln, only twenty miles from home. By the way my sister, brother and self <u>all</u> had <u>red</u> hair! I was very self-conscious about it and when I got to Lincoln School I was bullied. I was frightfully unhappy for a term or two, but after having had a fight behind the fives court and attained some measure of respect, I began to enjoy life. It was there that I became very keen on acting. I would really have liked to be an actor but of course such a thing would never have been allowed. My father's

Above: Studio portrait of William Crowder (date unknown.

word was law and in those days we would have never have thought of questioning it or been in the slightest rebellious."

ON ROBERT
"My brother Robert was very delicate as a boy and so was not sent away to school but went to the local Queen Elizabeth Grammar School until he was about sixteen and then he went off to train for the business as I had done before him (to Northampton). Unlike me, he was keenly interested in his work and was highly thought of in the firm of Perkins and Sons. I think he must have left before the end of his three years because the war would then have started.

My father suffered badly from asthma and wanted my brother's help [in the family firm of Crowder Nurseries] and that is what he did until he was called up in 1917. He was also fond of music and learnt to play the organ. We had a good small organ in our village church and so he used to play for the services.

"[Robert] was in the Artists Rifles and was killed at Passchendaele at the age of twenty-one. My parents got the news of his death on the day I sailed for France in 1917.

"My brother's death was a dreadful grief to my

parents and indeed to all of us. He was not at all the type to have been forced into the Army, a simple (in the best sense) home loving boy."

ON HIS WAR

"I was in the Yeomanry before getting my commission in the Gunners and missed going out to Egypt with the first line through illness. On their way out their ship "The Mercian" was shelled and they suffered quite a few casualties. I was quite young when I got my DSO (24) and I was a prisoner for 9 months in Germany. Not a very distinguished war I fear."

Now I think is the time to say how much I hate war and was thankful that my own family were not involved in WWII. However, when I was in the army I made up my mind to do my best and, in due course, I grew to be a lance corporal and from there eventually obtained a commission. I think I was pretty forward (in appearance) and in my work and when in the ranks was often chosen to act as troop leader etc."

AFTER THE GREAT WAR

"Between the wars I hunted a bit and we used to have marvellous tennis parties, starting in the afternoon and going on until after supper.

"I live in the house in which I was born and where my father and grandfather also were. My family are an old established firm of nurserymen and seed merchants. My son is the sixth generation to be involved all in direct line from father to son and my grandson is at the moment training to enter the business.

"It is and always has been a very happy and interesting life and the firm was established two hundred years ago."

Grace lived at home and, when her father died in 1922, she lived with her mother until her death in 1933. In 1938 she married William Brown. She died in 1958.

William went on to marry Violet Pearson in 1921 and they had 4 children, Roberta, Sheila, Janet and William. He died in 1979. Robert Holland is Roberta's son and William's grandson. — Liz

Top: Grace Crowder (date unknown). This is the photo that William carried with him throughout his service and imprisonment.

Middle: Robert Crowder (1911; age 15)

Bottom: William Crowder (ca. 1975)

Vintage Garments from Cast On to Finish

IMPORTANT NOTES ABOUT THESE PATTERNS • JUDITH BRODNICKI

The patterns in this book raised many questions for the knitters, and not just from the standpoint of interpreting vintage instructions. Patterns from the WWI era were written in a way that challenged our courage in the course of construction, and later again when it came to converting them to modern language and modern sizes. But early on we decided to preserve the unique characteristics of these garments, especially as regards the method of construction, while updating the way instructions were written. We hope that the following information will be of assistance when you work these patterns.

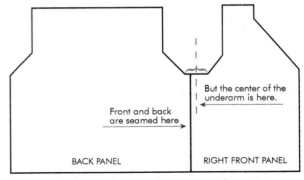

Illustration of typical proportions among these vintage patterns. The back and front panels are asymmetrical in armhole shaping but the sleeves are constructed in a symmetrical manner just as they are today. After seaming front to back at the side seams, fold in half to find the center of the underarm.

FLAT BACKS AND FULL FRONTS

Modern patterns for garments are the same width in front as in back. If the finished bust/chest circumference is to be 42 inches, then the back panel will be 21 inches wide and the front panel will be the same. A hundred years ago, however, the sensibility for garment fit was quite different. It started with the measurement at the hips instead of the chest, and the back panel measured 3/7 of the whole. Thus, a garment with a finished circumference of 42 inches would have a back panel that measured 18 inches wide, but the front panel would measure 24 inches wide. If you're working a pullover or cardigan and feel concerned (as many volunteers did) that the back was too narrow, check the measurement of the front panel(s).

All of this makes sense when you consider the adult figure because even the most slender among us has a rib cage that projects forward of the spine. Patterns for sewn garments have always reflected this difference (and still do today); it is only in knitting and crocheting that this sensibility has changed.

The "flat back" construction therefore has an effect on how armholes are shaped and how sleeves are set in. The armhole shaping on the back panel is often minimal whereas the front is fuller. With the front armhole cutting further into the torso, the side seam is more toward the back; thus, a set-in sleeve has an underarm seam that is forward of the side seam.

In order to find the placement of the underarm seam, we recommend that, after blocking and sewing the side seams, you fold the flat underarm portion in order to identify the center. Place a marker there as your guide for setting in the sleeve.

OVER-THE-SHOULDER FROM BACK TO FRONT

Both cardigans and pullovers tend to be constructed by starting at the bottom of the back panel Ⓐ (see illustration at right), working to the shoulders, and then continuing over the shoulder to each front Ⓑ, Ⓒ. It creates a smooth shoulder and a clean edge along the front neck.

In some garments constructed in this manner, the sleeves are worked separately (e.g., the Service Sweater, the Rough & Ready Cardi) then set into the armholes at the finishing stage. In other garments (e.g., the Sailor Sweater, the Tuxedo Jacket, Violet's Jacket), the sleeves are worked as extensions of the shoulder and cuffs are added afterward.

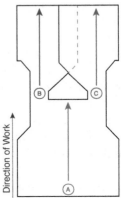

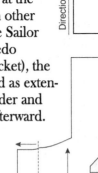

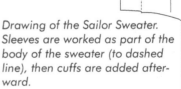

Drawing of the Sailor Sweater. Sleeves are worked as part of the body of the sweater (to dashed line), then cuffs are added afterward.

Translating Vintage Patterns

ELIZABETH LOVICK

Knitting and crochet patterns of 100 years ago were very different from what we are used to today, so if you want to 'translate' a vintage pattern you need to get into the mindset of the folk writing patterns all those years ago.

For example, here is a line from a crochet pattern from 1912, for which there were no abbreviations given:

36th: ^ {z}10 sq., 3 l., 3 sq., 6 l., 2 sq., 3 l ^ {z}., 79 sq., 3 l., 74 sq., ^ {&}6 l., 2 sq., 6 l., 3 sq., 6 l., 6 sq ^ {&}.

And here is a row from a knitted lace edging:

Thirteenth row.-K 3, o twice, p 2 to., k 2, o, n, o, n, k 6, o twice, p 2 to., n, o, n, o, k 9, o, n, o, n, o twice, p 2 to., k 2, o twice, n, k 6, o, k 2.

Knitting patterns in today's magazines tend to use many abbreviations and few line breaks to keep the pattern short. A hundred years ago, patterns were also usually kept short, but to save paper. During the Great War paper was in short supply, so small fonts were used, with very few spaces between patterns, let alone between pieces of the pattern. New rows were not started on a new line, and this can make for difficulties in working out exactly which section the instruction 'repeat' is referring to.

The process of reproducing illustrations was very different too. In the 19th Century illustrations were all hand drawn then engraved. This meant there were no charts, and very few pictures. Often patterns had no illustration, and there was never more than one.

During the first 15 years of the 20th Century the ability to print photos meant that patterns started to change. Instead of a line drawing of the garment in thin air, photos of garments on models stared to appear. And by the end of the War, the process of 'Colouration' had been developed, which allowed crude colours to be added to the photos.

PROBLEMS WITH PATTERNS

The translator has various problems to overcome when starting to produce a pattern intelligible to the modern reader.

WOOL THICKNESSES

Some patterns gave a brand of yarn, eg Columbia Lady Jane, Paton's Soft Knitting Wool, and some may give what looks like a yarn thickness, eg

Bell gauge made in England, with a modern 3 mm needle.

Paton's Rose Petticoat Sports wool, but wool thicknesses did not have the universal meanings they have today. For example, '3 ply vest fingering' is what today we would call a 2 ply/lace weight yarn!

YARN AMOUNTS

The most helpful publishers will note that 'a pound and a half' of wool is needed for a design, but more often, if given at all, the yarn amounts is given in 'hanks' or 'balls'. However, as today, not all brands and thicknesses of yarn were put up in the same sized hanks or balls.

NEEDLE SIZES

The practice of sizing knitting needles and crochet hooks started at about the turn of the Century. Before that, and in some books up to the 1920s, phrases like 'take a medium sized hook', or simply '4 needles will be needed', were common. The famous 'bell' gauges were common by 1914 - but unfortunately they were not of a consistent size. The same needle might measure 2.5mm on one gauge and 3.5mm on a different example of the same gauge!

FANCY AND PRACTICAL KNITTING.

NORMANDY LACE.

No. 66.—Cast on 36 stitches. Knit across plain.
First row.—K 12, n, o, k 3, o, n, k 10, n, o, k 3, o, k 2.

Second row.—K 2, o, k 5, o, n, k 8, n, o, k 5, o, n, k 11.

Third row.—K 10, n, o, k 1, n, o, k 1, o, n. k 1, o, n, k 6, n, o, k 1, n, o, k 1, o, n, k 1, o, k 2.

Fourth row.—K 2, o, k 1, n, o, k 3, o, n,

NO. 66.—NORMANDY LACE.

k 1, o, n, k 4, n, o, k 1, n, o, k 3, o, n, k 1, o, n, k 9.

Fifth row.—K 8, n, o, k 1, n, o, k 5, o, n, k 1, o, n, k 2, n, o, k 1, n, o, k 5, o, n, k 1, o, k 2.

Sixth row.—K 2, o, k 1, n, o, k 3, o, n, k 2, o, n, k 1, o, n, o, n, o, k 1, n, o, k 3, o, n, k 2, o, n, k 1, o, n, k 7.

Seventh row.—K 9, o, n, k 1, o, n, k 3, n, o, k 1, n, o, k 2, n, k 1, o, n, k 1, o, n, k 3, n, o, k 1, n, o, k 1, n.

Eighth row.—K 3, o, n, k 1, o, n, k 1, n, o, k 1, n, o, k 6, o, n, k 1, o, n, k 1, n, o, k 1, n, o, k 10.

Ninth row.—K 11, o, n, k 1, o, slip 1, n, pass the slipped stitch over, o, k 1, n, o, k 8, o, n, k 1, o, slip 1, n, pass slipped stitch over, o, k 1, n, o, k 2, n.

Tenth row.—N, k 2, o, n, k 3, n, o, k 10, o, n, k, 3, n, o, k 12.

Eleventh row.—K 13, o, n, k 1, n, o, k 12, o, n, k 1, n, o, k 2, n.

Twelfth row.—N, n, o, k 3 to, o, k 14, o, k 3 to, o, k 14. Repeat from first row.

TORCHON LACE.

No. 67.—Cast on 14 stitches and knit across plain.
First row.—Sl 1, o, n, k 2, o, n, k 1, n, o, n, o, k 1, o, k 1.
Second and every alternate row.—Knit plain.
Third row.—Sl 1, o, n, k 4, n, o, n, o, k, 3 o, k 1.
Fifth row.—Sl 1, o, n, k 3, n, o, n, o, k 5, o, k 1.

Seventh row.—Sl 1, o, n, k 2, n, o, n, o, k 7, o, k 1.
Ninth row.—Sl 1, o, n, k 1, n, o, n, o, k 4, o, n, k 3, o, k 1.
Eleventh row.—Sl 1, o, n, n, o, n, o, k 4, n, o, n, k 3, o, k 1.
Thirteenth row.—Sl 1, o, n, k 2, o, n, o, n, k 3, o, n, k 3, o, n.
Fifteenth row.—Sl 1, o, n, k 3, o, n, o, n, k 5, n, o, n.
Seventeenth row.—Sl 1, o, n, k 4, o, n, o, n, k 3, n, o, n.
Nineteenth row.—Sl 1, o, n, k 5, o, n, o, n, k 1, n, o, n.
Twenty-first row.—Sl 1, o, n, k 2, o, n, k 2, o, n, o, k 3 to., o, n.
Twenty-third row.—Sl 1, o, n, k 3, o, n, k 2, o, k 3 to., o, n.

KNITTED LACE.

No. 68.—Cast on 15 stitches.
First row.—Slip 1, k 2, o, n, o, n, k 4, o, n, over twice, k 2.

Second row.—Sl 1, k 2, p 1, k 2, o, n, k 6, o, n, k 1.

Third row.—Sl 1, k 2, o, n, k 1, o, n, k 3, o, n, k 4.

Fourth row.—Sl 1, k 5, o, n, k 6, o, n, k 1.

Fifth row.—Sl 1, k 2, o, n, k 2, o, n, k 2, o, n, o twice, n, o twice, k 2.

Sixth row.—Sl 1, k 2, p 1, k 2, p 1, k 2, o, n, k 6, o, n, k 1.

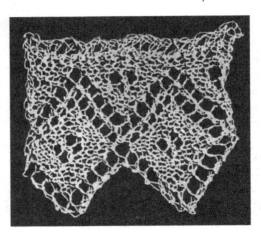

NO. 67.—TORCHON LACE.

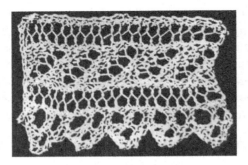

NO. 68.—KNITTED LACE.

Seventh row.—Sl 1, k 2, o, n, k 3, o, n, k 1, o, n. k 7.
Eighth row.—Bind off 5, k 3, o, n, k 6, o, n, k 1
Repeat from first row.

A page from Practical and Fancy Knitting, published by Butterick.

Bone and steel needles tended to have different thicknesses, even though they might have the same number. So a steel No 8 might be about a 4mm needle, while a bone No 8 might be about 5.5mm in diameter and a wooden No 8 about 7mm. To add to the confusion, steel needles get thinner as the number increases, but bone and wooden needles get thicker as the number increases.

In some books it looks as if the beginnings of the UK and US systems of numbering needles are coming in, but as several of the main publishers (eg Butterick) had printing works in London and New York, or who sold widely to different countries by post (eg Weldon's and Paton's) it is often not clear which system is in use.

TENSION

Inconsistencies in yarn thickness and needle size would be fairly straightforward to work with if a tension for the garment was given. However, usually no tension was given. Sometimes it is there, often hidden in a sentence part way down the column. Some publishers, like Paton's, gave a stitch tension, but row tensions were almost never given.

ABBREVIATIONS

In the early years of the Twentieth Century abbreviations in knitting and crochet were beginning to be used, but rarely explained! Again, there was no standardisation, and every company had its own way of describing the common actions.

The word 'narrow' or the letter n was used for 'narrowing' or decreasing. Rarely was the exact method to be used mentioned, and often the place and frequency of decreasing was also vague. 'Narrow from 66 to 52 stitches over the next few rows' is a quote from a glove with a long cuff.

SIZING

Almost always only one size was ever given, especially for sweaters and jackets. Gloves and socks might have more than one size, often noted at the cast on but not later in the pattern. 'Cast on 56 or 64 sts and make a round.' 'For the heel, knit half way and then work for 2 or 3 inches' was common.

Often the size was 'Lady's Sweater' or 'Man's Cardigan' with no further sizing mentioned. Sometimes the sizing was given as 'about 34 inches or 36 inches'. A very few patterns were written 'For a Matron' or 'For an Older Lady', even 'For a Lady of Fuller Figure'. These were usually to fit a 38" bust.

Garments for children were sized by age - 'To fit a 4 year old boy'. Baby garments were simply for 'infants'; no other sizing was mentioned.

LEFT AND RIGHT SIDES

These days knitters expect every stage of the pattern to be spelt out. A hundred years ago, the second glove, front etc wasn't even mentioned in the pattern!

It was usual to write the instructions for the right

SOCKS AND STOCKINGS.

No. 1.—SCALE FOR SOCKS AND STOCKINGS.

I worked out this scale some thirty years ago for the benefit of readers of the *Queen* newspaper. It is the plan used by the best firms in the hosiery trade, and has been adopted generally in elementary schools; it at once gives a worker a reliable scheme for her work.

Before commencing a stocking always knit a square with the wool and needles you propose using. If too coarse, use finer needles, or *vice versa*. From this, find the number of stitches to be cast on by multiplying the number of stitches in the inch by the length of foot.

For a stout and tall figure add 12 more stitches to the number thus acquired.

SCALE FOR MEN'S STOCKINGS.

Length of leg to bottom of heel = 3 times the length of foot for gartering above the knee, or 2¾ times for shooting stockings that have a turn over, which it includes.

Length to first intake = 1½ times the length of foot; from first to last intake ¾ of length of foot.

Length of ankle 1/5 of foot; length of heel 1/3 of foot.

Length of instep intakes 1/4 of foot.

From intake of instep 3/8 of foot to the commencement of toe.

Length of toe 1/8 of foot.

SCALE FOR WOMEN'S STOCKINGS.

To find out the number of stitches to set up in a stocking, determine the length of foot and multiply this by the number of stitches to the inch of knitting (*see* Lady's Stocking, page 60). A few extra stitches may be added for a very full size.

Average length of foot 9½ inches.

Length from casting-on to bottom of heel—2⅔ the length of foot.

Length to first intake = 1⅓ the length of foot; from first to last intake ⅔ of foot.

Other proportions same as for men's.

SCALE FOR SOCKS.

Determine length of foot, and find the number of stitches to be cast on. Divide this number by 16: the product gives the number of intakes for leg.

Deduct twice the number of intakes from the number found by the length of foot, and you have the number to be cast on.

Ribbing for top of leg = 1/3 of foot.

1st intake in row after the rib.

Length from first to last intake 1/3 of foot.

Other proportions as for stockings.

Typical size tables for the period.

glove or mitten. The knitter would know how to reverse the shaping to give the left hand. This was the sort of thing which was taught in schools, so it was not necessary to mention it.

The same was true of the right and left fronts on sweaters etc. If the construction was to work the back first, then over the shoulders and down to the front hem, then instructions were usually given for the right front. 'Work the left front to match' was sometimes written, but often it was simply implied.

MISTAKES IN THE PATTERN

The final problem the translator has with vintage patterns is that there were far more mistakes in the patterns than there are today. These days some mistakes get through, but very few. The designer writes the pattern, the technical editor checks it and makes corrections. Those words are then copied and pasted into the software which will be used to produce the magazine or book.

In the past, the letters were actually 'set' individually between wooden blocks, which were inked and pressed on to the paper. This meant that even if the person writing the pattern was careful, many mistakes could creep in at the type setting stage. Letters, words, or even whole lines of type might be omitted, and it was very easy, for example, to pick up a 5 instead of a 3.

TRANSLATION WORK ON CENTENARY STITCHES

For this book, the pattern translators started by guessing the yarn thickness, needle or hook size, and tension. We have used standard yarn thicknesses throughout so that yarn substitution is easy.

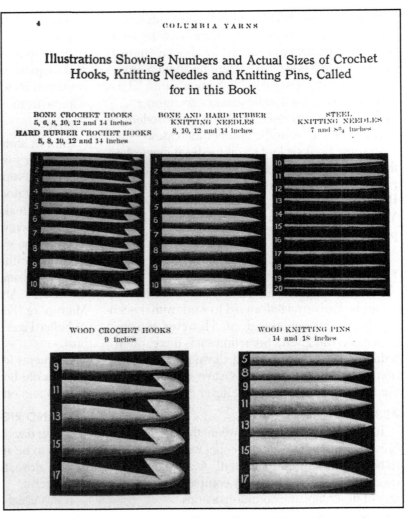

Pictures of some US needles and hooks from a US publication by Columbia yarns.

Complete pattern for a lady's sweater.

Common Name	Abbr.	Vintage Instruction
knit	k	plain
purl	p	pearl, seam
2 knit rows		ridge, rib
yarn over	o	over, or thread over (th o)
increase		make
decrease	n	narrow
together	to	

No. 2 — TABLE FOR SIZE OF FEET.

An exact table cannot be given for the size of the foot. Many of our most eminent artists have taken it, on an average, as $\frac{1}{7}$ part of the full height, but no reliance can be placed upon this for practical use, for it is well known that many people have small feet for their size—others, equally large.

This table has been carefully compiled by the sizes of shoes, and other measures, as used in large clothing establishments.

Babies' boots require a length from $3\frac{1}{2}$ to 4 inches.

AGE.	SIZE.	AGE.	SIZE.
About 1 year	$4\frac{1}{4}$ ins.	About 5 years	$6\frac{1}{2}$ ins.
„ $1\frac{1}{2}$ years	$4\frac{1}{2}$ „	„ $6\frac{1}{2}$ years	7 „
„ 2 years	5 „	„ 7 to 8 years	$7\frac{1}{2}$ „
„ $2\frac{1}{2}$ years	$5\frac{1}{2}$ „	„ $9\frac{1}{2}$ years	8 „
„ 3 to 4 years	$5\frac{3}{4}$ „	„ 12 years	$8\frac{1}{2}$ „
„ 4 years	6 „		

and about half-an-inch extra for every 18 months or 2 years additional age, up to 16.

TABLE FOR UNDER VESTS FOR YOUTHS AND MEN.

AVERAGE HEIGHT.	CIRCUMFERENCE OF BODY UNDER ARM.
3 feet $1\frac{1}{2}$ inches	20 inches.
3 „ $3\frac{1}{2}$ „	21 „
3 „ 5 „	22 „
3 „ $6\frac{1}{2}$ to 7 inches	23 „
3 „ 8 „ 9 „	24 „
3 „ 10 inches	25 „
4 „ —	26 „
4 „ $1\frac{1}{2}$ to $2\frac{1}{2}$ inches	27 „
4 „ $3\frac{1}{2}$ inches	28 „
4 „ 5 „	29 „
4 „ 7 „	30 „

After this you may allow 1 inch more in circumference for every inch of height.

The usual length of vest is about half the height for little children; for adults $\frac{2}{3}$ of height.

To find the length of arm-hole take $\frac{1}{4}$ of circumference of body.

Length of sleeve, $\frac{2}{3}$ of length of vest minus the cuff. Circumference of sleeve at top, $\frac{1}{2}$ the circumference of body. Length of gusset, $\frac{1}{3}$ of length of sleeve less cuff. Width of cuff, $\frac{1}{4}$ that of sleeve.

Once the yarn was decided the translator would knit a swatch to see whether her first idea of needle size was right. If the fabric was as required, then tension could be worked out from the swatch. If the fabric was not right, a different needle or hook size was tried.

Having decided on the yarn, needle and tension, the pattern was usually written out using the instructions given. If a lace pattern was involved, then it was charted exactly as the instructions were given before checking to see if any corrections were needed. The line-by-line instructions were then written out.

Now the translation began. The original pattern was written out and the wording was altered to suit modern preferences, but we tried whenever possible to keep to the original construction. The type and position of increases and decreases was spelt out, and both hands or fronts etc were written down.

At this stage we had a modern pattern, but only in one size. Where appropriate more sizes were added, and the pattern checked. It then came to me for checking and putting on to the style sheet we were using and once I had finished with it, it went to Elly Doyle, our 'tech ed'. Sometimes only one pass between Elly and I was needed, sometimes she sent it back to me for more work before she gave it a final check.

Only once we were satisfied did the pattern go to Judith for a final check as she did the 'type setting', making up the pages, leaving spaces between pieces and adding the photos to complete the thoroughly modern, easy-to-read patterns in the book.

Violet's Jacket

TRANSLATED BY ELIZABETH LOVICK • KNITTED BY SHEILA CUNNEA

INSPIRATION

This was one of the first garments to be knitted. When people saw it photographed, they asked for the pattern, so we obliged! — Liz

MATERIALS

Aran weight yarn in the following colours:

400 (500, 600, 800) g MC

200 (200, 300, 400) g CC1

50 (50, 100, 100) g CC2

Pairs 3.75 and 4 mm (US 4 and 6) needles

Stitch holders or lengths of thread

2 stitch markers

Row counter

4 buttons, about 1" diameter

Sheila used Rowan Creative Focus Worsted; 75% Wool, 25% Alpaca; 220 yds / 200 m per 100g ball; MC shade Charcoal heater, CC1 shade Nickel, CC2 shade Ebony.

SIZE

Sizes are designated 1 (2, 3, 4)

To fit bust: 32 (40, 50, 55)"

Actual bust: 35 (43, 53, 58)"

Length: 25 (26, 27, 28)"

Sleeve: 16 (17, 18, 19)"

TENSION

17 sts and 40 rows to 4" over garter stitch

NOTES

To get the given measurements, the row tension must be correct as well as the stitch tension.

CONSTRUCTION

The jacket is worked from the back hem up, increasing for the sleeves, over the shoulders. The fronts are then worked down from the shoulder, casting off the sleeves as they are worked. The cuffs are then picked up from the ends of the sleeves. The collar and pockets are worked separately.

PATTERN

BACK

Peplum

With larger needles and MC, cast on 80 (101, 122, 144) sts. Knit 8 (9, 10, 11)" in garter stitch, noting number of rows worked. Adjust length here.

Change to CC2 and k 5 rows.

Row 6: K0 (5, 3, 0), *k7 (7, 7, 7), k2tog, k7 (7, 8, 7). Repeat from * to end of row. 75 (95, 115, 135) sts

Waist

Change to smaller needles and CC1 and work from the Back Waist Chart. Work through the chart twice, then Rows 1 to 8 once more.

Change to larger needles and CC2, and knit 6 rows.

Change to MC and knit 16 (20, 24, 28) rows.

SLEEVES

Row 1: K1, m1, k to last st, m1, k1.

Row 2: K.

Repeat Rows 1 and 2 four times more.

Row 11: Cast on 10 (11, 12, 13) sts, k to end of row.

Repeat Row 11 nine times more. 185 (215, 245, 275) sts

Now work in garter stitch for 5.5 (6, 6.5, 7)".

Divide for the neck:

Knit 85 (100, 110, 125) and place these sts onto a length of yarn; cast off 15 (15, 25, 25) sts for the back of the neck; k to end of row. 85 (100, 110, 125) sts remain on the needle. Continue on these sts only.

LEFT FRONT AND SLEEVE

Knit 0 (38, 62, 64) rows straight.

Decrease for the sleeve and increase on the front edge:

Rows 1 to 3: K.

Row 4: K1, m1, k to end of row.

Repeat Rows 1 to 4 14 (6, 1, 2) times more.

Decrease the sleeve:

Row 1: Cast off 10 (11, 12, 13), k to end of row.

Row 2: K.

Row 3: As Row 1.

Row 4: K1, m1, k to end of row.

Repeat Rows 1 to 4 once more, then Rows 1 and 2 again.

Row 11: K2tog, k to end of row.

Row 12: K1, m1, k to end of row.

Row 13: As Row 11.

Row 14: K.

Repeat Rows 11 to 14 once more, then Rows 11 and 12 again. 50 (70, 80, 95) sts

Change to CC2 and work 6 rows.

Waist

Change to smaller needles and CC1 and work from the Front Waist Chart for your size. Work through the chart twice, then Rows 1 to 8 once more.

Peplum

Change to larger needles and CC2 and knit 6 rows.

Change to MC and work for the same number of rows as the back.

Cast off.

RIGHT FRONT AND SLEEVE

Place the 85 held sts onto a 4 mm needle, with the neck edge nearest the point.

Knit 0 (38, 62, 64) rows straight.

Decrease for the sleeve and increase on the front edge:
Rows 1 to 3: K.

Row 4: K to last st, m1, k1.

Repeat Rows 1 to 4 14 (6, 1, 2) times more.

Decrease the sleeve:
Row 1: K.

Row 2: Cast off 10 (11, 12, 13), k to end of row.

Row 3: As Row 1.

Row 4: Cast off 10 (11, 12, 13), k to last st, m1, k1.

Repeat Rows 1 to 4 once more, then Rows 1 and 2 again.

Row 11: K.

Row 12: K2 tog, k to last st, m1, k1.

Row 13: K.

Row 14: K2tog, k to end of row.

Repeat Rows 11 to 14 once more, then Rows 11 and 12 again. 50 (70, 80, 95) sts

Work in garter stitch for 16 rows, finishing at the front edge.

Change to CC2 and work 6 rows.

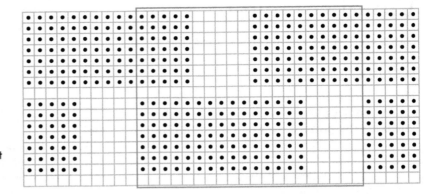

Waist

Change to smaller needles and CC1, and work from the Front Waist Chart for your size. Work through the chart twice, then Rows 1 to 8 once more.

Peplum

Change to larger needles and CC2 and knit 6 rows.

Change to MC and work for the same number of rows as the back.

Cast off

CUFFS

With larger needles and CC2, and with RSF, pick up and knit 50 (60, 70, 80) sts from the bottom of the sleeve. Knit 5 more rows.

Change to smaller needles and CC1, and work through the Cuff Chart for your size twice, then rows 1 to 8 once more.

Change to CC2 and knit 5 rows. Cast off.

LEFT BORDER

With larger needles and CC2, with RSF and starting from the beginning of the neck shaping, pick up and knit 1 st from every garter stitch ridge to the belt, 25 sts from the basket stitch central section, then 1 st from every ridge of the garter stitch section to the hem.

Knit 4 rows. Cast off.

RIGHT BORDER

With larger needles and CC2, with RSF and starting from the hem, pick up and knit 1 sts from every ridge from the garter stitch section, then 25 sts for the basket stitch central section, then 1 st for every garter stitch ridge to the start of the neck shaping.

Row 1 (WSF): K2tog, k to end of

row.

Row 2: K44, *cast off 3 sts for the first button hole, k7 (9, 11, 13). Repeat from * twice more, cast off 3 sts, k to end of row.

Row 3: K2tog, k the rest of the row, casting on 3 sts over the ones cast off on the last row.

Row 4: K.

Cast off.

COLLAR

Start with the left side of the collar. With smaller needles and CC1, cast on 95 (98, 101, 104) sts.

Row 1: K.

Row 2: Cast off 2, k3 (6, 9, 12), *p5, k15. Repeat from * to last 10 (13, 16, 19) sts, p5, k5 (8, 11, 14).

Row 3: P5 (8, 11, 14), *k5, p15. Repeat from * to last 8 (11, 14, 17), sts, k5, p3 (6, 9, 12).

This sets the pattern. Continuing in pattern, cast off 2 sts at the start of even numbered rows until 65 (68, 71, 74) sts remain. Then cast off 3 sts at the start of even numbered rows until 50 sts remain.

Work straight for 24 (24, 40, 40) rows.

Now cast on 3 sts at the start of alternate rows until there are 65 (68, 71, 74) sts on the needle, then cast on 2 sts at the start of alternate rows until there are 95 (98, 101, 104) sts on the needle.

Finish with a knit row, and cast off.

COLLAR BORDER

With smaller needles and CC2, with RSF pick up and knit 95 (98, 101, 104) sts along the long edge of the collar, PM, pick up and knit 65 (65, 76, 76) sts from the straight edge, PM, pick up and knit 95 (98, 101,

104) sts along the other edge.

Row 1: K1, m1, k to M, m1, SM, k to M, SM, m1, k to last st, m1, k1.

Row 2: K1, m1, k to M, SM, m1, k to M, m1, SM, k to last st, m1, k1.

Rows 3 and 4: As Rows 1 and 2.

Cast off.

POCKETS With larger needles and MC, cast on 25 sts and knit 30 rows.

Change to CC2 and knit 6 rows.

Change to smaller needles and CC1 and work as follows:

Row 1: K.

Row 2: K10, p5, k10.

Row 3: P10, k5, p10.

Rows 4 to 7: Repeat Rows 2 and 3 twice more.

Row 8: As Row 2.

Change to CC2 and knit 6 rows. Cast off.

FINISHING

Fold the main piece with RSF and sew the body and sleeve seams. Turn to right side. Pin collar in place, then sew. Pin pockets in place and sew. Wash and dry flat. Sew on buttons.

RIGHT FRONT WAIST • SIZE 3

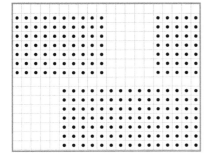

LEFT FRONT WAIST • SIZE 3

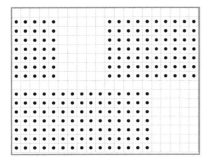

RIGHT FRONT WAIST • SIZES 1 AND 2
CUFFS (ALL SIZES)

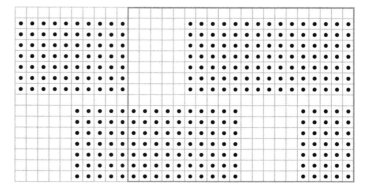

LEFT FRONT WAIST • SIZES 1 AND 2

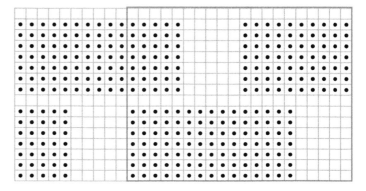

RIGHT FRONT WAIST • SIZE 4

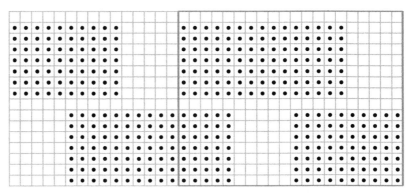

LEFT FRONT WAIST • SIZE 4

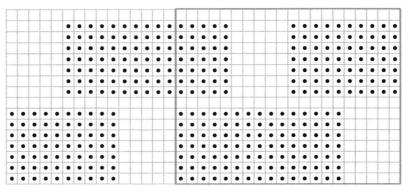

William's Waistcoat

TRANSLATED BY JUDITH BRODNICKI • KNITTED BY CATHERINE HOPKINS

MATERIALS

300 (350, 400, 450, 500, 600, 700) g aran weight yarn

Pair 4.5 mm (US 7) needles, or size to achieve tension

Row counter

2 Stitch markers

Stitch holders

6 (6, 7, 7, 8, 8, 8) Buttons, 0.5" diameter,

Catherine used British Breeds Blue-faced Leicester Aran; 100% BFL wool; 65 yds / 58 m per 100g ball; shade Sienna.

SIZE

Men's Sizes: XS (S, M, L, 1X, 2X, 3X)

Actual Chest: 32 (36.5, 40, 44.5, 48, 52.5, 56)"

Back Length: 20 (21, 22, 24, 25, 26, 28)"

TENSION

20 sts and 28 rows to 4" over stocking stitch

3/1 Garter Rib Stitch (multiple of 4 sts)

Row 1(RS): K.

Row 2: [K1, p3] to end of row.

PATTERN

BACK
Cast on 80 (90, 100, 110, 120, 130, 140) sts.

Knit 8 rows.

Work in reverse stocking stitch until piece measures 10 (10, 10, 11, 12, 12, 13)" ending after working a WS row. *Adjust length here.*

Back Armhole Shaping
Row 1 (RS): Cast off 0 (2, 3, 4, 5, 7, 9) sts, patt to end of row.

Row 2: As Row 1. 80 (86, 94, 102, 110, 116, 122) sts

Row 3: Slp, k3, PM, k2tog, p to 6 sts before the end of the row, ssk, PM, k4.

Row 4: Slp, patt to end of row.

Repeat Rows 3 and 4 until 56 (60, 66, 70, 74, 76, 80) sts remain.

*Patt 6 rows.

Next Row (RS): S1p, k to M, SM, m1, p to M, m1, SM, k4.

Next Row: In patt.

Repeat from * 4 more times. 66 (70, 76, 80, 84, 86, 90) sts

Work straight until piece measures 10 (11, 12, 13, 13, 14, 15)" from the start of the armhole shaping.

Shape Shoulders
Row 1: Cast off 3 (3, 3, 3, 4, 4, 5), patt to end of row.

Rows 2 to 4: As Row 1.

Row 5: Cast off 3 (3, 3, 4, 4, 4, 4), patt to end of row.

Row 6: As Row 5.

Row 7: Cast off 3 (3, 4, 4, 4, 4, 4), patt to end of row.

Rows 8 to 12: As Row 7.

Row 13: Cast off 3 (4, 4, 4, 4, 4, 4), patt to end of row.

Row 14: As Row 13.

Cast off remaining 24 (26, 26, 28, 28, 30, 30) sts.

LOWER POCKETS
Cast on 19 (19, 19, 23, 23, 23) sts and work in stocking stitch for 3". Leave sts on a stitch holder.

UPPER POCKETS
Cast on 15 (15, 15, 19, 19, 19) sts and work in stocking stitch for 3". Leave sts on a stitch holder.

RIGHT FRONT
NOTE: When shaping, work in pattern as far as possible while maintaining 2 garter sts at the Center Front.

Cast on 32 (36, 40, 44, 48, 52, 56) sts and knit 3 rows.

Row 1(RS): S1p, k1, PM, m1, k to 4 sts before the end of the row, W&T.

Row 2: K.

Change to 3/1 Garter Rib pattern.

Row 3: S1p, k1, SM, m1, k to 8 sts before the end of the row, W&T.

Row 4: Patt to M, SM, k2.

Row 5: S1p, k1, SM, m1, patt to 12 sts before the end of the row, W&T.

Row 6: As Row 4.

Continue in this way, adding 4 sts before the W&T on each odd numbered row until there are 36 (41, 45, 50, 54, 59, 63) sts on the needle.

Next Row (RS): S1p, k1, PM, m1, patt to end of row.

Next Row: In patt.

Repeat these 2 rows until there are 40 (46, 50, 56, 60, 66, 70) sts on the needle, ending after a WS row.

Work 12 (10, 10, 8, 6, 4, 2) more rows in patt.

Lower Pocket:

Row 1 (RS): In patt.

Row 2: Patt 4 (4, 4, 4, 8, 12, 16), k21 (21, 21, 25, 25, 25, 25), patt to end of row.

Rows 3 and 4: As Rows 1 and 2.

Row 5: S1p, k1, SM, patt 16 (22, 26, 28, 28, 30, 30),

cast off 19 (19, 19, 23, 23, 23, 23) sts, patt to end of row.

Row 6: Patt 5 (5, 5, 5, 9, 13, 17) sts, k19 (19, 19, 23, 23, 23, 23) sts from the Lower Pocket, patt to end of row.

Work in patt until piece measures 7.5 (7.5, 8, 8, 8.5, 8.5, 9)" from hem at side edge.

Upper Pocket:
Row 1 (RS): In patt.

Row 2 (WS): Patt 4 (4, 4, 4, 8, 12, 16) sts , k17 (17, 17, 21, 21, 21, 21), patt to end of row.

Rows 3 and 4: As Rows 1 and 2.

Row 5: S1p, k1, SM, patt 21 (26, 30, 32, 32, 34, 34), cast off 15 (15, 15, 19, 19, 19, 19) sts, patt to end of row.

Row 6: Patt 5 (5, 5, 5, 9, 13, 17), k15 (15, 15, 19, 19, 19, 19) sts from the Upper Pocket, patt to end of row.

Work in patt until piece measures same length as Back to armhole along the side edge, ending after working a WS row.

Shape Armhole & Front Neck Edge
Row 1 (RS): Patt to last 6 sts, ssk, PM, k4.

Row 2: S1p, k3, SM, patt to end of row.

Rows 3 and 4: In patt.

Repeat from Rows 1 to 4 until 30 (40, 44, 52, 56, 64, 68) sts remain.

Shape Neck
Row 1 (RS): Patt 2, k2tog, patt to last 6 sts, ssk, k4.

Row 2: In patt.

Row 3: Patt 2, k2tog, patt to end of row.

Row 4: In patt.

Repeat Rows 1 to 4 until 30 (34, 38, 40, 41, 43, 47) remain.

Next Row (RS): Patt 2, SM, k2tog, patt to last 4 sts, m1, k4.

Next Row: In patt.

Next Row: Patt 2, SM, k2tog, patt to end of row.

Next Row: In patt.

Repeat these 4 rows until 25 (26,

29, 30, 32, 32, 34) sts remain, removing markers on final row.

Shape Right Front Shoulder
Row 1: In patt.

Rows 2: Cast off 3 (3, 3, 3, 4, 4, 5), patt to end of row.

Rows 3 and 4: As Rows 1 and 2.

Row 5: In patt.

Row 6: Cast off 3 (3, 3, 4, 4, 4, 4), patt to end of row.

Row 7: In patt.

Row 8: Cast off 3 (3, 4, 4, 4, 4, 4), patt to end of row.

Rows 9 to 12: As Rows 7 and 8.

Row 13: In patt.

Row 14: Cast off 3 (4, 4, 4, 4, 4, 4), patt to end of row.

Cast off remaining 24 (26, 26, 28, 28, 30, 30) sts.

Place Right Front flat, and mark the positions of the buttons with pins. Place the first 1" from the hem and the last 1" down from the start of the neck shaping with the others evenly spaced between.

LEFT FRONT
NOTE: When shaping, work in pattern as far as possible while maintaining 2 garter sts at the Center Front.

Buttonholes
Work the buttonholes to correspond with the button placements as follows:

Row 1 (RS): Patt to last 4 sts, cast off 2, patt 2.

Row 2: Patt 2, cast on 2, patt to end of row.

Cast on 32 (36, 40, 44, 48, 52, 56) sts and knit 3 rows.

Row 1 (RS): K to 2 sts before the end of the row, m1, PM, k2.

Row 2: S1p, k to 4 sts before end of row, W&T.

Row 3: K to 2 sts before the end of the row, m1, k2.

Row 4: S1p, k1, SM, work WS row of 3/1 Garter St to 8 sts before the end of the row, W&T.

Continue in this way, adding 4 sts before the W&T on each even

numbered row 3 (4, 4, 5, 5, 6, 6) times more. 36 (41, 45, 50, 54, 59, 63) sts

Next Row (RS): K to 2 sts before end of row, m1, SM, k2.

Next Row: In patt.

Repeat these 2 rows until there are 40 (46, 50, 56, 60, 66, 70) sts on the needle, ending after a WS row.

Work 12 (10, 10, 8, 6, 4, 2) more rows in patt.

Lower Pocket:
Row 1 (RS): In patt.

Row 2: S1p, k1, SM, patt 13 (19, 23, 25, 25, 27, 27), k21 (21, 21, 25, 25, 25, 25), patt to end of row.

Rows 3 and 4: As Rows 1 and 2.

Row 5: Patt 5 (5, 5, 5, 9, 13, 17), cast off 19 (19, 19, 23, 23, 23, 23) sts, patt to end of row.

Row 6: S1p, k1, SM, patt 14 (20, 24, 26, 26, 28, 28), k19 (19, 19, 23, 23, 23, 23) sts from the Lower Pocket, patt to end of row.

Work in patt until piece measures 7.5 (7.5, 8, 8, 8.5, 8.5, 9)" from hem at the side edge.

Upper Pocket
Row 1 (RS): In patt.

Row 2: S1p, k1, SM, patt 17 (23, 27, 29, 29, 31, 31), k17 (17, 17, 21, 21, 21, 21), patt to end of row.

Rows 3 and 4: As Rows 1 and 2.

Row 5: K5 (5, 5, 5, 9, 13, 17), cast off 15 (15, 15, 19, 19, 19, 19), patt to end of row.

Row 6: S1p, k1, SM, patt 18 (24, 28, 30, 30, 32, 32), k15 (15, 15, 19, 19, 19, 19) sts from the Upper Pocket, patt to end of row.

Work in patt until piece measures same length as Back to armhole along the side edge, ending after working a WS row.

Shape Left Armhole and Front Neck Edge
Row 1 (RS): S1p, k3, PM, k2tog, patt to end of row.

Row 2: Patt to last 4 sts, k4.

Rows 3 and 4: In patt.

Repeat from Rows 1 to 4 5 (5, 5, 3, 3, 1, 1) times more. 30 (40, 44, 52,

56, 64, 68) sts

Shape Neck

Row 1 (RS): Patt 4, k2tog, patt to last 4 sts, ssk, k2.

Row 2: In patt.

Row 3: Patt to last 4 st, ssk, k2.

Row 4: In patt.

Repeat Rows 1 to 4 until 30 (34, 38, 40, 41, 43, 44, 47) sts remain.

Continue decreasing at the neck on alternate rows, keeping the armhole straight until 30 (34, 38, 40, 41, 43, 47) st remain.

Next Row (RS): Patt 4, m1, patt to last 4 sts, ssk, k2.

Next Row: In patt.

Next Row: Patt to last 4 st, ssk, k2.

Next Row: In patt.

Repeat these 4 rows until 25 (26, 29, 30, 32, 32, 34) sts remain, removing markers on final row.

Shape Left Front Shoulder

Row 1: Cast off 3 (3, 3, 3, 4, 4, 5), patt to end of row.

Row 2: In patt.

Rows 3 and 4: As Rows 1 and 2.

Row 5: Cast off 3 (3, 3, 4, 4, 4, 4), patt to end of row.

Row 6: In patt.

Row 7: Cast off 3 (3, 4, 4, 4, 4, 4), patt to end of row.

Row 8: In patt.

Rows 9 to 12: As Rows 7 and 8.

Row 13: Cast off 3 (4, 4, 4, 4, 4, 4), patt to end of row.

Row 14: In patt.

Cast off remaining 24 (26, 26, 28, 28, 30, 30) sts.

FINISHING

Sew pockets in place. Sew side and shoulder seams. Weave in all ends. Sew on buttons. Wash and dry flat.

Grace Crowder at Bridlington (Yorkshire), date unknown. © Robert Holland

Grace's Jacket

DESIGNED AND KNITTED BY ELIZABETH LOVICK

INSPIRATION

This jacket was my introduction to the project. Pauline had a photo of Grace sitting on a wall wearing a knitted jacket, and she wondered whether it would be possible to recreate it. So here it is! — Liz

MATERIALS

600 (650, 750, 800, 900, 950, 1000, 1100, 1200, 1300, 1400) g DK yarn

Pairs 3.5 and 4 mm (US 4 and 6) needles, or size to achieve tension

Row counter

Crochet hook, about 4 mm

5 buttons about 1" diameter

2 medium sized press-studs if required

Liz used Rowan Pure Wool DK; 100% Superwash Merino Wool, 130 m per 50 g ball; shade 007, Cypress.

SIZE

To Fit Bust: 26 (30, 33, 36, 40, 44, 49, 53, 57, 61, 66)"

Actual Bust: 29 (33, 37, 41, 45, 49, 54, 57, 61, 65, 70)"

Length: 22.5 (25.5, 26.5, 28, 29.5, 31, 32, 32.5, 33, 33.5, 34)"

Sleeve: 16.5 (17, 17.5, 18, 18, 18, 18, 18.5, 18.5, 19, 19)"

Length and sleeve length are easily adjustable

TENSION

21 sts and 36 rows to 4" over pattern

CONSTRUCTION

The jacket is worked in the conventional, modern, way, in pieces and is then seamed together.

PATTERN

BACK

With smaller needles, cast on 86 (96, 106, 116, 126, 136, 146, 156, 166, 176, 186) sts. Knit 7 rows.

Change to larger needles and pattern. Work straight for 8 (9, 10, 11, 12, 13, 13.5, 14, 14.5, 15, 15.5)" finishing after an even numbered row. *Adjust length below waist here.*

Next Row (RS): *K6 (7, 8, 9, 10, 11, 12, 13, 14, 15, 16), k2tog. Repeat from * to last 6 sts, k to end of row. 76 (86, 96, 106, 116, 126, 136, 146, 156, 166, 176) sts

Change to smaller needles, and work 11 (11, 11, 11, 11, 15, 15, 15, 15, 15, 15) rows in k1, p1 rib.

Change to larger needles and pattern. Work straight until for a further 7 (7.5, 8, 8, 8, 8, 8, 7.5, 7, 6.5, 6.5)", noting the number of rows worked. *Adjust length above waist here.*

Shape Armholes

Row 1: Cast off 2 (3, 4, 6, 8, 10, 12, 14, 16, 18, 20) sts, work to end of row.

Row 2: As Row 1.

Row 3: K2tog, patt to last 2 sts, ssk.

Row 4: P2tog, patt to last 2 sts, p2tog.

Repeat Rows 3 and 4 until 68 (76, 80, 86, 88, 94, 96, 102, 104, 110, 112) sts remain.

Work straight for 7.5, (8, 8.5, 9, 9.5, 10, 10.5, 11, 11.5, 12, 12)".

Next Row: Cast off 22 (25, 26, 28, 28, 30, 30, 32, 34, 34, 34), work 24, (26, 28, 30, 32, 34, 36, 38, 40, 42, 44), cast off 22 (25, 26, 28, 28, 30, 30, 32, 34, 34, 34). Leave sts on stitch holder for the back neck.

POCKET LININGS (MAKE 2)

With larger needles, cast on 21 (23, 25, 25, 25, 27, 27, 27, 27, 27, 27) sts. Work in stocking stitch for 4". Leave sts on stitch holder.

LEFT FRONT

With smaller needles, cast on 65 (72, 79, 84, 89, 96, 101, 106, 111, 116, 121) sts. Knit the same number of rows as the back.

Change to larger needles and pattern as follows:

Row 1 (RS): Patt to last 19 (21, 23, 25, 25, 27, 27, 27, 27, 27, 27), PM, k to end of row.

Row 2: K to M, SM, patt to end of row.

Row 3: Patt to M, SM, k to end of row.

Repeat Rows 2 and 3 for 4", finishing after a RS row.

Place Pocket

Next row (WS): Patt 8 (9, 8, 13, 18, 17, 20, 23, 26, 29, 32), put next 21 (23, 25, 25, 25, 27, 27, 27, 27, 27, 27) sts onto holder, patt the 21 (23, 25, 25, 25, 27, 27, 27, 27, 27, 27) sts from the Pocket Lining, work to end of row.

Continue straight until the peplum measures the same as the back, ending with WSF for next row.

Next Row: [K6 (7, 8, 9, 10, 11, 12, 13, 14, 15, 16), k2tog] five times, p to end of row. 60 (67, 74, 79, 84, 91, 96, 101, 106, 111, 116) sts

Change to smaller needles.

Next Row: K to M, SM, work in k1, p1 rib to end of row.

Next Row: Rib to M, SM, k to end of row.

Repeat these two rows 4 (4, 4, 4, 4, 6, 6, 6, 6, 6, 6) times more, then the first row again.

Change to larger needles and pattern. Work straight for the same number of rows as the back.

Shape Armholes

Row 1: Cast off 2 (3, 4, 6, 8, 10, 12, 14, 16, 18, 20) sts, work to end of row.

Row 2: In patt.

Row 3: K2tog, patt to end of row.

Row 4: Patt to last 2 sts, p2tog.

Repeat Rows 3 and 4 until 56 (62, 66, 69, 70, 75, 76, 79, 80, 83, 84) sts remain.

Work straight for 5.5 (5.5, 6, 6, 6.5, 6.5, 6.5, 7, 7, 7, 7)", finishing at the lapel edge.

Next Row: Cast off 19 (21, 23, 25, 25, 27, 27, 27, 27, 27, 27), work to end of row.

Next Row: Patt to last 2 sts, ssk.

Next Row: P2tog, patt to end of row.

Repeat the last two rows until 22 (25, 26, 28, 28, 30, 30, 32, 34, 34, 34) sts remain.

Work straight to the same number of rows to the shoulder as for the back. Cast off.

Above: Grace's Jacket worked in a different yarn.
Opposite: The original design by Elizabeth Lovick, created from the photograph of Grace.

GRACE'S JACKET PATTERN STITCH

Row 1: P1, *p2, k2, p1. Repeat from * to end of row.

Row 2: *K1, p2, k2. Repeat from * to last st, k1.

Row 3: P1, *k2, p3. Repeat from * to end of row.

Row 4: *K3, p2. Repeat from * to last st, k1.

Emma Louise Clarke (left) in Grace's Jacket and Kate Loven in the Fitted Sweater during filming of the Armistice Day celebration.

RIGHT FRONT

With smaller needles, cast on 65 (72, 79, 84, 89, 65, 72, 79, 84, 89) sts. Knit 7 rows.

Change to larger needles and pattern as follows:

Row 1 (RS): K19 (21, 23, 25, 25, 27, 27, 27, 27, 27, 27), PM, patt to end of row.

Row 2: Patt to M, SM, k to end of row.

Row 3: K to M, SM, patt to end of row.

Repeat Rows 2 and 3 for 4".

Place Pocket

Next Row: Patt 38 (43, 46, 48, 48, 25, 27, 29, 31, 33, 35) sts, put next 21 (23, 25, 25, 25, 27, 27, 27, 27, 27, 27) sts onto holder, work the 21 (23, 25, 25, 25, 27, 27, 27, 27, 27, 27) sts from the Pocket Lining, work to end of row.

Continue straight until the peplum measures the same as the back ending with RSF for next row.

Next Row: K to M, SM, k1 (2, 3, 4, 5, 6, 7, 8, 9, 10, 11), k2tog, k5] five times, k to end of row. 60 (67, 74, 79, 84, 91, 96, 101, 106, 111, 116) sts

Change to smaller needles.

Next Row: Rib to M, SM, k to end of row.

Next Row: K to M, SM, rib to end of row.

Repeat these two rows 4 (4, 4, 4, 4, 6, 6, 6, 6, 6, 6) times more, then the first row again.

Change to larger needles and pattern. Work straight for the same number of rows as the Left Front.

Shape Armholes

Row 1: In patt.

Row 2: Cast off 2 (3, 4, 6, 8, 10, 12, 14, 16, 18, 20) sts, work to end of row.

Row 3: Patt to last 2 sts, k2tog.

Row 4: P2tog, patt to end of row.

Repeat Rows 3 and 4 until 56 (62, 66, 69, 70, 75, 76, 79, 80, 83, 84) sts remain.

Work straight for 5.5 (5.5, 6, 6, 6.5, 6.5, 6.5, 7, 7, 7, 7)", finishing at the lapel edge.

Next Row: Cast off 19 (21, 23, 25, 25, 27, 27, 27, 27, 27, 27), work to end of row.

Next Row: Patt to last 2 sts, p2tog.

Next Row: K2tog, pattern to end of row.

Repeat the last two rows until 22 (25, 26, 28, 28, 30, 30, 32, 34, 34, 34) sts remain.

Work straight to the same number of rows to the shoulder as for the back. Cast off.

POCKET TOPS

Return to the 21 (23, 25, 25, 25, 27, 27, 27, 27, 27, 27) held stitches, and place on a smaller needle. Knit 5 (5, 5, 5, 5, 7, 7, 7, 7, 7, 7) rows. Cast off.

COLLAR

Join shoulder seams.

With smaller needles and RSF, pick up and knit 19 (22, 25, 28, 31, 34, 37, 40, 43, 46, 46) sts from the right front neck, knit the 24 (26, 28, 30, 32, 34, 36, 38, 40, 42, 44) sts from the back neck, knitting twice into the last stitch, pick up and knit 19 (22, 25, 28, 31, 34, 37, 40, 43, 46, 46) sts from the left front neck. 63 (71, 79, 87, 95, 103, 111, 119, 1267 135, 137) sts

Next Row: K3, PM, *p1, k1. Repeat from * to last 4 sts, p1, PM, k3.

Shape collar:

Row 1 (RS): K to M, m1, SM, *k1, p1. Repeat from * to 1 st before M, k1, SM, m1, k to end of row.

Row 2: K to M, SM, *p1, k1. Repeat from * to 1 st before M, p1, SM, k to end of row.

Row 3: K to M, SM, *k1, p1. Repeat from * to M, SM, k to end of row.

Row 4: As Row 2.

Repeat these 4 rows 5 (6, 7, 7, 7, 8, 8, 8, 8, 8, 8) times more.

Knit 5 rows. Cast off.

SLEEVES

With larger needles, cast on 48 (52, 56, 60, 64, 64, 68, 72, 76, 80, 84) sts and work 3 (3.5, 4, 4, 4, 4.5, 4.5, 4.5, 4.5, 4.5, 4.5)" in rib.

Change to smaller needles and k 1 row, p 1 row. Mark the end of this row.

Work 3 (3.5, 4, 4, 4, 4.5, 4.5, 4.5, 4.5, 4.5, 4.5)" in rib, finishing after an odd numbered row.

Next Row: K2, m1, k2, *m1, k4. Repeat from * to last 4 sts, m1, k2, m1, k2. 61 (66, 71, 76, 81, 81, 86, 91, 96, 101, 106) sts

Change to larger needles and patt for 8 rows.

Shape Sleeve:

Row 1: K1, m1, patt to last st, m1, k1.

Rows 2 to 8: In patt.

Continue in pattern, incorporating the extra sts into the pattern, until there are 71 (82, 91, 102, 111, 111, 116, 121, 126, 131, 136) sts on the needle.

Work straight until the work measures 16.5 (17, 17.5, 18, 18, 18, 18, 18.5, 18.5, 19, 19)" from the marked row.

Shape armholes:

Row 1: Cast off 2 (3, 4, 6, 8, 10, 12, 14, 16, 18, 20) sts, work to end of row.

Row 2: As Row 1.

Row 3: K2tog, patt to last 2 sts, ssk.

Row 4: P2tog, patt to last 2 sts, p2tog.

Repeat Rows 3 and 4 until 63 (72, 75, 82, 83, 79, 76, 77, 74, 75, 72) sts remain, finishing after a RS row.

Next Row: As Row 3.

Next Row: In patt.

Repeat these two rows until 39 (37, 35, 34, 31, 35, 32, 31, 30, 27, 24) sts remain.

Repeat Rows 3 and 4 until 11 (13, 15, 16, 19, 15, 16, 15, 16, 15, 16) sts remain.

Cast off.

BELT

With smaller needles, cast on 3 sts.

Row 1: K1, m1, k to end of row.

Repeat this row until there are 21 (23, 25, 25, 25, 27, 27, 27, 27, 27, 27) sts on the needle.

Work straight in garter stitch for 2".

Make buttonhole:

Next Row: K9 (10, 11, 11, 11, 12, 12, 12, 12, 12, 12), cast off 3, k to end of row.

Next Row: K9 (10, 11, 11, 11, 12, 12, 12, 12, 12, 12), cast on 3, k to end of row.

Continue straight for another 22 (24, 28, 32, 34, 36, 38, 40, 42, 44, 46)".

Shape end:

Row 1: K1, ssk, k to last 3 sts, k2tog, k1.

Row 2: K.

Repeat Rows 1 and 2 until 5 sts remain.

Next Row: K1, s1, k2tog, psso, k1.

Cast off.

BELT LOOPS (MAKE 2)

With smaller needles, cast on 4 (4, 5, 5, 5, 6, 6, 6, 6, 6, 6) sts.

Work in garter stitch until the piece measures 3 (3, 3.5, 3.5, 3.5, 4, 4, 4, 4, 4, 4)" long.

Cast off.

FINISHING

Pin the pocket linings in place then sew carefully. Sew the edges of the pocket tops in place. With RSF, sew the side seams, and the sleeve seams. Turn the sleeves right way out and insert into the armholes so that the right sides are together. Pin, matching the underarm seams, and sew in place. Sew the belt loops to the side seams at the waist. Weave in all ends. Wash and dry flat.

Make the button hole loops (either by working blanket stitch loops or using crochet chains) on the outer edge of the cast off edges of the lapels, and on the outer edges of the lapels 2" above the waist ribbing. Sew on buttons to correspond. Sew button on to the belt just before the shaped end. If desired, sew press studs to the fold of the lapels at the neck and waist.

Choose The Best For All Your Charting Needs! We Did!

Stitchmastery

Fitted Sweater

TRANSLATED BY JUDITH BRODNICKI • KNITTED BY WENDY WALL

MATERIALS

650 (750, 850, 1000, 1100, 1300, 1400, 1600) g aran weight yarn

Pairs 3.5 mm and 4.5 mm needles, or size to achieve tension

Stitch holder or length of waste yarn

SIZE

Sizes: XXS (XS, S, M, L, 1X, 2X, 3X)

Actual Bust: 30 (35, 39.5, 42, 47, 51.5, 56.5, 60)"

Length: 23.5 (23.5, 24, 24.5, 25, 26.5, 27, 27.5)"

The length is adjustable above and below the waist

TENSION

20 sts and 32 rows to 4" over the garter rib pattern.

ABBREVIATIONS

Garter Rib (multiple of 2 sts, plus 1)

Row 1 (RS): K.

Row 2: *K1, p1. Repeat to last st, k1.

CONSTRUCTION

This garment is worked flat starting at the lower back and then up and over the shoulders where each front is worked separately from the top down. Sleeves are worked flat from the top down. The collar is worked as one rectangular piece that is sewn on.

PATTERN

BACK

Skirt

With larger needles, cast on 113 (121, 137, 153, 169, 177, 185, 201) sts and knit 3 rows.

Work in lace patt until piece measures 7 (7, 7.5, 7.5, 8, 8.5, 9, 9)" from the cast on edge, ending after working a 4th row. ***Adjust length below the waist here.***

Work the decrease row for your size:

Size XXS: *K2tog, k1. Repeat from * to last 2 sts, k2tog. 75 sts

Size XS: *K1, k2tog, k2, k2tog. Repeat from * to last 2 sts, k2. 87 sts

Size S: [K2, k2tog] 5 times, [k1, k2tog, k2, k2tog] 15 times, [k2, k2tog] 3 times. 99 sts

Size M: *[K1, k2tog] 4 times, k2, k2tog. Repeat from * 9 times, [k1, k2tog] 3 times. 105 sts

Size L: K5, *K1, k2tog. Repeat from * to last 6 sts, k6. 117 sts

Size 1X: *[K2, k2tog] twice, k1, k2tog. Repeat from * 15 times, [k2, k2tog] 3 times. 129 sts

Size 2X: K4, *k2, k2tog. Repeat from * to last 5 sts, k5. 141 sts

Size 3X: *K2, k2tog. Repeat from * to last st, k1. 151 sts

Ribbed Waist

Change to smaller needles.

Row 1 (WS): [K1, p1] to last st, k1.

Row 2: [P1, k1] to last st, p1.

Repeat these two rows for 2".

Upper Back

Change to larger needles and work Garter Rib over all sts until work measures approx. 17" from cast on edge, ending after working a WS row. ***Adjust length above the waist here.***

Back Armholes

Row 1 (RS): Cast off 2 (4, 4, 4, 6, 10, 16, 16) sts, patt to end of row.

Row 2: As Row 1. 71 (79, 91, 97, 105, 109, 109, 119) sts

Row 3: Ssk, patt to end of row.

Repeat Row 3 until 63 (67, 75, 81, 85, 87, 87, 91) sts remain.

Work straight until the armholes measure 6.5 (6.5, 7, 7.5, 8.5, 9.5, 10, 10.5)" ending after a WS row.

Divide Back from Front

Next Row: K22 (22, 26, 28, 30, 30, 30, 32) and place on holder, cast off the next 19 (23, 23, 25, 25, 27, 27, 27) sts for the back neck. The remaining 22 (22, 26, 28, 30, 30, 30, 32) sts are worked as the Upper Left Front.

UPPER LEFT FRONT

Work 0 (0, 0, 0, 0, 0, 4, 10) rows straight.

Increase at the neck edge:

Row 1 (RS): In patt.

Row 2: In patt.

Row 3: K1, m1, patt to end of row.

Row 4: In patt.

Repeat these 4 rows until there are 32 (29, 36, 38, 40, 41, 42, 43) sts on the needle.

Increase for the armhole:

Row 1: Patt to last st, m1, k1.

Row 2: In patt.

Continue increasing 1 st on the armhole edge of every other row, and AT THE SAME TIME increase on the neck edge as before 0 (2, 3, 3, 3, 2, 0, 0) times more, until there are 37 (43, 47, 51, 56, 61, 57, 61) sts on the needle, finishing after a WS row.

Next Row (RS): In patt.

Next Row: Cast on 8 (9, 10, 14, 15, 16, 24, 27) sts, patt to end of row. 45 (52, 57, 65, 71, 77, 81, 88) sts

Place sts on a stitch holder.

UPPER RIGHT FRONT

Return to held sts from the back.

Work 0 (0, 0, 0, 0, 0, 4, 10) rows straight.

Increase at the neck edge as follows:

Row 1 (RS): In patt.

Row 2: In patt.

Row 3: Patt to last st, m1, k1.

Row 4: In patt.

Repeat these 4 rows until there are 32 (29, 36, 38, 40, 41, 42, 43) sts on the needle.

Increase for the armholes:
Row 1: K1, m1, patt to end of row.

Row 2: In patt.

Continue increasing 1 st on the armhole edge of every other row, and AT THE SAME TIME increase on the neck edge as before 0 (2, 3, 3, 3, 2, 0, 0) times more, until there are 37 (43, 47, 51, 56, 61, 57, 61) sts on the needle, finishing after a WS row.

Next Row (RS): Cast on 8 (9, 10, 14, 15, 16, 24, 27) sts, patt to end of row; cast on 15 (15, 17, 17, 17, 19, 23, 25) sts; work the sts held from the Left Front. 105 (119, 131, 147, 159, 173, 185, 201) sts

FRONT

Work in patt across all sts until the front measures the same length as the back from the bottom of the armhole to the start of the waist-band ribbing.

Ribbed Waist
Change to smaller needles and work in k1, p1 rib as for the back, ending with a WS row.

Work the increase row for your size:
Size XXS: K12, *k2, m1. Repeat from * to last 13 sts, k13. 145 sts

Size XS: *K3, m1, k4, m1. Repeat from * to end of row. 153 sts.

Size S: K5, *k3, m1. Repeat from * to last 6 sts, k6. 161 sts

Size M: K4, m1, k3. Repeat from * to last 7 sts, k1, m1, k3, m1, k3. 169 sts

Size L: K3, *k4, m1, k5. Repeat from * to last 3 sts, m1, k3. 177 sts

Size 1X: K2, *k7, m1, k7. Repeat from * to last 3 sts, k3. 185 sts

Note that on Row 2 two stitches are decreased per pattern repeat, and on Row 3 two stitches are increased per pattern repeat.

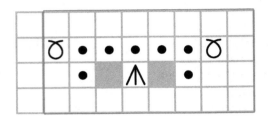

Row 1 (RS): K.

Row 2: P1, *p1, k1, k3tog, k1, p2. Repeat from * to end of row.

Row 3: *K1, m1, p5, m1. Repeat from * to last st, k1.

Row 4: P.

Size 2X: K1, *k7, m1, k7. Repeat from * to last 2 sts, m1, k2. 199 sts

Size 3X: K2, m1, *k7, m1, k7. Repeat from * to last 3 sts, m1, k3. 217 sts

All sizes: Purl 1 row.

Skirt
Change to larger needles and work in Marlboro Lace for the same number of rows as for the back. Knit 3 rows. Cast off.

LEFT SLEEVE

With RSF, count 5 (6, 7, 8, 11, 13, 19, 21) sts in along the cast on edge at the front underarm, then join new yarn. Pick up and knit 70 (76, 80, 88, 100, 118, 128, 132) evenly around the armhole edge, then cast on 5 (6, 7, 10, 11, 13, 19, 21) sts. Work the second row of the Garter Rib pattern. 75 (82, 87, 98, 111, 131, 147, 153) sts.

Decrease sleeve:
Row 1: K1, k2tog, patt to last 3 sts, ssk, k1.

Work 5 (5, 3, 3, 2, 2, 2) rows in pattern.

Repeat these 6 (6, 6, 4, 4, 3, 3, 3) rows until 34 (38, 38, 40, 40, 44, 46, 50) sts remain. Work straight until sleeve measures 16.5 (17, 27, 17.5, 17.5, 18, 18 18.5)" *Adjust*

length here.

Change to smaller needles and work k1, p1 rib for 3". Cast off loosely.

RIGHT SLEEVE

Cast on 5 (6, 7, 8, 11, 13, 19, 21) sts. Beginning at the edge of the back underarm, pick up and knit 70 (76, 80, 88, 100, 118, 128, 132) evenly around the armhole edge, ending 5 (6, 7, 8, 11, 13, 19, 21) sts before the front underarm edge. Work the second row of the Garter Rib pattern. 75 (82, 87, 98, 111, 131, 147, 153) sts

Complete as for the Left Sleeve.

COLLAR

With larger needles, cast on 30 sts and work in garter st as follows:

Row 1: S1p, k to end of row.

Repeat Row 1 until the piece is long enough to fit the front sides and back neck, about 15.5 (16.5, 17.5, 18.5, 20.5, 22.5, 24.5, 26)". Cast off.

FINISHING

Sew side seams. Sew the sleeve seams, then sew the cast on stitches of the sleeve to the front armhole edge. Sew collar to neck edge. Weave in all ends. Wash and dry flat.

Old Shale Wrap

DESIGNED BY GLADYS WALLIS AND DOROTHY POTTS • KNITTED BY GLADYS WALLIS

MATERIALS

250 g DK yarn

Pair 4 mm needles, or size to achieve tension

Gladys used Ice Souffle Alpaca; 40% baby alpaca, 30% wool, 30% polymide; 180 yds / 165 m per 50 g ball, shade Light Maroon

TENSION

21 sts and 32 rows to 4" over pattern

NOTES

This pattern can be made narrower or wider by subtracting or adding multiples of 18 sts. The length is also easily adjustable.

PATTERN

Cast on 116 sts and knit 4 rows.

Rows 1 to 24: Work through the chart 6 times.

Rows 25 to 28: K.

These 28 rows form the pattern. Repeat them until the wrap measures about 60" or desired length, finishing at the end of a pattern repeat.

Cast off.

FINISHING

Weave in all ends. Wash and dry flat.

SIZE

22" by 56"

GLADYS WALLIS

My mother turned 85 in July and has been knitting for years. She has knitted mainly for the family, which she has kept supplied with baby items. The items that she knitted for the group have been the biggest things she has done in the last few years because of the weight. But she did enjoy doing them. Julie Speed asked if she would like to do them and sent the wool for her. — Dorothy

OLD SHALE

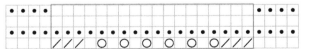

Row 1: K4, *k2tog three times, [yo, k1] six times, k2tog three times. Repeat from * to last 4 sts, k4.

Row 2: K.

Row 3: K.

Row 4: K4, p to last 4 sts, k4.

Old Shale Wrap (left) and Rose Leaf Lace Wrap.

Rose Leaf Lace Wrap

DESIGNED BY ELIZABETH LOVICK • KNITTED BY MELANIE SMITH

MATERIALS

Pair 5 mm (US 8) needles, or size to achieve tension

200 g 4 ply/fingering wool

2 Stitch markers

Stitch holder or waste yarn

Melanie used J&S 2 ply jumper weight; 100% Shetland wool; 125 yds / 115 m per 25 g ball; shade FC22

SIZE

To fit toddler (child, teen, adult, plus)

Width: 20 (25, 30, 36, 41)"
Length: 32 (40, 48, 56, 64)"

TENSION

15 sts and 12 rows to 4" over central pattern

CONSTRUCTION

One tail is knitted and the stitches left live. The other tail is then knitted, and the centre is knitted on to it. The two pieces are then grafted together. Note that if preferred, the two sections can be cast off and sewn together.

INSPIRATION

I came across this lace pattern in a Weldon's booklet, with no picture. I started to chart it, and realised there were mistakes in the written pattern. Several attempts later I had the pattern 'right'. Melanie liked the pattern and had the perfect, rose-coloured yarn for it. — Liz

PATTERN

FIRST TAIL

Cast on 75 (95, 115, 135, 155) sts LOOSELY.

Foundation Row: K5, PM, k to last 5 sts, PM, k5.

Work straight, keeping the 5 st borders in garter stitch, and working the central section from the Rose Leaf Chart, until the work measures about 8 (10, 12, 14, 16)", finishing at the end of a pattern repeat. Break yarn, and place sts on a thread.

SECOND TAIL

Work as for the First Tail, but do not break yarn. Continue with these stitches.

CENTRE

Work across the whole piece:

Row 1: K.

Row 2: K.

Row 3: K5, [k wrapping the yarn round the needle twice] to last 5 sts, k5.

Row 4: K5, [k dropping the second loop] to last 5 sts, k5.

These four rows form the pattern. Repeat them until the centre section measures 16 (20, 24, 28, 32)", finishing after a second row. *Adjust length here.* Break yarn leaving a long tail.

FINISHING

Graft the two sets of live stitches together. Weave in all ends. Wash and dry flat, preferably on wires.

ROSE LEAF CHART

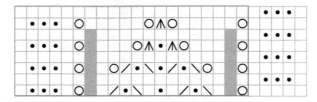

Note that the pattern starts and finishes with 20 sts in the repeat, but from the 2nd to the 6th row there are 18 sts per repeat.

Row 1: K1, p3, k1, *yo, k1, ssk, p1, k2tog, k1, p1, k1, ssk, p1, k2tog, k1, yo, k1, p3, k1. Repeat from * to end of row.

Row 2 and all alternate rows: P.

Row 3: K1, p3, k1, *yo, k1, yo, ssk, p1, k2tog, p1, ssk, p1, k2tog, yo, k1, yo, k1, p3, k1. Repeat from * to end of row.

Row 5: K1, p3, k1, *yo, k3, yo, k3togtbl, p1, k3togtbl, yo, k3, yo, k1, p3, k1. Repeat from * to end of row.

Row 7: K1, p3, k1, *yo, k5, yo, k3togtbl, yo, k5, yo, k1, p3, k1. Repeat from * to end of row.

Row 8: P.

These eight rows form the pattern. Repeat them as required.

Ann's Cloud

DESIGNED AND KNITTED BY ELIZABETH LOVICK

MATERIALS

Wrap: 60 (100, 160, 240) g / 330 (550, 880, 1350) yds lace weight mohair yarn

Scarf: 30 (50, 65, 90) g / 170 (275, 360, 500) yds lace weight mohair yarn

Pair 5 mm (US 8) needles, or size to achieve tension

Row counter

Tapestry needle

1 yd 1" ribbon

Liz used Ice Yarns Premium mohair, 80% mohair, 20% acrylic, 550 yds / 495 m; shade Ivory

SIZE

To fit child (teen, woman, plus sizes)

Wrap: 13 (17, 21, 25)" wide by 40 (55, 70, 85)" long

Scarf: 7 (9, 11, 13)" wide by 36 (48, 54, 60)" long

The length of the wrap and the scarf is easily adjustable.

TENSION

16 sts and 26 rows to 4" over lace pattern on 5 mm needles

NOTES

Note the pattern will also work with sock weight yarn, but will need a greater weight of yarn.

PATTERN

WRAP

Cast on 61 (77, 93, 109) sts.

Row 1: S1p, k to end of row.

Repeat Row 1 six times more.

Change to pattern. Work from the chart until the piece measures about 39 (54, 69, 84)", finishing after an 8th row.

Next Row: S1p, k to end of row.

Repeat this row six time more. Cast off.

SCARF

Cast on 37 (45, 53, 61) sts. Work as for the wrap until the piece measures 35 (47, 53, 59)". Finish as for the wrap.

FINISHING

Weave in all ends. Wash and dress, preferably on wires. When dry, cut off all ends. Make one large tassel. Gather one end of the wrap and attach the tassel to it firmly. Fold the other short end of the wrap in half and sew the edges together. Place a large bow at the end of the seam.

In wear, the end with the bow is placed on the head like a hood, with the bow over the forehead. The rest of the cloud is wrapped once or twice round the neck with the tassel hanging down the front or the back.

Alternatively, place the non-tasselled end on the right shoulder, take the cloud over the head, then wrap it round the neck and shoulders, covering the first end. Again the tassel may be at the front or the back.

If preferred, the piece may be used with no tassels as a regular wrap, or with two tassels as a scarf.

INSPIRATION

This is a Victorian 'cloud'. I found it in one of the Weldon's leaflets. There was no picture, just the row-by-row instructions, which I charted. Clouds had a tassel on one end and the other end was folded in half and sewn up, with a bow attached. This could then be worn as a hood if required, as well as a scarf or wrap. I have also sized the pattern as a scarf for modern day use.

— Liz

ANN'S CLOUD

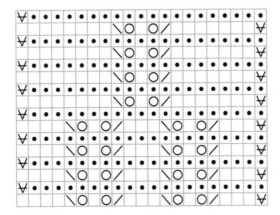

Row 1: S1p, k3, *k2tog, yo, k1, yo, ssk, k3. Repeat from * to last st, k1.

Row 2: S1p, k to end of row.

Rows 3 to 8: Repeat Rows 1 and 2 three times more.

Row 9: S1p, k7, *k2tog, yo, k1, yo, ssk, k3. Repeat from * to last 5 sts, k5.

Row 10: S1p, k to end of row.

Rows 11 to 16: Repeat Rows 9 and 10 three times more.

These 16 rows form the pattern. Repeat them as required.

Shoulder Cape

TRANSLATED BY ELIZABETH LOVICK
CROCHETED BY SAM BRAID

MATERIALS

300 g lace weight yarn

4 mm crochet hook, or size to achieve tension

Sam used a lace weight yarn which was only labeled as 'cotton blend'.

SIZE

Length from neck to bottom edge: 18"

Bottom edge: 56"

TENSION

12 st and 5 rows of trebles to 3"

NOTES
First treble of each round is worked as 3 chain.

PATTERN
Chain 3, sl-st to join.

Rnd 1: 14 tr; sl-st to join.

Rnd 2: 2 tr between each treble; sl-st to join. 14 groups

Rnd 3: 4 tr between the 2 tr of each group; sl-st to join. 14 groups of

Rnd 4: *4 tr into space between 2nd and 3rd tr of group, 2 tr into space between groups; sl-st to join. 28 groups

Rnd 5: *4 tr into space between 2nd and 3rd tr of group, 4 tr into space between 2 tr; sl-st to join. 56 groups

Rnd 6: 1 dc into space between 2nd and 3rd tr of group *4 tr into space between 2nd and 3rd tr of group; sl-st to join.

Rnds 7 to 9: As Rnd 6.

Rnd 10: As Rnd 4; sl-st to join.

Rnds 11 to 15: As Rnds 5 to 9.

Fold the circle in half so that the sets of 4 tr lie over each other forming an upper and lower layer. Now work in ROWS not rounds.

Row 1: *Working into both layers at the same time, dc into space between groups; taking upper and lower layers; 8 ch. Repeat from * to last group, 1 dc into fold, turn. 56 groups. Chain loops will be worked later.

Row 2: Working into both layers, *4 tr into space between 2nd and 3rd tr of group. Repeat from * to end of row. Turn.

Repeat Row 2 5 times more.

Row 8: 1 dc into first tr of last row, *8 ch, 1 dc into space between groups. Repeat from * to last group, 8 ch 1, dc into last tr of last row. Turn. Chain loops will be worked later.

Row 9: *4 tr into space between 2nd and 3rd tr of group, 2 tr into space between groups. Turn.

Row 10: *4 tr into space between 2nd and 3rd tr of group, 4 tr into space between 2 tr. Turn.

Row 11: *4 tr into space between 2nd and 3rd tr of group. Turn.

Rows 14 to 16: As Row 10.

Row 17: As Row 8.

Row 18: Work 11 tr into each 8 ch loop. Fasten off.

Repeat Row 18 on each of the other two rows of 8 ch loops.

FINISHING
Weave in all ends. Wash and dry flat.

INSPIRATION
I inherited a copy of The Lady's World 1909 from my grandmother and have used several of the crochet lace patterns from it over the years. This is a shawl from that book. The introduction says: "This is one of the prettiest capes I have seen. It looks so charming on and does not have the effect of making one look older as some wool capes have. It is a crochet cape and made using Paton's 2ply Pearl Wool, and a large hook is required." — Sam

Three Point Shawl (left) and Shoulder Cape.

Three Point Shawl

DESIGNED BY ELIZABETH LOVICK • KNITTED BY MELANIE SMITH

MATERIALS

150 g lace weight mohair

Pair 5 mm (US 8) needles, or size required to achieve tension

One smaller needle for picking up stitches

4 Stitch markers

Row counter

Melanie used Ice Angora Premium Mohair; 80% mohair, 20% acrylic; 550 yds / 495 m; shade Ivory

SIZE

36" deep and 72" across

TENSION

16 sts and 24 rows to 4" over garter stitch

CONSTRUCTION

The lace edging is worked first, then the loops along the straight edge are picked up for the border. The border and centre are worked decreasing in the middle, finishing at the centre back. The long edge is then finished with picots.

INSPIRATION

Although most shawls of the time were square, there were some triangular ones. I found this one in one of Columbia Yarn books. Like many patterns of the time, this one had several mistakes in the lace section. These have been corrected! — Liz

PATTERN

LACE EDGING

Cast on 12 sts and knit 1 row.

Now work through the Lace Chart a total of 71 times.

Cast off.

THE BORDER

With the smaller needle, pick up all the slipped stitch loops on the straight side of the lace. 356 sts

Foundation Row (RSF): K172, k3togtbl, k2togtbl three times, k3togtbl, k172. 349 sts

Next Row: K 174, PM, k1, PM, k to end of row.

Work through the Border Chart, placing it as follows:

Row 1: S1p, work from Row 1 of the chart to M, SM, k1, SM, work from Row 1 of the chart until 1 st remains, k1.

Row 2: S1p, work from Row 2 of the chart to M, SM, p1, SM, work from Row 2 of the chart until 1 st remains, k1.

Continue in this way, working the chart twice on each row, until all 28 rows of the chart have been worked.

THE CENTRE

Row 1: S1p, ssk, k to 2 sts before M, k2tog, SM, k1, SM, ssk, k to last 3 sts, k2tog, k1.

Row 2: S1p, k to end of row.

Repeat these two rows until 7 sts remain, finishing after a 2nd row.

Next Row: S1p, k3tog twice.

Next Row: K3tog. Fasten off.

THE EDGING

With RSF, pick up the 12 sts cast off for the lace, then every s1p loop along the long edge of the shawl, then the 12 sts cast on for the lace.

Work the picot edging as follows:

*Cast on 2 sts, cast off 4 sts. Repeat from * until all the sts have been worked off.

FINISHING

Weave in all ends. Wash and dry flat, pulling into shape.

THREE POINT SHAWL • BORDER CHART

Note that 'last x sts' refers to the end of that repeat (ie before the marker or before the end of the whole row).

Row 1: Ssk, k to last 2 sts, k2tog.

Row 2: P.

Row 3: Ssk, k to last 2 sts, k2tog.

Row 4: K.

Row 5: P2tog, p to last 2 sts, p2tog.

Row 6: K.

Row 7: *Ssk, k1, k2tog, yo, k1, yo. Repeat from * to last 5 sts, ssk, k1, k2tog.

Row 8: P.

Row 9: *K3togtbl, yo, k3, yo. Repeat from * to last 3 sts, k3togtbl.

Row 10: P.

Row 11: Ssk, k2, *k2tog, yo, k1, yo, ssk, k1. Repeat from * to last 9 sts, k2tog, yo, k1, yo, ssk, k2, k2tog.

Row 12: P.

Row 13: Ssk, k2tog, *yo, k3, yo, k3togtbl. Repeat from * to last 7 sts, yo, k3, yo, ssk, k2tog.

Row 14: P.

Row 15: Ssk, *yo, ssk, k1,

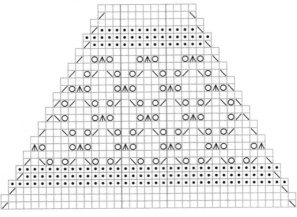

k2tog, yo, k1. Repeat from * to last 7 sts, yo, ssk, k1, k2tog, yo, k2tog.

Row 16: P.

Row 17: Ssk, *yo, k3togtbl, yo, k3. Repeat from * to last 5 sts, yo, k3togtbl, yo, k2tog.

Row 18: P.

Row 19: Ssk, *k1, yo, ssk, k1, k2tog, yo. Repeat from * to last 3 sts, k1, k2tog.

Row 20: P.

Row 21: Ssk, k1, *yo, k3togtbl, yo, k3. Repeat

from * to last 6 sts, yo, k3togtbl, yo, k1, k2tog.

Row 22: P.

Row 23: P2tog, p to last 2 sts, p2tog.

Row 24: K.

Row 25: P2tog, p to last 2 sts, p2tog.

Row 26: P.

Row 27: Ssk, k to last 2 sts, k2tog.

Row 28: P.

THREE POINT SHAWL LACE CHART

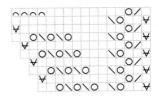

Row 1 (RS): S1p, k2, yo, ssk, k1, [yo, ssk] twice, yo, k2. 13 sts

Row 2: S1p, k9, yo, k2tog, k1.

Row 3: S1p, [k2, yo, ssk] twice, yo, ssk, yo, k2. 14 sts

Row 4: S1p, k10, yo, k2tog, k1.

Row 5: S1p, k2, yo, ssk, k3, [yo, ssk] twice, yo, k2. 15 sts

Row 6: S1p, k11, yo, k2tog, k1.

Row 7: S1p, k2, yo, ssk, k4, [yo, ssk] twice, yo, k2. 16 sts

Row 8: S1p, k12, yo, k2tog, k1.

Row 9: S1p, k2, yo, ssk, k11.

Row 10: Cast off 4, k9, yo, k2tog, k1. 12 sts

48

Tassel Tie

TRANSLATED BY ELIZABETH LOVICK
CROCHETED BY GAIL LEE

MATERIALS

35 g 3 ply yarn

If desired, a sliding buckle

Gail used two ColourMart yarns together - a 1 ply silk/cashmere in green and a 2 ply silk/wool in turquoise.

SIZE

1" wide and 45" long

TENSION

14 sts to 1" over Tunisian crochet

PATTERN

Chain 14.

Work in Tunisian crochet, changing colours as desired, until the tie measures 45" long. Fasten off.

THE BUCKLE

Wrap the thread round your first three fingers 18 times. Slip off. Now work dcs into the ring, pushing them close together, making a stiff ring. Fasten off and weave in ends. Shape the ring into an oval. Take a 40" length of thread and pass it across the oval several times. Now cover this with buttonhole stitch, again pushing the stitches close together. Fasten off and weave in ends.

THE TASSELS

Make 6 small tassels about 2" long, each using 15 lengths of yarn.

FINISHING

Fold the corners of each end inwards to form a point. Stitch in place. Weave in all ends. Attach the tassels on the end of the tie as shown.

Ann Crowder (Susan Thorpe) and her daugher Grace (Victoria Rigby) looking fashionable for an afternoon party. Grace is wearing the Tassel Tie.

MATERIALS

40 g 4 ply/fingering yarn

3 mm crochet hook

Stitch marker

Liz used ColourMart 6/20; 50% silk, 50% linen; shade medium green

SIZE

1" wide round the neck and 40" long

TENSION

9 sts to 1"

NOTES

The turning chain is counted as a dc. Work is turned after each row.

CONSTRUCTION

The tie is worked in two parts then joined at the centre back.

PATTERN

Chain 9.

Row 1: Miss 1 ch, dc into each ch. 9 sts

Row 2: 1 ch, miss 1 dc, dc into each dc, working into the BACK loop ONLY.

Repeat Row 2 until the piece measures 9".

Place a marker in the centre st.

Shape end as follows, working into the back loop only:

Row 1: 1 ch, miss 1 dc, dc to centre st, 3 dc into centre st, dc to end. (2 sts inc)

Row 2: Dc across row.

Repeat Rows 1 and 2 until there are 53 sts. Fasten off.

Make a second piece the same.

FINISHING

Join the two tails together. Weave in all ends.

Make a fringe using 3 pieces of yarn. Then knot as in the photo. Wash and dry flat.

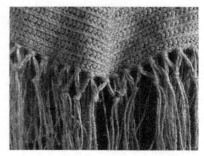

Crocheted Tie with Fringe

TRANSLATED AND CROCHETED BY ELIZABETH LOVICK

INSPIRATION

Another tie from the Needlework booklet. I love the clever shaping of this, and the knotted fringe takes it to the next level. — Liz

Scarf Vest

TRANSLATED AND KNITTED BY JUDITH A. BRODNICKI

INSPIRATION

When I saw this pattern in the Bear Brand book I was immediately intrigued by three things: the construction of it, the lovely stripe pattern, and the fact that the design looked like something a 21st century woman would want in her wardrobe.

The first time I worked the pattern, it was pretty much an act of faith because I had no idea how it would work out. The second time I worked it I had the Juvell yarn on hand. I was testing out a few modifications, among them the armhole edge treatment.

The original pattern calls for all of the edges (around the armhole and along the fronts) to be worked in single crochet, but I was concerned that it would constrain the natural elasticity of the garter edge, so I changed the armhole finishing to a few rounds of ribbing and then work the first stitch of every row along the sloped front edge and bottom band as a purl stitch to give those edges a smooth finish. — Judith

MATERIALS

450 (500, 500, 550, 600, 600, 650, 650, 650) g DK yarn

Pair 3.5 mm (US 4) needles, or size required to achieve the correct tension

Set 3.5 mm (US 4) dpns

Spare dpns for picking up stitches

Waste yarn

2 Stitch markers

2 strips of fabric, each 1 to 2 inches wide and long enough to go around your hips (optional)

3.75 mm (US F) crochet hook and stuffing for embellishment at tie-ends (optional)

Judith used Rowan Purelife Organic DK; 100% organic wool; 137 yds / 125 m per 50g ball; shade 603 Black Tea for the first scarf vest. The second one was worked in

Schachenmayr Juvel; 100% super-wash wool; 118 yds / 106 m per 50g ball; shade Pistachio.

SIZE

Sizes: XXS (XS, S, M, L, 1X, 2X, 3X, 4X)

Chest: 28 (32, 36, 40, 44, 48, 52, 56, 60)"

Length: 17.5 (17.5, 18, 18, 18.5, 18.5, 18.5, 18.5, 18.5)"

Shoulder Width: 12 (13, 13.5, 14, 15, 15.5, 16, 17, 17)"

This garment is made to wrap around the body (with zero or negative ease) and has a lot of stretch to the fabric. Work the size that is closest to your shoulder width (measured shoulder-to-shoulder across the back neck), less 1".

TENSION

22 sts and 40 rows to 4" in garter stitch

CONSTRUCTION

This garment is worked sideways, starting at the lower Right Front, through the back and armholes, and ending at the lower Left Front. Back and Fronts are stitched together at the shoulder seams, then the armholes are finished with a few rounds of ribbing. Finally the ties are knitted and embellishments added if required.

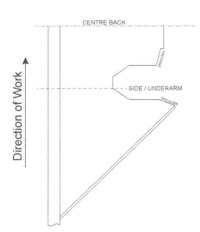

PATTERN

RIGHT FRONT

With waste yarn, cast on 15 sts.

Row 1 (RS): P1, k to end of row.

Row 2 and all alternate rows: P1, k to end of row.

Row 3: P1, kfb, k to end of row. 16 sts

Row 5: P1, k1, kfb, k to end of row. 17 sts

Row 7: P1, k2, kfb, k to end of row. 18 sts

Row 9: P1, k3, kfb, k to end of row. 19 sts

Row 11: P1, k4, PM, kfb, k to end of row. 20 sts

Front border increases and stripe patt st:

Row 13 (RS): P1, k4, PM, yo, SM, k to end of row.

Row 14: P1, k to M, SM, patt to M, SM, k5.

Row 15: P1, k to M, SM, yo, patt to M, SM, k to end of row.

Row 16: P1, k to M, SM, patt to M, SM, k5.

Repeat Rows 15 and 16, working the Garter Stitch Stripe pattern between the markers, until there are a total of 109 (112, 115, 116, 120, 121, 124, 126, 125) sts on the needle, finishing after the WS row.

Right Shoulder
Maintaining the 15 sts garter border and Garter Stitch Stripe,

continue as follows:

Row 1 (RS): Cast off 5 (5, 6, 7, 6, 7, 6, 7, 6) sts removing marker; patt to end of row.

Row 2 and alternate rows: In patt.

Rows 3, 5 and 7: Cast off 4 (5, 5, 5, 6, 6, 7, 7, 7) sts, patt to end of row. 92 (92, 94, 94, 96, 96, 98, 98, 98) sts

Row 9: Cast off 1 st, k35 (35, 31, 33, 27, 31, 27, 29, 25) sts; place these sts on a stitch holder; patt to end of row.

Right Front Armhole
Cast off 2 sts at the beg of the next 2 (3, 5, 5, 8, 8, 10, 10, 12) RS rows. 52 (50, 52, 50, 52, 48, 50, 48, 48) sts

Next Row (WS): In patt.

Work in garter stitch for 6 (8, 12, 24, 24, 32, 30, 36, 42) rows.

BACK PANEL

Back Right Armhole
Return to the Garter Stripe pattern with 15 st garter stitch border and shape back armhole edge as follows:

Cast on 2 sts at beg of next 2 (3, 5, 5, 8, 8, 10, 10, 12) RS rows, working as set to end of row.

With waste yarn, cast on 35 (35, 31, 33, 27, 31, 27, 29, 25) sts to a spare needle.

Next Row (WS): Patt to the end of row, then k the sts on the spare needle.

Next Row: Kfb into the first st, then work as set to the end of the row. 91 (91, 93, 93, 95, 95, 97, 97, 97) sts

Right Shoulder
Inc 1 st at the shoulder every 6 (6, 8, 8, 8, 10, 10, 10, 10) rows four times as follows:

Next Row (WS): Patt to last st, m1, work 1.

Work 5 (5, 7, 7, 7, 9, 9, 9, 9) rows in patt as set.

Repeat these 6 (6, 8, 8, 8, 10, 10, 10, 10) rows three times more. 96 (96, 98, 98, 100, 100, 102, 102, 102) sts

Work 0 (6, 0, 2, 6, 0, 2, 6, 4) more rows in patt.

Centre Back
Row 1 (RS): Cast on 5 for neck border, p1, k4, PM, yo, k2tog, patt to end of row.

Row 2: P1, k to M, SM, patt to M, SM, k to end of row.

Row 3: P1, k4, SM, yo, k2tog, patt to end of row.

Row 4: As Row 2.

Repeat Rows 3 and 4 a total of 35 (35, 35, 35, 37, 37, 37, 37, 39) times.

Next Row: Cast off 5, RM, patt to end of row.

Next Row: P1, k to M, patt to end of row.

Work 0 (6, 0, 2, 6, 0, 2, 6, 4) rows in patt.

Left Shoulder
Next Row: K1, k2tog, patt to end of row.

Work 5 (5, 7, 7, 7, 9, 9, 9, 9) rows in patt.

Repeat these rows 3 times more. 92 (92, 94, 94, 96, 96, 98, 98, 98) sts

Left Armhole
Next Row: Cast off 1, k35 (35, 31, 33, 27, 31, 27, 29, 25); place these sts on a stitch holder; patt to end of row.

Keeping the pattern correct, cast off 2 sts at the beg of the next 2 (3, 5, 5, 8, 8, 10, 10, 12) RS rows. 52 (50, 52, 50, 52, 48, 50, 48, 48) sts

Knit 6 (8, 12, 24, 24, 32, 30, 36, 42) rows.

LEFT FRONT

Left Armhole
Return to the Garter Stripe patt with 15 st garter stitch border and shape armhole edge as follows:

Cast off 2 at beg of next 2 (3, 5, 5, 8, 8, 10, 10, 12) RS rows.

With waste yarn, cast on 25 (35, 31, 33, 27, 31, 27, 29, 25) sts to a spare needle.

Next Row (WS): Patt to end of row, then k the sts on the spare needle.

Next Row: Kfb, patt to end of row. 92 (92, 94, 94, 96, 96, 98, 98, 98) sts

Work 1 row.

Left Shoulder
Cast on 4 (5, 5, 5, 6, 6, 7, 7, 7) sts at the beg of the next 3 RS rows.

Work 1 row.

Row 7: Cast on 5 (5, 6, 7, 6, 7, 5, 7, 6), p1, patt to end of row. 109 (112, 115, 116, 120, 121, 124, 126, 125) sts

Row 8: P1, k to M, patt to end of row.

Row 9: P1, k3, k2tog, yo, k2tog, patt to end of row.

Row 10: P1, k to M, patt to last 5 sts, k5.

Repeat Rows 9 and 10 until 22 sts remain, removing M on last row.

Continue as follows:

Row 1 (RS): P1, k3, k2tog, yo, k2tog, k to end of row. 21 sts

Row 2 and all alternate rows: P1, k to end of row.

Row 3: P1, k3, k2tog, yo, k2tog, k to end of row. 20 sts

Row 5: P1, k4, k2tog, k to end of row. 19 sts

Row 7: P1, k3, k2tog, k to end of row. 18 sts

Row 9: P1, k2, k2tog, k to end of row. 17 sts

Row 11: P1, k1, k2tog, k to end of row. 16 sts

Row 13: P1, k2tog, k to end of row. 15 sts

Row 14: As Row 2.

Place sts on holder, but DO NOT BREAK YARN.

Sew shoulder seams, matching up the upper borders.

LEFT ARMHOLE EDGING

Place armhole sts from holders on to spare dpns, and carefully unpick the waste yarn.

With RS facing, join new yarn to start of the Left Front. Pick up and knit sts along the angled edge between underarm and front straight armhole edge; knit the sts from spare dpns; pick up and knit sts along angled edge between back straight armhole edge and underarm; pick up and knit 1 st from each garter ridge at the underarm, making sure you finish with an even number of stitches.

Work 3 rounds in k1, p1 rib. Cast off loosely in pattern.

RIGHT ARMHOLE EDGING

Work as for Left Edging, but rejoining yarn before the garter stitch panel.

TIE-ENDS

According to the original pattern, each tie-end was 1.5 times the total back width.

Left Tie

Return to the 15 held sts from the Left Front, and work in garter stitch for the desired length. Cast off.

Right Tie

Remove the waste yarn from the right front and work as for the Left Tie.

NOTE: If you are working the optional crocheted embellishment, do not pull thread through the last loop and break the yarn. Instead, proceed to the next section of instructions.

OPTIONAL CROCHETED ORNAMENTATION ON THE TIE-ENDS

Using the final loop of the tie-end, work embellishment as follows:

Row 1: 5 ch, miss 4 sts, 1 dc into next st, 5 ch, miss 3 sts, 1 dc into next st, 5 ch, miss 4 sts, 1 dc into last st. Turn.

Row 2: Sl sts to get to top of ch loop, 1 dc into loop, [5 ch, 1 dc in the top of the next loop] twice. Turn.

Row 3: Sl sts to get to the top of the ch loop, 1 dc into loop, 5 ch, 1 dc in the top of the next loop. Cut yarn, pull loop through, work in ends.

To make the dangle, 3 ch and join with sl st to form a ring.

Rnd 1: 6 dc into the ring.

Rnd 2: 2 dc in each st. 12 sts

Rnds 3 to 11: 1 dc in each st.

Rnd 12: [1 dc, miss 1] all around. 6 sts

Rnd 13: [1 dc, miss 1] all round. 3 sts

Cut end, leaving about 6" of yarn tail. Pull yarn through.

Stuff the dangle. Draw yarn through the 3-stitch opening and pull to close it. Sew to last chain loop on tie-end.

FINISHING

Weave in ends. If desired, line tie-ends with strips of material. Wash and dry flat.

Molly Marie Buckley models the Crossover. © Thomas Hinckley

Crossover

TRANSLATED AND KNITTED BY JUNIPER ASKEW

INSPIRATION

This 'knitted crossover' comes from the Third Edition of "The Book of Hows, or What May be Done with Wool in Every Home Edited by Miss Loch, Needlework Examiner to the London School Board", published in 1900. — Juniper

MATERIALS

300 g DK yarn for MC

30 g DK yarn for CC

Pair 4 mm (US 6) needles, or size to achieve tension

3 mm crochet hook

1 Stitch marker

Row counter

1 m ribbon, about 1" wide

Juniper used MC - Debbie Bliss Cashmerino; 55% merino, 33% PA,12% cashmere; 240 yds / 216 m per 100 g; colour Graphite. CC - , as MC in Debbie Bliss Rialto DK Solids; 100% merino, 230 yds / 207 m per 200 g; colour Duck Egg

SIZE

Fronts: 26" from point to where it joins for the back

Back: 27.5"

TENSION

22 sts and 30 rows to 4" over garter stitch

CONSTRUCTION

The two fronts are knitted first, then joined at the back of the neck before knitting down the back.

PATTERN

RIGHT FRONT

Cast on 2 sts.

Row 1 (RS): K1, m1, k1.

Row 2: Knit.

Row 3: K to last st, m1, k1.

Row 4: Knit.

Repeat Rows 3 and 4 until there are 67 sts on the needle.

Knit 128 rows straight, finishing at the straight edge. Break yarn and leave sts on a stitch holder.

LEFT FRONT

Cast on 2 sts.

Row 1 (RS): K1, m1, k1.

Row 2: Knit.

Row 3: K1, m1, k to end of row.

Row 4: Knit.

Repeat Rows 3 and 4 until there are 67 sts on the needle.

Knit 128 rows straight, finishing at the shaped edge. Do not break yarn.

BACK

Knit across the stitches of the Left Front, PM, then the stitches of the Right Front.

Shape the back as follows:

Row 1: K to 2 sts before the M, k2tog, k to end of row.

Repeat Row 1 until 3 sts remain. Remove marker and k3tog.

Fasten off.

EDGING

With CC, and starting at the back of the neck, crochet right round the edge as follows, working the dc into the fabric between every other ridge:

*1 dc into the edge of the crossover, 5 ch, l dc into first ch, 1 dc into the crossover. Repeat from * all round the crossover.

FINISHING

Weave in all ends. Wash and dry flat. Cut the ribbon in half and attach one piece to the tip if each front.

In wear, cross one front over the other and tie behind the back.

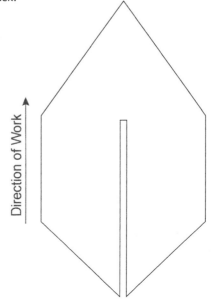

Direction of Work

Fila Lace. No. 26

ABBREVIATIONS.—Ch., chain ; tr., treble ; d.tr., double treble ; s.c., single crochet ; d.c., double crochet ; sht. tr., short treble.
Dewhurst's Sylko, 40.

1st row.—14 ch. 1 tr. in eighth ch. (from hook), 2 ch. 1 tr. in eleventh ch., 2 ch. 1 tr. in fourteenth ch., turn.

2nd row.—9 ch. 1 tr. in seventh ch. (from hook), 2 ch. 1 tr. on tr below. Repeat 2 ch. 1 tr. on tr. below, turn.

3rd row.—5 ch. 1 tr. on tr. below, 2 ch. 1 tr. on next, 2 tr. in space, 1 tr. on tr., 2 ch. 1 tr. on next tr., 2 ch. 1 tr. in next space, turn.

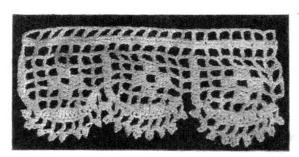

4th row.—5 ch. 1 tr. on tr. below, 2 tr. in space, 1 tr. on tr., 2 ch. miss 2 tr., 1 tr. on next tr., 2 tr. in space, 1 tr. on tr., 2 ch. 1 tr. on next tr., turn.

5th row.—5 ch. 1 tr. on tr., 2 ch. miss 2 tr., 1 tr. on next, 2 tr. in space, 1 tr. on next tr., 2 ch. miss 2 tr., 1 tr. on next tr., 2 ch. 1 tr. in next space, turn.

6th row.—3 ch. 1 tr. on tr. below, twice 2 ch. 1 tr. on tr. below, turn.

7th row.—5 ch. 1 tr. on tr. below, twice 2 ch. 1 tr. on tr. below, 3 ch. 1 d.c. on next tr., now work along edge, 2 sht. tr. in next space, 1 sht. tr. on tr. stitch, 2 tr. in next space, 1 tr. on tr., 2 tr. in next space, 1 tr. on tr., 2 tr. in next space, 1 tr. in next tr., 3 sht. tr. in next space (as at beginning), 3 d.c. in last space (leaving the side of first row space free), turn. (There will be 18 sht. tr., tr., and d.c. stitches in all.)

8th row.—1 ch. 1 picot. 5 ch.), miss 2 d.c. below, 1 tr. in third d.c., 1 picot, miss one stitch below, 1 tr. in next. Repeat picot and tr., missing one stitch below till there are 8 picots, then 1 picot. 1 ch. 1 d.c. on d.c. stitch (after the 3 ch. of *7th row*), 3 d.c. in next space of 3 ch. 1 d.c. on tr. stitch. 2 d.c. in each space, 1 d.c. on each tr., turn.

9th row.—5 ch. miss 2 d.c., 1 tr. on third 2 ch. (miss 1 d.c.), 1 tr. on third, 2 ch. miss 2 d.c., 1 tr. on third. Repeat from second row. After length worked add the heading along the top.

10th row.—2 ch. 1 tr. in the end stitch of each row, turn, 2 d.c. in each space, 1 d.c. on each tr., turn. Again 2 ch. 1 tr. (missing 2 d.c. below) in each third d.c.

Ladies' Crocheted Auto Hood

MATERIAL

8 Fold Columbia Germantown
3 hanks

or 8 Fold Columbia Imported Germantown
4 hanks
1 Celluloid Crochet Hook No. 6
3 yards Ribbon No. 16

INSTRUCTIONS

Hood is started at the back, work back and forth in Sg. C taking the back stitch to form a rib. Chain 13, turn.

Row 1—1 Sg. C in each of the first 5 stitches, increase by making 3 Sg. C in each of 6th and 7th stitches, 1 Sg. C in each of the remaining stitches, chain 1, turn.

Row 2—1 Sg. C in each stitch, except in centre stitch of increases, make 3 Sg. C in each of these, chain 1, turn. Repeat 2d row until there are 6 ribs.

Now work back and forth without increasing until you have 11 more ribs. Finish the edge by making 1 slip stitch in each stitch. Sew up the back, work across the bottom with 1 slip stitch in each rib.

Turn back 3 ribs, trim as illustrated.

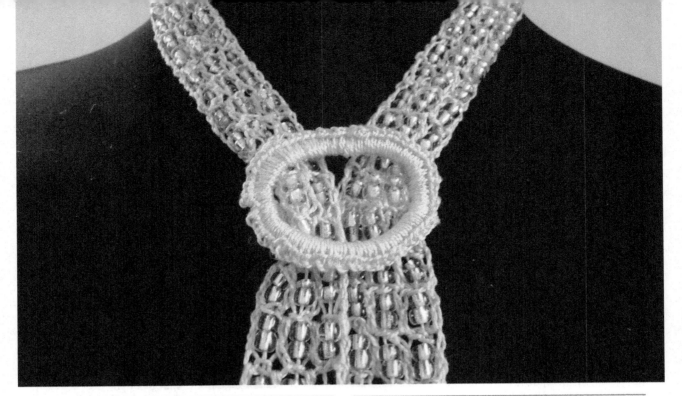

Beaded Tie

TRANSLATED AND CROCHETED
BY ELIZABETH LOVICK

INSPIRATION

From the original pattern:

"Crochet and Bead Tie for wear with a smart lace or silk blouse. A little beaded crochet tie, such as we illustrate, forms an exceedingly smart finish to a dainty blouse, and is, moreover, simplicity itself so far as the making thereof is concerned.

"The colour to be selected is entirely a matter of individual necessity, the model being shown being worked in pale blue silk decorated with fine cut beads in two colors, viz., green and gold. The tie measures half and inch wide and as 1 yard and 4 inches long. A half ounce ball of silk is ample, with one bunch of each shade of beads."

MATERIALS

10g Crochet Cotton No 8

2 mm crochet hook, or size to achieve tension

Seed beads in 2 colours to tone with thread

Tapestry needle to fit through the beads

Liz used Anchor Pearl Cotton No 8; 100% cotton; shade 291 Gold.

SIZE

About 1.5" wide and 40" long

TENSION

6 sts to 1"

CONSTRUCTION

The filet framework is crocheted first, then the beads are added using a tapestry needle. The buckle is worked separately.

PATTERN

Chain 10.

Row 1: 1 tr into 6th ch from hook, [1 ch, miss 1 ch, 1 tr in next ch] twice. Turn.

Row 2: 4 ch, [1 tr into top of tr, 1ch] twice, 1 tr into 3rd of 4 ch. Turn.

Repeat Row 2 until the tie measures 40" or the length required.

FINISHING

The Beading

Cut a length of thread at least 12" longer than the tie and thread into a beading needle. Tie one seed bead to the long end, then thread beads for about 3 or 4" for the tassel. Sew to the bottom chain of the tie.

Thread 2 beads, put the needle through the 1 ch space on the next row. Repeat for the whole length of the tie, occasionally taking a stitch through the chain space to stablise the beading thread. Take a stitch on the final 1 ch space, then thread beads to match the starting tassel. Finish the tassel off by passing the thread through the final bead as second time and tying off.

Repeat for the other two lines of chain spaces.

The Buckle

Wrap the thread round your first and second fingers 15 times. Slip off. Work dc into the ring, pushing them close together, making a stiff ring. Fasten off. Take a 40" length of thread and pass it across the ring several times. Cover this with buttonhole stitch, again pushing the stitches close together. Fasten off.

Grace's Mourning Shawl

TRANSLATED AND KNITTED BY JUNIPER ASKEW

INSPIRATION

This is a simple rectangular wrap with decorative borders at each end. Updated from the original pattern Martha Washington scarf, found in one of the Fleisher's Manuals.
— Juniper

MATERIALS

500 g 4 ply / fingering yarn

Pair 2.25 mm (US 1) needles, or size to achieve tension

One 5 mm (US 8) needle, or size to achieve tension

Row counter

Juniper used Rowan pure wool 4ply; 100% wool; 174 yds / 159 m per 50 g ball; shade 404 black

SIZE

16" by 81"

TENSION

31 sts and 28 rows to 4" over central pattern

NOTES

The texture of the main part of the wrap is achieved through alternation of thin and thick needles.

CONSTRUCTION

The centre of the wrap is worked first, from end to end. The lace borders are then knitted separately, from side to side, and sewn on.

PATTERN

CENTRE

With smaller needles, cast on 125 sts and knit 5 rows.

Row 1: With the smaller needle, knit.

Row 2: With the larger needle, knit.

Repeat Rows 1 and 2 until the piece measures 60".

On the smaller needles, knit 5 rows.

Cast off.

LACE BORDERS

With smaller needles cast on 26 sts. Work from the Lace Border Chart until the piece is the same length as the width of the centre, finishing after a 10th row.

Cast off.

Make a second piece the same.

FINISHING

Sew the Lace Borders to each end of the centre. Weave in all ends. Wash and dry flat, pinning the peaks of the lace out.

GRACE'S MOURNING SHAWL • LACE BORDER CHART

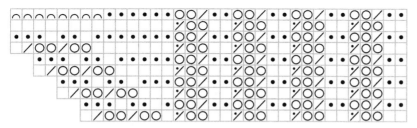

Row 1: [K2, yo, yo, p2tog] four times, k1, [yo, yo, k2tog] twice, k1.

Row 2: K3, p1, k2, p1, k1, [yo, yo, p2tog, k2] four times.

Row 3: [K2, yo, yo, p2tog] four times, k3, [yo, yo, k2tog] twice, k1.

Row 4: K3, p1, k2, p1, k3, [yo, yo, p2tog, k2] four times.

Row 5: [K2, yo, yo, p2tog] four times, k5, [yo, yo, k2tog] twice, k1.

Row 6: K3, p1, k2, p1, k5, [yo, yo, p2tog, k2] four times.

Row 7: [K2, yo, yo, p2tog] four times, k7, [yo, yo, k2tog] twice, k1.

Row 8: K3, p1, k2, p1, k7, [yo, yo, p2tog, k2] four times.

Row 9: [K2, yo, yo, p2tog] four times, k14.

Row 10: Cast off 8, k6, [yo, yo, p2tog, k2] four times.

Crocheted Shetland Shawl

TRANSLATED AND CROCHETED BY SAM BRAID

INSPIRATION

I stumbled across the Centenary Stitches project whilst researching early 19th century clothing. I cannot take any credit for this shawl, other than the translation into modern UK terminology. It was originally published in Beehive Knitting Booklet No. 9, Woolcraft, A Practical Guide to Knitting & Crochet [c.1915] — Sam

MATERIALS

200 g lace weight yarn

Sam used J&S 2 ply lace weight; 100% wool; 185 yds / 169 m per 25 g ball; shade Black

4 mm crochet hook, or size to achieve tension

Stitch marker

SIZE

30" deep by 60" wide

TENSION

2 shells to 3.5" in width

ABBREVIATIONS

Shell - 3 tr, 1 ch, 3 tr

NOTES

Do not turn at the end of a round.

Note that the start of a new round is in the middle of one side.

CONSTRUCTION

The shawl is worked in the round from the centre out.

PATTERN

CENTRE

Commencing at the centre of the shawl, 4 ch, join with a sl-st to form a ring.

Rnd 1:   3 ch, 2 tr into ring, *1 ch, 3 tr into ring. Repeat from * until there are 8 groups of trebles with the ch between each. Dc into first st of rnd.

Rnd 2:   *Work 3 tr, 1 ch, 3 tr, 1 ch, 3 tr into the next ch-sp, dc into next ch-sp. Repeat from * to end of rnd; dc into first dc.

Rnd 3:   *Work Shell into next ch-sp, 1 ch, work Shell into next ch-sp, dc into dc. Repeat from * to end of rnd.

Place marker to mark beginning of rnds.

Rnd 4:   *Work Shell into ch-sp, [1 ch, Shell into next ch-sp] twice, dc into dc. Repeat from * to the end of the rnd.

Rnd 5:   *Work Shell into ch-sp of first shell, dc into ch-sp, work 3 tr, 1 ch, 3 tr, 1 ch and 3 tr into ch-sp of next shell, dc in ch-sp after shell, Shell into ch-sp of next shell, dc into dc. Repeat from * to end of rnd.

Rnd 6:   *Shell into ch-sp, dc into dc. Repeat from * to corner (the 3 tr, c1 ch, 3 tr, 1 ch, 3tr of previous round). Shell into first ch-sp, ch, Shell into second ch-sp, dc into dc. Repeat from *. Finish by working [Shell into ch-sp, dc into dc] to end of rnd.

Rnd 7:   *Shell into ch-sp, dc into dc. Repeat from * to corner, Shell into ch-sp of first shell, 1 ch, Shell into ch-sp between shells, 1 ch, Shell into ch-sp of 2nd shell, dc into dc. Repeat from *. Finish by working [Shell into ch-sp, dc into dc] to end of rnd.

Rnd 8:   *Shell into ch-sp, dc into dc. Repeat from * to the corner, Shell into ch-sp of first shell, dc into ch-sp between shells, 3 tr, 1 ch, 3 tr, 1 ch, 3 tr into second shell, dc into ch-sp between shell, Shell into ch-sp of third shell. Repeat from *. Finish by working [Shell into ch-sp, dc into dc] to end of rnd.

Repeat Rnds 6 to 8 until the shawl measures 36" square, or the desired size. Finish after Rnd 8.

BORDER

Rnd 1:   Work Shell into each ch-sp (do not work dc between). Sl st into first st.

Rnd 2:   Into ch-sp of each shell work [4 tr, 1 ch, 4 tr; dc] between shells to end of rnd.

Rnd 3:   3 ch *1 tr into ch-sp, 5 ch, 1 dc in the first ch to make a picot, repeat from * until 7 tr and picots are worked, 3 ch, dc into dc, 3 ch, repeat from beginning of rnd.

Fasten off.

FINISHING

Weave in all ends. Wash and dry flat.

Whilst staying with my Grandma, (an avid knitter) at the tender age of eight, I picked up the needles for the first time and learnt along side her. I made my Grandad a very long, thin scarf in blue, brown and orange (colours of the 70's) and although I don't think he ever wore it, years later when we where sorting through things we found it neatly folded in his chest of drawers. I picked up the hook a little later, learnt the basics from my mum and haven't looked back since. As the years ebb and flow, I alternate in favour between the two. — Sam

Fife Collarette and Muff

TRANSLATED BY ELIZABETH LOVICK
COLLARETTE KNITTED BY KATY-JAYNE LINTOTT • MUFF KNITTED BY KIRSTY JOHNSTON

INSPIRATION

The collarette was in one of the Weldon's booklets and the Muff was in the 1900 edition of The Book of Hows. They belong together! The Ice yarn gives a lovely 'fur' look, but they can be knitted in plain aran weight yarn if preferred. — Liz

MATERIALS

Collarette

100 g DK eyelash or boucle yarn

Pair 6 mm (US 10) needles, or size to achieve tension

2 large hooks and eyes

1 m 3" wide ribbon

Muff

250 g DK eyelash or boucle yarn

Pair 5 mm (UK 8) needles, or size to achieve tension

2 m 3" wide ribbon

Polyester wadding about 14" by 24"

SIZE

Collarette, with a circumference of 21" at the top, fits most women. Muff is about 14" across and 24" in circumference

TENSION

14 sts and 22 rows over stocking stitch

ABBREVIATIONS

Loop st - insert the needle tip as if to knit. Pass the yarn anticlockwise round the needle tip and your finger twice, then round the needle only. Complete the stitch as usual. There are three loops on the needle for each stitch knitted

NOTES

The exact tension is not crucial as the fabric is stretchy.

CONSTRUCTION

The collarette is a single piece knitted in short rows. The muff consists of an outer in loop stitch and a stocking stitch inner, with wadding between.

PATTERN

MUFF

MAIN PIECE
Cast on 40 sts and knit 1 row.

Row 1: K1, loop st to last st, k1.

Row 2: K, knitting all three loops from each loop stitch together

Repeat Rows 1 and 2 until the piece measures 24", finishing with a knit row.

Cast off.

LINING
Cast on 36 sts. Work in stocking stitch for 18". Cast off.

Finishing
Sew the cast on and cast off edges of the main piece together. Sew the row ends of the lining to the row ends of the main piece together, stretching the lining to fit.

Cut a piece of wadding to size and

insert between the main piece and the lining. Sew the cast on and cast off edges of the lining together.

Attach ribbons and bows as desired.

COLLARETTE

Using the yarn double throughout, cast on 12 sts.

Row 1:   Loop st.

Row 2:   K.

Row 3:   Loop st 1; increase in next st by working 1 loop st into each of the two strands, loop stitch to end of row.

Row 4:   K.

Rows 5 and 6:   As Rows 3 and 4.

Row 7:   As Row 3.   15 sts

Row 8:   K2, turn.

Row 9:   Loop st 2.

Row 10:   K4, turn.

Row 11:   Loop st 4.

Row 12:   K6, turn.

Row 13:   Loop st 6.

Rows 14 and 15:   As Rows 10 and 11.

Rows 16 and 17:   As Rows 8 and 9.

Row 18:   K to last 2 sts, k2tog.   14 sts

Row 19:   Loop st across row.

Rows 20 to 23:   Repeat Rows 18 and 19 twice.   12 sts

Row 24:   K.

Repeat Rows 3 to 24 six times more.

Cast off.

FINISHING

Weave in ends. Sew two hooks and eyes to the short ends.

Originally the collarette was worn with the longer edge upwards, framing the face. It can also be worn as a collar with the longer edge down.

Angora Cape & Hat

CAPE TRANSLATED & HAT DESIGNED BY ELIZABETH LOVICK

INSPIRATION

I was flicking through one of my Bear Brand books and saw this cape. I thought it would look equally good in the film and on the street today. I designed the hat to match it. — Liz

KNITTED BY
AILEEN YORKE

MATERIALS

For the Cape:

40 (45, 50, 60, 70, 90) g 4 ply angora yarn

Pair 5 mm (US6) needles, or size to achieve tension

3 mm crochet hook and a small amount of stuffing OR two buttons about 0.75" diameter

For the Hat:

30 (40, 50, 60, 70, 90) g 4 ply angora yarn

Pair 3.5 mm (US 4) needles, or size to achieve tension

6 stitch markers

Aileen used Rowan Angora Haze; 69% angora, 20% PA, 11% wool; shade Cuddle

SIZE

Toddler (child, teen, adult, plus)

TENSION

Cape: 20 sts and 28 rows to 4" over garter stitch on larger needles

Hat: 28 sts and 48 rows to 4" over garter stitch on smaller needles

NOTES

The cape looks scraggy while being knitted, but comes together once the buttons and fringe have been added!

CONSTRUCTION

The cape is knitted from the left front, round the back to the right front. The band of the hat is knitted first, then stitches are picked up along one edge for the crown.

PATTERN

CAPE

Cast on 4 (5, 5, 7, 8) sts and knit 1 row.

Row 1:   Cast on 3 (3, 4, 5, 6) sts, knit to end of row.

Row 2:   Knit.

Repeat Rows 1 and 2 twice more. 13 (14, 18, 22, 26) sts

Knit 28 (32, 38, 44, 44) rows straight. *Adjust right front length here.*

Next Row: Cast on 17 (26, 32, 38, 44) sts. 30 (40, 50, 60, 70) sts

Knit straight for another 12 (14, 17, 22, 25)", finishing at the shaped edge. *Adjust back width here.*

Next Row: Cast off 17 (26, 32, 38, 44) sts. 13 (14, 18, 22, 26) sts

Knit 29 (33, 39, 45, 45) rows straight. *Adjust left front length here.*

Next Row: Cast off 3 (3, 4, 5, 6) sts, k to end of row.

Next Row: Knit.

Repeat these rows twice more. 4 (5, 6, 7, 8) sts

Cast off.

Finishing

Weave in all ends. Make a fringe about 4" long and attach to the

edges as shown in the photo. Either make two crocheted buttons of about 0.75" diameter or use bought buttons. Sew in place on the fronts. Crochet a 3" chain and sew the ends under one button, forming a loop for the other button.

HAT

Band

Cast on 24 (28, 30, 34, 38) sts and work in garter stitch until the strip measures 11 (12, 14, 16, 18)" unstretched. Cast off.

Crown

Pick up and knit 76 (80, 92, 100, 116) sts along one long edge of the band.

Foundation Row (WS): *K1, kfb. Repeat from * to end of row. 114 (120, 138, 150, 174) sts

Work in garter stitch until the Crown measures 6 (7, 8, 10, 12)", finishing after an odd numbered row.

Next Row (WS): *K19 (20, 23, 25, 29), PM. Repeat from * to end of row.

Shape the top of the crown as follows:

Row 1 (RS): *K2tog, k to M, SM. Repeat from * to end of row.

Row 2: K.

Repeat these two rows until 36 sts remain.

Next Row: K2tog along row.

Next Row: K2tog along row.

Break yarn and thread through remaining stitches.

Finishing

Sew the band and crown seam.

Run a thread up the back seam from the top of the band to the start of the crown shaping. Pull to gather, then run back down the seam to stabilise. Make three crocheted buttons about 2 cm diameter and sew to this gathered section, arranging and sewing through the gathers as desired. Wash and dry as flat as possible.

In wear, turn the band in half. The hat may be worn with the buttons at the front, the back or the side.

Poppy Shawl

DESIGNED AND KNITTED BY ELIZABETH LOVICK

INSPIRATION

Pauline asked me to design a shawl for giving away at the exhibition. I wanted something of the period, but which could be worn today. I was thinking of the Flander's poppies, so I took two stitch patterns from a Butterick book 'The Art of Knitting' 1897, which suggested to me the texture of the flower's centre and the ruffled petals.

MATERIALS

100g 4 ply/fingering yarn

Pair 5 mm (US 8) needle, or size to achieve tension

32" or longer circular 5 mm (US 8) needle

Row counter

Liz used Jamieson's Spindrift; 100% wool; 117 yds / 105 m per 25 g ball; shade 524, Poppy

SIZE

Centre 13" deep by 46" wide; border 3" deep

TENSION

18 sts and 28 rows to 4" over centre pattern

CONSTRUCTION

The centre is knitted first from the tip up. Stitches are picked up and the border is knitted outwards.

PATTERN

THE CENTRE

Cast on 8 sts loosely.

Work from Centre Chart until there are 208 sts on the needle.

Next Row: S1p, k1, yo, k to last 2 sts, yo, k2.

Repeat this row once more. 212 sts

Cast off.

THE BORDER

With WSF, and using the circular needle, pick up 52 sts from the first edge, pick up 8 sts from the cast on edge, pick up 52 from the other edge. Work to and fro as follows.

Row 1 (RS): S1p, k1, yo, *k1, yo, k1. Repeat from * to last 2 sts, yo, k2. 168 sts

Row 2: S1p, k3, *p4, k2. Repeat from * to last 4 sts, k4.

Row 3: S1p, k1, *p2, k4. Repeat from * to last 4 sts, p2, k2.

Row 4: As Row 2.

Now work through the 18 rows of the Border Chart.

POPPY SHAWL • CENTRE CHART

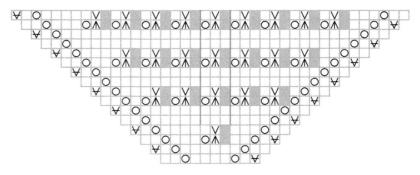

Row 1: Slp, k1, yo, k4, yo, k2.

Row 2: Slp, k1, yo, k6, yo, k2.

Row 3: Slp, k1, yo, k2, k3togtbl, yo, k3, yo, k2.

Row 4: Slp, k1, yo, k5, kfb, k3, yo, k2.

Row 5: Slp, k1, yo, knit to last 2 sts, yo, k2.

Row 6: As Row 5.

Row 7: Slp, k1, yo, [k3togtbl, yo] to last 3 sts, k1, yo, k2.

Row 8: Slp, k1, yo, k3, [kfb, k1] to last 2 sts, yo, k2.

Rows 9 and 10: As Row 5.

Row 11: Slp, k1, yo, k1, [k3togtbl, yo] to last 4 sts, k2, yo, k2.

Cast off loosely.

FINISHING

Weave in all ends. Wash and dress/block flat. If you have them, run dressing wires through the edges of the centre, and let the border form ruffles. Otherwise, pin out, or lay the wet shawl on fluffy towels and smooth out into shape, again allowing the border to form ruffles.

Row 12: Slp, k1, yo, k4, [kfb, k1] to last 3 sts, k1, yo, k2.

Rows 13 and 14: As Row 5.

Row 15: Slp, k1, yo, k2, [k3togtbl, yo] to last 5 sts, k3, yo, k2.

Row 16: Slp, k1, yo, k5, [kfb, k1] to last 4 sts, k2, yo, k2.

Rows 5 to 16 form the pattern. Repeat them as required.

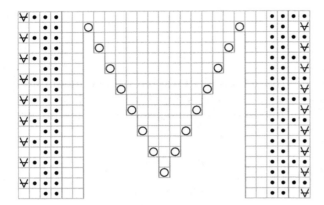

Row 1: S1p, k1, *p2, k4. Repeat from * to last 4 sts, p2, k2.

Row 2: S1p, k3, *p4, k2. Repeat from * to last 2 sts, k2.

Row 3: S1p, k1, *p2, k2, yo, k2. Repeat from * to last 4 sts, p2, k2.

Row 4: S1p, k3, *p5, k2. Repeat from * to last 2 sts, k2.

Row 5: S1p, k1, *p2, k2, yo, k1, yo, k2. Repeat from * to last 4 sts, p2, k2.

Row 6: S1p, k3, *p7, k2. Repeat from * to last 2 sts, k2.

Row 7: S1p, k1, *p2, k2, yo, k3, yo, k2. Repeat from * to last 4 sts, p2, k2.

Row 8: S1p, k3, *p9, k2. Repeat from * to last 2 sts, k2.

Row 9: S1p, k1, *p2, k2, yo, k5, yo, k2. Repeat from * to last 4 sts, p2, k2.

Row 10: S1p, k3, *p11, k2. Repeat from * to last 2 sts, k2.

Row 11: S1p, k1, *p2, k2, yo, k7, yo, k2. Repeat from * to last 4 sts, p2, k2.

Row 12: S1p, k3, *p13, k2. Repeat from * to last 2 sts, k2.

Row 13: S1p, k1, *p2, k2, yo, k9, yo, k2. Repeat from * to last 4 sts, p2, k2.

Row 14: S1p, k3, *p15, k2. Repeat from * to last 2 sts, k2.

Row 15: S1p, k1, *p2, k2, yo, k11, yo, k2. Repeat from * to last 4 sts, p2, k2.

Row 16: S1p, k3, *p17, k2. Repeat from * to last 2 sts, k2.

Row 17: S1p, k1, *p2, k2, yo, k13, yo, k2. Repeat from * to last 4 sts, p2, k2.

Row 18: S1p, k3, *p19, k2. Repeat from * to last 2 sts, k2.

Baby Lace (Pattern No. 10)

Abbreviations.—Ch., chain; d.c., double crochet; tr., treble.

Ardern's Lace Cotton, No. 20. In No. 30 lace cotton the pattern is particularly dainty for babies' linen.

1st row.—3 ch. 1 picot (5 ch. 1 d.c. in first ch.), 3 ch. 1 picot, for length desired, turn.

2nd row.—11 ch. 1 d.c. on first picot, * 4 ch. 2 picots, 4 ch. miss 1 picot below (of *1st row*), 1 d.c. in next picot. Repeat from *.

|Fig. 10.

3rd row.—7 ch., * 1 d.c. in first picot below, 3 picots, 1 d.c. in second picot below, 4 ch. 1 tr. on next picot, 1 picot, 1 tr. in same place, 1 picot, 1 tr. in next picot, 1 picot, 1 tr. in same place, 4 ch. Repeat from * to end.

4th row.—Along the top work 1 tr. in picot below, 3 ch. 1 tr. in next picot. * 3 ch. 1 tr. in next picot. Repeat from *.

Villager's Shawl

DESIGNED BY ELIZABETH LOVICK • KNITTED BY KIRSTY JOHNSTON

MATERIALS

200 (300, 500) g 4 ply yarn

Pair 5 mm (US 8) needles, or size to achieve tension

5 mm (US 8) circular needle

Contrast waste yarn

Stitch holders or lengths of thread

8 stitch markers

Row counter

Kirsty used Texere Jura; 100% wool; 400 yds / 360 m per 100 g; shade Walnut

Above: Villager Shawl worked in an alternate yarn. Following page: Villager Shawl worked in Texere Jura.

SIZE

Approx 48 (60, 72)" square

TENSION

18 sts and 36 rows to 4" over garter stitch

CONSTRUCTION

The centre square is knitted first to and fro. Stitches are picked up round the centre and the border is knitted outwards in the round. Finally the lace is knitted to and fro, removing 5 sts from the border for each pattern repeat.

PATTERN

THE CENTRE

With 5 mm needles and MC, cast on 101 (119, 137) sts.

Row 1: S1p, k to end of row.

Repeat Row 1 until you have worked 202 (238, 274) rows.

Do not break yarn.

PREPARATION FOR THE BORDER

Using the 5 mm circular needle, knit the 101 (119, 137) live sts, pick up and knit 101 (119, 137) sts down the side of the centre, pick up and knit 101 (119, 137) sts from the cast on edge, pick up and knit 101 (119, 137) sts from the other side of the centre. Now knit the first 5 sts. This will be start of subsequent rounds.

Next Rnd: *PM, k90 (108, 126), PM, k2, [yo, k1] four times, [k1, yo] three times, k2. Repeat from * three times more.

You now have four sides of 90 (108, 126) sts and four corners of 18 sts with markers between.

BORDER

Work from the Side Border and Corner Border Charts, repeating the Side Border Chart as necessary, and working the Corner Border Chart once between the markers. If using several colours, change colour on the knit row after the purl row.

If you are NOT working the Lace Chart, purl one round, then cast off loosely.

LACE

With 5 mm needles and a length of waste yarn of a different colour, cast on 17 sts.

Change to the working yarn and work through the Lace Chart, using one straight needle and the end of the circ. Once through the Lace Chart forms one point. Continue in this way until you have removed all the border stitches, finishing after a 9th row.

FINISHING

Sew in ends, leaving tails of about 3". Wash and dress the shawl, placing a pin in each peak of the edging to accentuate the points. Once dry, remove and trim the long ends.

INSPIRATION

Throughout the Nineteenth and early Twentieth Centuries, woman of all classes wore shawls. For everyday wear, triangular or square shawls were worn over the shoulders and tied or pinned to the breast. The centre of these shawls was usually garter stitch, but many knitters substituted their own patterns. Sometimes the lace was added round the edge, sometimes the border was left to form scallops. — Liz

VILLAGER SHAWL • LACE CHART

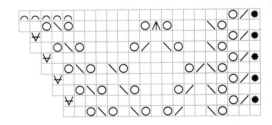

Row 1: K3, yo, ssk, k2, k2tog, yo, (k1, yo, ssk) twice, yo, k2.

Row 2: S1p, k to last 5 sts, yo, ssk, ktb.

Row 3: K3, yo, ssk, k1, k2tog, yo, k3, yo, ssk, k1, yo, ssk, yo, k2.

Row 4: As Row 2.

Row 5: K3, yo, ssk, k2tog, yo, k4, k2tog, yo, ssk, k1, yo, ssk, yo, k2.

Row 6: As Row 2.

Row 7: K3, yo, ssk, k2, yo, ssk, k1, k2tog, yo, k4, yo, ssk, yo, k2.

Row 8: As Row 2.

Row 9: K3, yo, ssk, k3, yo, k3togtbl, yo, k6, yo, ssk, yo, k2.

Row 10: Cast off 5, k to last 5 sts, yo, ssk, ktbl.

These 10 rows form the pattern. Repeat them as required.

SIDE BORDER CHART

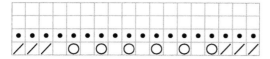

Rnd 1: K2tog three times, [yo, k1] six times, k2tog three times.

Rnd 2: P.

Rnd 3: K.

Rnd 4: K.

These 4 rounds form the pattern. Repeat them as required.

TEXERE YARNS LTD

Texere Jura is a 4-ply yarn spun from 90% Wool with 10% Nylon giving it Strength and Durability. It is available in a range of Bright and Soft Shades all with a Natural Soft Lustre. Not only is Jura a great knitting yarn for Garments and Socks, but it's ideal for Weaving in the warp and weft, Tapestry and tablet weaving, braiding into Strong Braids and cords and will Crochet into Vessels, Bags and Throws.

"Texere Jura is the very best, sir. You can count on that."

Texere Yarns Ltd
College Mill
Barkerend Road
Bradford
BD1 4AU
www.texere-yarns.co.uk

CORNER BORDER CHART

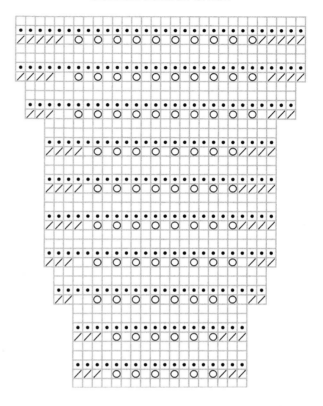

Rnd 1: [Yo, k2tog] nine times.

Rnd 2: P.

Rnd 3: K.

Rnd 4: K.

Rnd 5: K2tog three times, [yo, k1] six times, k2tog three times.

Rnd 6: P.

Rnd 7: K.

Rnd 8: K.

Rnds 9 to 16: Repeat Rnds 5 to 8 twice more.

Rnd 17: K2tog twice, [k1, yo] eight times, k2, k2tog twice.

Rnd 18: P.

Rnd 19: K.

Rnd 20: K.

Rnd 21: K2tog three times, [k1, yo] eight times, k2, k2tog three times.

Rnd 22: P.

Rnd 23: K.

Rnd 24: K.

Rnd 25: K2tog four times, [yo, k1] eight times, k2tog four times.

Rnd 26: P.

Rnd 27: K.

Rnd 28: K.

Rnds 29 to 36: Repeat Rnds 25 to 28 twice more.

Rnd 37: K2tog three times, [k1, yo] ten times, k2, k2tog three times.

Rnd 38: P.

Rnd 39: K.

Rnd 40: K.

Rnd 41: K2tog four times, [k1, yo] ten times, k2, k2tog four times.

Rnd 42: P.

Rnd 43: K.

Rnd 44: K.

Rnd 45: K2tog five times, [yo, k1] ten times, k2tog five times.

Rnd 46: P.

Rnd 47: K.

Pine Cone Shawl

DESIGNED BY ELIZABETH LOVICK
KNITTED BY CATHERINE HOPKINS

INSPIRATION

I found the pattern for the centre in one of my pattern books from about 1900. It is very different from most stitch patterns we use today. The original had some errors in the instructions, and I worked with Catherine to sort out what the correct stitch pattern was. The edging is another stitch pattern from the period.

MATERIALS

350 g DK yarn

Pair 5 mm (US 8) needles, or size to achieve tension

2 Stitch markers

Row counter

Catherine used an old yarn, Falcon Wools 4 ply; 100% wool; shade Shrimp. Note that it is labelled a 4 ply but is the thickness of a modern DK.

SIZE

42" square excluding fringe; fringe is 6" long

TENSION

15 sts and 22 rows to 4" over Pine Cone pattern

CONSTRUCTION

The centre is knitted first. The fringe is knitted separately and sewn on.

PATTERN

CENTRE

Cast on 168 sts and knit 5 rows.

Next Row: K3, PM, k to last 3 sts, PM, k3.

Work from the chart, placing it as follows:

Row 1:   K3, SM, work from the chart to M, SM, k3.

Continue in this way until the piece measures about 41", finishing after a 24th row of the pattern.

Knit 5 rows. Cast off.

FRINGE

With waste yarn, cast on 14 sts. Change to main yarn and work in garter stitch until the strip is long enough to go round centre, including an extra 30 rows for each corner.

Next Row: Cast off 4, slip other 10 sts off the needle.

Break yarn.

FINISHING

Sew the edging to the shawl centre, using whip stitch or other flat stitch. Remove the waste yarn at the start of the edging, and sew the 4 cast off sts to the inner 4 live sts st the start of the fringe. Now pull the remaining 10 sts of the edging back to form the fringe.

Weave in all ends. Wash and dry flat.

PINE CONE CHART

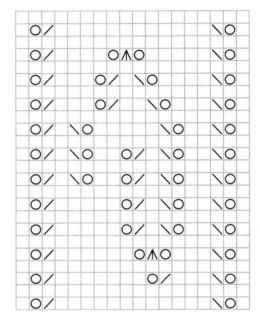

Row 1 (RS):   K1, yo, ssk, k12, k2tog, yo, k1.

Row 2 and all WS rows: P.

Row 3:   K1, yo, ssk, k3, k2tog, yo, k7, k2tog, yo, k1.

Row 5:   K1, yo, ssk, k3, yo, k3togtbl, yo, k6, k2tog, yo, k1.

Row 7:   K1, yo, ssk, k2, yo, ssk, k1, k2tog, yo, k5, k2tog, yo, k1.

Row 9:   As Row 7.

Row 11:   K1, yo, ssk, [k2, yo, ssk, k1, k2tog, yo] twice, k1.

Row 13:   As Row 11.

Row 15:   K1, yo, ssk, k2, yo, ssk, k5, yo, ssk, k1, k2tog, yo, k1.

Row 17:   K1, yo, ssk, k3, yo, ssk, k2, k2tog, yo, k3, k2tog, yo, k1.

Row 19:   K1, yo, ssk, k4, yo, ssk, k1, k2tog, yo, k3, k2tog, yo, k1.

Row 21:   K1, yo, ssk, k5, yo, k3togtbl, yo, k4, k2tog, yo, k1.

Row 23:   As Row 1.

Row 24:   P.

Nubia Scarf

TRANSLATED AND CROCHETED BY ALISON CASSERLY

Molly Marie Buckley models the Nubia Scarf. © Thomas Hinckley

MATERIALS
150 g 4ply/fingering yarn
3.5 mm hook

SIZE
45" wide including ties by 15" deep at the point

TENSION
5 shells to 4"

ABBREVIATIONS
Shell - [4 tr, 4 ch, sl st into the top of the 4th tr, 3 tr] into the same st

NOTES
A chain loop is made in the middle stitch of each cluster, and the next row is worked into that loop.

CONSTRUCTION
The scarf is length-wise, making the ties first, adding the triangular piece after. Finally the border is worked round the whole scarf.

PATTERN
Ch 278 sts.

Row 1: Miss 3 sts, work shell, miss 3 sts, 1 tr into next st, Repeat from * to end of row. 4 ch. Turn.

Row 2: *Work shell into the chain loop of shell on previous row, 1 tr into top of tr of previous row. Rep from * to the end of the row. Turn.

Repeat Row 2 3 times more.

Break yarn & rejoin at the top of the 6th shell, work as set until 6 shells from the end. Work one less shell on every row until there are just 2 shells on the row. Turn. Do not break yarn.

BORDER
4 ch. * 5 tr into next 4 ch loop, 5ch, sl st into the top of the 5th tr, 4 tr. Work 1 tr into each of the next 2 ch spaces. Rep from * along the sides of the triangle edge.

Along the straight edge work 1 tr into each tr and a shell into each 4 ch loop.

In corners, work 7 tr, 5 ch loop, 6 tr. Work in this way round the whole scarf.

Fasten off.

FINISHING
Weave in ends. Wash gently in warm water, and block to shape.

Print of the Wave Wrap

DESIGNED BY ELIZABETH LOVICK • KNITTED BY SAM BRAID

INSPIRATION

This wrap, in a version of the popular Print of the Wave pattern, was adapted from a shawl in one of the early Paton's Woolcraft books.

MATERIALS

125 g 640 yds / 575 m DK yarn

Pair 5.5 mm (US 9) needles, or size to achieve tension

Row counter

Crochet hook for fringe

Sam used The Little Knitting Company DK; 50% angora, 30% wool, 20% nylon; 128 yds / 115 m per 25g ball.

SIZE

40" by 80" excluding the fringe

TENSION

6.5 sts and 8.5 rows to 4" over pattern

NOTES

The pattern can be used for a shawl by adding multiples of 26 sts to the number cast on, and working until the piece is square.

PATTERN

Cast on 64 sts loosely, and knit 10 rows.

Change to the pattern, and work from the chart until the work measures 78" or desired length.

Knit 10 rows.

Cast off.

FINISHING

Weave in all ends. Make a fringe about 4" long across the short ends of the wrap. Wash and dry flat, pinning to size.

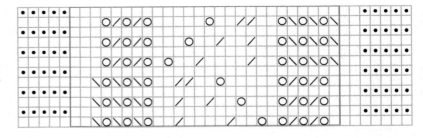

PRINT OF THE WAVE

Row 1: K5, *k3, [yo, k2tog] twice, yo, k1, yo, k2, k2tog, k4, k2tog, k2, [yo, ssk] three times. Repeat from * to last 7 sts, k7.

Row 2 and all alternate rows: K5, p to last 5 sts, k5.

Row 3: K5, *k3, [yo, k2tog] twice, yo, k3, yo, [k2, k2tog] twice, k2, [yo, ssk] three times. Repeat from * to last 7 sts, k7.

Row 5: K5, *k3, [yo, k2tog] twice, yo, k5, yo, k2, k2tog twice, k2, [yo, ssk] three times. Repeat from * to last 7 sts, k7.

Row 7: K5, *k2, [ssk, yo] three times, k2, k2tog, k4, k2tog, k2, yo, k1, [yo, k2tog] twice, yo. Repeat from * to last 8 sts, k8.

Row 9: K5, *k2, [ssk, yo] three times, [k2, k2tog] twice, k2, yo, k3, [yo, k2tog] twice, yo. Repeat from * to last 8 sts, k8.

Row 11: K5, *k2, [ssk, yo] three times, k2, k2tog twice, k2, yo, k5, [yo, k2tog] twice, yo. Repeat from * to last 8 sts, k8.

Row 12: As Row 2.

These 12 rows form the pattern. Repeat as required.

MATERIALS

450 g DK yarn

Pair 4 mm (US 6) needles, or size to achieve tension

Tina used Rowan Pure Wool DK; 100% wool; 142 yds / 130 m per 50 g ball; shades 052 and 030

SIZE

23" wide and 46" long

TENSION

21 sts and 40 rows to 4" over garter stitch

ABBREVIATIONS

m1f - lift the strand before next stitch and knit into the front of it.

NOTES

If you want to add broad bands of colour, as Tina did, knit a whole ball of yarn and switch to the different colour at an end of row.

PATTERN

Cast on 120 and knit 25 rows.

Start pattern as follows:

Row 1 (RS): K10, p100, k10.

Row 2: K11, k2tog 49 times, k11.

Row 3: K11, [m1f, k1] 49 times, k11.

Row 4: K.

Repeat Rows 1 to 4 until the pattern section measures 41", finishing after a 4th row. Adjust length here.

Knit 25 rows.

Cast off.

FINISHING

Weave in all ends. Wash and dry flat.

Mersey Wrap

TRANSLATED AND KNITTED BY TINA KINNAR

INSPIRATION

The pattern comes from one of the Fleicher's Knitting and Crocheting Manuals. I was taught to knit by my Mum and Grandmother. I recall doing some as a small child, but I really got interested in it in my early 20s, when I knitted a few jumpers for myself. Then interest waned and I didn't pick up needles again until about 20 years later, when a friend reminded me of the basics, and I was hooked. I prefer making small items like gloves and hats, and this is one of the biggest items I've knitted. — Tina

Cabled Cardi

TRANSLATED BY JUDITH A BRODNICKI • KNITTED BY KAREN EVANS

MATERIALS

600 (700, 800, 900, 1100, 1200, 1400, 1500) g DK
weight yarn

Pair 4 mm (US 6) needles, or size to achieve tension

1 stitch marker

4 row markers

*Karen used Rowan Pure Wool DK; 100% wool; 136
yds/124 m per 50 g ball; shade Black*

SIZE

Sizes: XS (S, M, L, 1X, 2X, 3X, 4X)

Actual Chest: 36 (40, 44, 48, 52, 56, 60, 64)"

Back Length: 23.5 (23.5, 23.5, 24.5, 25, 25, 25.5,
25.5)"

Sleeve Length: 16 (16, 16, 16, 18, 18, 18, 18)"

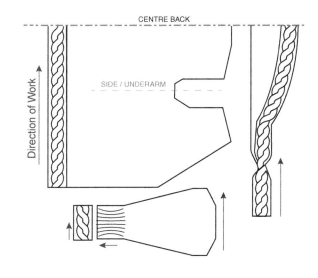

TENSION

22 sts and 40 rows to 4" in garter stitch

CONSTRUCTION

The body is worked sideways from the Right Center Front to the Left Center Front. Sleeves are initially worked sideways, then cuff ribbing is picked up from the edge; a cabled border is worked separately. Cabled Front Bands and Collar are worked separately, then sewn onto the cardigan.

PATTERN

RIGHT FRONT

Cast on 82 sts for all sizes. Note that right side rows start at the neck and finish at the hem.

Row 1(RS): K58, PM, work the Cable Chart over the next 18 sts, PM, k to end of row.

Row 2 (WS): K to M, SM, work the Cable Chart over the next 18 sts, SM, k to end of row.

This sets the pattern.

Keeping the pattern correct, increase 1 st at the neck edge on every row (every row, two rows in three, two rows in three, two rows in three, two rows in three, two rows in three, every other row) until there are a total of 124 (126, 126, 130, 132, 132, 136, 136) sts, ending after working a WS row.

Right Front Shoulder
*Work 8 (8, 8, 8, 8, 10, 10, 10) rows in patt.

Next Row: K1, k2tog, patt to end of row.

Next Row: In patt.

Repeat from * 3 times more. 120 (122, 122, 126, 128, 128, 132, 132) sts

Right Armhole
Row 1: Cast off 28 (26, 30, 30, 32, 32, 36, 38) sts, patt to end of row.

Row 2: In patt.

Row 3: Cast off 2 sts patt to end of row.

Row 4: In patt.

Repeat Rows 3 and 4 6 (8, 6, 8, 8, 8, 8, 7) times more. 78 sts remain.

Work straight in patt for 16 (24, 22, 26, 30, 42, 48, 40) rows.

Next Row: Cast on 2 sts, patt to end of row.

Next Row: In patt.

Repeat these two rows 1 (2, 3, 3, 4, 4, 6, 6) times more.

Next Row: Cast on 38 (38, 36, 40, 40, 40, 40, 40) sts, patt to end of row. 120 (122, 122, 126, 128, 128, 132, 132) sts

Next Row: In patt.

BACK

Right Back Shoulder
*Row 1: K1, kfb, patt to end of row.

Work 9 (9, 9, 9, 9, 9, 11, 11, 11) rows in patt.

Repeat from * 3 more times.

124 (126, 126, 130, 132, 132, 136, 136) sts

Work 25 (27, 30, 33, 34, 35, 35, 38) rows in patt. Place row marker at neck edge to signify center back, then work 25 (27, 30, 33, 34, 35, 35, 38) more rows in patt.

Left Back Shoulder
*Work 8 (8, 8, 8, 8, 10, 10, 10) rows in patt.

Next Row: K1, k2tog, patt to end of row.

Next Row: In patt.

Repeat from * 3 times more. 120 (122, 122, 126, 128, 128, 132, 132) sts

Left Armhole
Row 1 (RS): Cast off 38 (38, 36, 40, 40, 40, 40, 40) sts, patt to end of row.

Row 2: In patt.

Row 3: Cast off 2 sts, patt to end of row.

Row 4: In patt.

Repeat Rows 3 and 4 1 (2, 3, 3, 4, 4, 6, 6) times more. 78 sts remain.

Work in patt for 16 (24, 22, 26, 30, 42, 48, 40) rows.

Next Row: Cast on 2, patt to end of row.

Next Row: In patt.

Repeat these two rows 6 (8, 6, 8, 8, 8, 8, 7) times more.

Next Row: Cast on 28 (26, 30, 30, 32, 32, 36, 38) sts. 120 (122, 122, 126, 128, 128, 132, 132) sts

LEFT FRONT

Shape Left Front Shoulder
Row 1: K1, kfb, patt to end of row.

Row 2: In patt.

Work 8 (8, 8, 8, 8, 10, 10, 10) rows in patt.

Repeat from * 3 more times. 124 (126, 126, 130, 132, 132, 136, 136) sts

Keeping the pattern correct, decrease 1 st at the neck edge on every row (every row, two rows in three, two rows in three, two rows in three, two rows in three, two rows in three, every other row) until there are a total of 82 sts, ending after working a WS row.

Cast off all sts.

SLEEVES

Cast on 9 (9, 9, 9, 10, 10, 10, 10) sts and knit 1 row.

Increase to the wrist as follows:

Row 1 (RS): Cast on 9 (9, 9, 9, 10, 10, 10, 10), k to end of row.

Row 2: Knit.

Repeat Rows 1 and 2 six times more. 72 (72, 72, 72, 80, 80, 80, 80) sts

Shape the sleeve cap as follows:

Row 1: K to last 2 sts, kfb, k1.

Row 2: Knit.

Repeat these 2 rows 21 (23, 23, 27, 22, 29, 34, 39) times more. 94 (96, 96, 100, 103, 110, 115, 120) sts

Knit 24 (24, 32, 32, 72, 20, 44, 40) rows.

Next Row: K to last 3 sts, ssk, k1.

Next Row: Knit.

Repeat these 2 rows 21 (23, 23, 27, 22, 29, 34, 39) times more. 72 (72, 72, 72, 80, 80, 80, 80) sts

Decrease sleeves:
Row 1 (RS): Knit.

Row 2: Cast off 9 (9, 9, 9, 10, 10,

10, 10), k to end of row.

Repeat Rows 1 and 2 six more times.

Cast off remaining stitches.

Wrist
With RS facing, pick up and knit 56 (60, 64, 72, 82, 90, 102, 108) sts along the wrist edge.

Work 32 rows in k1, p1 rib.

Cast off in rib.

CABLED TURN-BACK CUFF

Cast on 21 sts and work in garter stitch with the Cable Chart:

Row 1 (RS):   K3, PM, work the Cable Chart over the next 18 sts.

Row 2:   Work the Cable Chart to M, SM, k3.

This sets the pattern.

Keeping the pattern correct, work until the piece measures 10 (11, 11.5, 13, 15, 16.5, 18.5, 19.5)".

Cast off.

FRONT BANDS AND COLLAR

Right Front Band
Cast on 24 sts and work in garter stitch with the Cable Chart:

Row 1 (RS):   K6, PM, work the Cable Chart over the next 18 sts.

Row 2:   Work the Cable Chart to M, SM, k6.

This sets the pattern.

Keeping the pattern correct, work through the Cable Chart a total of 13 times, then Rows 1 to 5 again.

Now reverse the knit side of the cable as follows:

Row 1 (RS):   Work the 1st row of the Reversed Cable Chart to M, SM, k to end of row.

Row 2:   K to M, SM, work the 2nd row of the Reversed Cable Chart.

Rows 3 to 10:   Work through the chart as set.

Collar Increases
Keeping the 6 st garter stitch border and Reversed Cable Chart correct, increase for the collar as follows, working the increased stitches in garter stitch:

Row 1 (RS):   Kfb, PM, patt to end

The original pattern calls for an additional 3 or 4 stitches on one edge of all of the cabled pieces. These were worked in garter stitch and then turned under for a hem on the coat, front bands and cuffs.

CABLE CHART

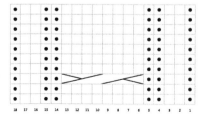

Row 1 (RS):   P1, k2, p2, k8, p2, k2, p1.

Row 2 and all WS rows: K1, p2, k2, p8, k2, p2, k1.

Row 3: P1, k2, p2, C8B, p2, k2, p1.

Rows 5 to 10:   Repeat Rows 1 and 2 three times.

REVERSED CABLE CHART

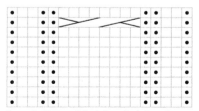

Row 1 (RS):   P1, k2, p2, k8, p2, k2, p1.

Row 2 and all WS rows: K1, p2, k2, p8, k2, p2, k1.

Rows 3 to 8:   Repeat Rows 1 and 2 three times.

Row 9:   P1, k2, p2, C8B, p2, k2, p1.

Row 10:   As Row 2

NATURALLY NAZARETH
is a four-ply yarn made
of **100% domestic wool.** It is a *versatile yarn*
with GREAT STITCH DEFINITION.
It is **study** and **warm**, perfect for *anything*
from a **cozy winter sweater**,
to **mittens,** *hats,* scarves, *pillows,*
and even STUFFED ANIMALS!!

Designed with felters in mind,
this yarn also makes lovely bags, hats,
and other felted items.

whether you are looking for **TEXTURE** *colour work* or **felting ability,** NATURALLY NAZARETH gives *beautiful results.*

Made in the U.S.A.

KRAEMER

KRAEMERYARNS.COM

of row.

Row 2 and all alternate rows: In patt.

Row 3:   K1, kfb, k to M, SM, patt to end of row.

Row 5:   K to M, SM, patt to end of row.

Row 7:   K1, kfb, k to M, SM, patt to end of row.

Row 9:   K1, kfb, k to M, SM, patt to end of row.

Row 10:   In patt.

Repeat Rows 5 to 10, until piece measures 8.5 (9, 9, 9.5, 10, 10, 10.5, 10.5)" from the beginning of the collar increases. Place a row marker to designate the Right Shoulder.

Work straight for 50 (54, 60, 66, 68, 70, 70, 76) rows. Break yarn, leaving a 36" tail for grafting. Leave sts on a stitch holder.

Left Front Band

Cast on 24 sts and work in garter stitch with the Cable Chart as follows:

Row 1 (RS):   Work the Cable Chart over the first 18 sts, PM, k6.

Row 2:   K6, PM, work the Cable Chart over the next 18 sts.

This sets the pattern.

Keeping the pattern correct, work through the Cable Chart a total of 13 times, then Rows 1 to 5 again. 135 rows worked.

Now reverse the RS for the collar as follows:

Row 1 (RS):   K to M, SM, work the 1st row of the Reversed Cable Chart.

Row 2:   Work the 2nd row of the Reversed Cable Chart to M, SM, k to end of row.

Rows 3 to 10:   Work through the chart as set.

Collar Increases

Keeping the 6 st garter stitch border and Reversed Cable Chart correct, increase for the collar as follows, working the increased stitches in garter stitch.

Row 1 (RS): Patt to last st, PM, kfb.

Row 2 and all alternate rows: In patt.

Row 3:   Patt to second M, K1, kfb, k to M, SM, patt to end of row.

Row 5:   K to M, SM, patt to end of row.

Row 7:   K1, kfb, k to M, SM, patt to end of row.

Row 9:   K1, kfb, k to M, SM, patt to end of row.

Row 10:   In patt.

Repeat Rows 5 to 10, until piece measures 8.5 (9, 9, 9.5, 10, 10, 10.5, 10.5)" from the beginning of the collar increases. Place a row marker to designate the Left Shoulder.

Work straight for 50 (54, 60, 66, 68, 70, 70, 76) rows. Break yarn, leaving a 36" tail for grafting. Leave sts on a stitch holder.

FINISHING

Sew the shoulder seams. With the RIGHT side of the collar to the WRONG side of the jacket, match the center back and shoulder markers, easing the fullness along the back, and pin in place. Pin the rest of the front band in place, starting at the bottom and working up to the V of the neck. Check that the bands are even, then sew in place.

Sew the WRONG side of the cuffs to the RIGHT side of the wrists along the edge without garter stitches, then sew the sleeve seam. Sew the sleeves into the arm-holes. Turn back the cuffs. Weave in all ends. Wash and dry flat.

Driving Coat

TRANSLATED BY ELLY DOYLE
KNITTED BY SALLY BLACK

INSPIRATION

The new passion for motor cars meant warm clothes were needed. This coat is lovely and long, and knitted quite tightly in aran weight yarn to keep the wearer cosy in open cars. — Sally

MATERIALS

1.5 (1.6, 1.75, 1.8, 1.9, 2, 2.2, 2.4, 2.6) kg aran weight yarn

Pairs 4 mm and 4.5 mm (US 6 and 7) needles, or size to achieve tension

12 buttons, about 1" diameter

6 large press studs

Sally used Kraemer Yarns Nazareth; 100% wool; 184 yds / 166 m per 100 g ball; shade Ice Skate

SIZE

To fit Chest: 28 (32, 36, 40, 44, 48, 52, 56, 60)"

Actual Chest: 32 (36, 40, 44, 48, 52, 56, 60, 64)"

Length: 40 (40, 42, 44, 45, 46, 48, 50, 50)" or as desired.

TENSION

20 sts and 36 rows to 4" over pattern stitch.

CONSTRUCTION

Back and fronts are worked up from the hem. Sleeves are worked flat from the top down.

DRIVING COAT

Row 1: K3, *k4, moss 5, k3. Repeat from * to last 4 sts, k4.

Row 2: P4, *p3, moss 5, p4. Repeat from * to last 3 sts, p3.

Row 3: P3, *p4, moss 5, p3. Repeat from * to last 4 sts, p4.

Row 4: K4, *k3, moss 5, k4. Repeat from * to last 3 sts, k3.

PATTERN

BACK

With smaller needles, cast on 111 (121, 131, 141, 151, 161, 171, 181, 191) sts. Work 3" garter stitch.

Change to larger needles.

Next Row (RS): Knit 46 (51, 56, 61, 66, 71, 76, 81, 86), patt 18, W&T.

Next Row: Patt 30, W&T.

Repeat last row, working 12 sts extra in each row until 10 (3, 8, 1, 6, 11, 4, 9, 2) sts remain at each side.

Next Row: Patt to end of row.

Next Row: Patt to end of row.

Work patt as set until work measures 6" from cast on.

Shape Waist

Row 1: K2tog, patt to last 2 sts, ssk.

Rows 2 to 5: In patt.

Repeat last 6 rows until 81 (91, 101, 111, 121, 131, 141, 151, 161) sts remain.

Work patt until piece measures 33.5 (33, 34.5, 36, 36.5, 37, 38.5, 40, 39.5)" or until desired length to underarm, ending after a WS row. *Adjust length here.*

Shape Armhole

Row 1: Cast off 3 (5, 5, 7, 9, 11, 13, 15, 17), patt to end of row.

Row 2: As Row 1.

Row 3: Moss 3, k2tog, patt to last 5 sts, ssk, Moss 3.

Row 4: Moss 3, patt to last 3 sts, Moss 3.

Repeat Rows 3 and 4 until 71 (73, 81, 85, 87, 91, 91, 93, 93) sts remain.

Work patt until piece measures 6.5 (7, 7.5, 8, 8.5, 9, 9.5, 10, 10.5)" from start of armhole shaping.

Shoulder Shaping

Rows 1 and 2: Cast off 8 (8, 9, 9, 9, 9, 9, 9, 9), work patt to end of row.

Rows 3 and 4: Cast off 8 (8, 9, 9, 9, 10, 10, 10, 10), work patt to end of row.

Rows 5 and 6: Cast off 7 (7, 9, 9, 10, 10, 10, 10, 10), work patt to end of row.

Cast off remaining sts for neck.

RIGHT FRONT

With smaller needles, cast on 63 (65, 69, 73, 74, 77, 77, 79, 79) sts. Work 3" garter stitch.

Change to larger needles.

Next Row (RS): K15 (17, 14, 13, 14, 17, 17, 17, 17), patt 11 (11, 6, 11, 11, 11, 11, 18, 18), W&T.

Next Row: In patt, keeping the garter stitch border.

Repeat these 2 rows, working 12 sts more on each RS row until 12 (12, 12, 12, 12, 12, 12, 7, 7) sts remain.

Next Row: In patt across all sts.

Work patt as set until piece measures 6" from cast on edge.

Shape Waist

Row 1 (RS): Patt to last 3 sts, ssk, k1.

Rows 2 to 6: In patt.

Repeat last 6 rows until 48 (50, 54, 58, 59, 62, 62, 64, 64) sts remain.

Work patt until piece measures same as Back to underarm.

Shape armhole and neck:

Row 1 (WS): Cast off 3 (5, 5, 7, 9, 11, 13, 15, 17), patt to end of row.

Row 2: Work to last 3 sts, ssk, k1.

Row 3: Work in patt.

Repeat Rows 2 and 3 1 (3, 4, 5, 7, 8, 11, 13, 16) more times. AT THE SAME TIME when work measures 2 (2.5, 2.5, 3, 3, 3.5, 3.5, 3.5, 3.5)" from the start of the armhole shaping, work 25 (27, 27, 31, 31, 33, 33, 35, 35) sts at centre front in garter st.

Work a further 2" of garter st, then cast off these 25 (27, 27, 31, 31, 33, 33, 35, 35) sts. Continue working remaining sts until piece measures 6.5 (7, 7.5, 8, 8.5, 9, 9.5, 10, 10.5)" from start of armhole shaping.

Shoulder Shaping

Row 1 (WS): Cast off 8 (8, 9, 9, 9, 9, 9, 9, 9), patt to end of row.

Row 2: In patt.

Row 3: Cast off 8 (8, 9, 9, 9, 10, 10, 10, 10), patt to end of row.

Row 4: In patt.

Cast off remaining 7 (7, 9, 9, 10, 10, 10, 10, 10) sts.

LEFT FRONT

With smaller needles, cast on 63 (65, 69, 73, 74, 77, 77, 79, 79) sts. Work 3" garter stitch.

Change to larger needles.

Next Row (WS): K15 (17, 14, 13, 14, 17, 17, 17, 17),

patt 11 (11, 6, 11, 11, 11, 11, 18, 18), W&T.

Next Row: In patt, keeping the garter stitch border.

Repeat these 2 rows, working 12 sts more on each WS row until 12 (12, 12, 12, 12, 12, 12, 7, 7) sts remain.

Next Row: In patt across all sts.

Work patt as set until piece measures 6" from cast on edge.

Shape Waist

Row 1 (RS):   K1, k2tog, patt to end of row.

Rows 2 to 6:   In patt.

Repeat last 6 rows until 48 (50, 54, 58, 59, 62, 62, 64, 64) sts remain.

Work patt until piece measures same as Back to underarm.

Shape armhole and neck:

Row 1 (RS):   Cast off 3 (5, 5, 7, 9, 11, 13, 15, 17), patt to end of row.

Row 2:   Work to last 3 sts, p2tog, p1.

Row 3:   Work in patt.

Repeat Rows 2 and 3 1 (3, 4, 5, 7, 8, 11, 13, 16) more times. AT THE SAME TIME when work measures 2 (2.5, 2.5, 3, 3, 3.5, 3.5, 3.5, 3.5)" from the start of the armhole shaping, work 25 (27, 27, 31, 31, 33, 33, 35, 35) sts at centre front in garter st.

Work a further 2" of garter st, then cast off these 25 (27, 27, 31, 31, 33, 33, 35, 35) sts. Continue working remaining sts until piece

measures 6.5 (7, 7.5, 8, 8.5, 9, 9.5, 10, 10.5)" from start of arm-hole shaping.

Shoulder Shaping

Row 1 (RS):   Cast off 8 (8, 9, 9, 9, 9, 9, 9, 9), patt to end of row.

Row 2:   In patt.

Row 3:   Cast off 8 (8, 9, 9, 9, 10, 10, 10, 10), patt to end of row.

Row 4:   In patt.

Cast off remaining 7 (7, 9, 9, 10, 10, 10, 10, 10) sts.

SLEEVES

With larger needles, cast on 79 (87, 89, 95, 103, 109, 119, 127, 137) sts.

Shape Sleeve Cap

Row 1 (RS):   K37 (41, 42, 45, 49, 52, 57, 61, 66) sts, moss 4. W&T. Keep these 5 sts in moss stitch as the central panel.

Row 2:   Patt 9, W&T.

Row 3:   Patt 14, W&T.

Continue in this way working 5 more sts each row until 5 (9, 10, 13, 17, 20, 25, 29, 34) sts rem each side.

Work 1 extra stitch each row until 3 (5, 5, 7, 9, 11, 13, 15, 17) sts rem each side.

Work 2 rows in patt across all sts.

Shape Sleeve

Next Row (RS):   K1, k2tog, patt to last 3 sts, ssk, k1.

Work 5 (5, 5, 5, 3, 3, 3, 3, 3) rows in patt.

Repeat these 6 (6, 6, 6, 4, 4, 4, 4) rows until 45 (45, 51, 51, 55, 55, 55, 61, 61) sts remain.

Work patt until sleeve measures 14.5 (15, 15, 15.5, 15.5, 16, 16, 16.5, 17)" from start of sleeve shaping. *Adjust length here.*

Change to smaller needles and work in garter stitch for 5".

Cast off.

COLLAR

Sew shoulder seams. Pick up sts around vertical edge of neck on front (1 st for every garter ridge), across the back, down side of other front. With smaller needles work in garter st for 2.5 (3, 3, 3.5, 3.5, 4, 4, 4.5, 4.5)" or desired length. Cast off

POCKETS

With smaller needles, cast on 37 sts.

Starting with moss 3, work in patt for 5".

Knit 8 rows. Cast off.

FINISHING

Sew side and sleeve seams. Set in sleeves. Lay flat and place buttons as desired. Sew buttons on. Make buttonhole loops for the outer buttons, and sew a press stud behind each of the inner buttons and on the edge of the Left Front. Pin, then sew, pockets in place.

Weave in all ends. Wash and dry flat.

Baby Lace (Pattern No. 11)

Abbreviations :—Ch., chain ; tr., treble ; d.c., double crochet.
Ardern's Crochet Cotton, 50.

1st row.—Chain length required, turn. 5 ch. miss 2 ch. below, 1 tr. in third ch., * 2 ch. miss 2 ch. below, 1 tr. in third ch. Repeat from *, turn.

2nd row.—5 ch. 1 tr. in space below (of 2 ch.), 1 picot (5 ch. 1 d.c. in first ch.), 1 tr. in same space, * miss one space below, 1 tr., 1 picot, 1 tr. in next space. Repeat from * to end, turn.

Pattern 11.

3rd row.—5 ch., * 1 tr. in first picot below, 1 picot, 1 tr., 1 picot, 1 tr., 1 picot, 1 tr. in same place, 3 ch. 1 d.c. in next picot below, 3 ch. Repeat from * to end.

Tam o'Shanter

TRANSLATED AND KNITTED BY ANGELA BANNISTER

INSPIRATION

This tam is very tightly knitted, but it has a lovely shape and is worth the effort! — Angela

MATERIALS

300 g 4 ply/fingering yarn

Pairs of 2.25 and 2.75 mm (US 1 and 2) needles, or size to achieve tension

Angela used Rowan Pure Wool 4 ply; 100% wool, 160 m per 50 g ball; shade 451 Porcelaine

SIZE

To fit an adult head

TENSION

25 sts and 25 rows to 4" over Garter Rib on larger needles with 2 strands of yarn

CONSTRUCTION

The band is knitted first with a single strand of yarn. The yarn is then doubled for the crown.

PATTERN

With smaller needles and ONE strand of yarn, cast on 192 sts. Work in k2, p2 rib for 1.5".

Change to larger needles. Using TWO strands of yarn work 18 rows in Garter Rib, then knit 64 rows.

Decrease Row: *K2, k2tog. Repeat from * to end of row.

Break one strand of yarn. Continue with ONE strand of yarn only.

Change to 2.25 mm needles and work 3" in k2, p2 rib.

Next Row: k2tog along row.

Repeat this row once more. 36 sts

Break yarn and draw through remaining sts, passing the yarn through them twice, and pulling tight.

FINISHING

Sew up back seam. Weave in all ends. Make a pom-pom and sew to the top. In wear, fold the brim in half.

Sports Sweater

TRANSLATED BY MARY LOU EGAN AND ELLY DOYLE KNITTED BY MARY LOU EGAN

MATERIALS LIST:

500 (550, 600, 700, 800, 950, 1050, 1200, 1350) g DK yarn

Pairs 3.5 and 4 mm (US 4 and 6) needles, or size to achieve tension

Circular 16" size 3.5 mm (US 4) needle, or set dpns

Row counter

Stitch holders

Mary Lou used Artesano DK; 100% Superfine Alpaca; 109 yds /100 m per 50 g skein; shade 743 Fern

SIZE

To Fit Bust: 26 (30, 34, 39, 42, 46, 50, 54, 58)"

Actual Bust: 30 (34, 38, 43, 46, 50, 54, 58, 62)"

Length: 27.5 (28, 29, 29.5, 30, 30.5, 31,5, 32, 32.5)"

Sleeve Length: 16 (17, 17, 18, 18, 18, 19, 19, 19)"

TENSION

22 sts and 30 rows to 4" over stocking stitch

CONSTRUCTION

The sweater is worked in pieces and then sewn together.

PATTERN

BACK

With smaller needles, cast on 88 (100, 110, 120, 132, 144, 154, 166, 176) sts.

Rows 1 to 9: K1, p1 rib.

Row 10 (WS): K.

Rows 11 to 20: Repeat Rows 1 to 10.

Change to larger needles and, beginning with a knit row, work in patt for 4 rows.

SPORTS SWEATER PATTERN STITCH

Row 1: K.

Row 2: P.

Rows 3 to 8: Repeat Rows 1 and 2 three times more.

Rows 9 and 10: K.

Keeping patt correct, shape waist:

Row 1: K2, k2tog, patt to last 2 sts, ssk, k2.

Rows 2 to 6: In patt.

Grace (Victoria Rigby) in Tam o'Shanter and Sports Sweater.
© Nick Loven

William (Adam Fox) and his sister Grace (Victoria Rigby) in a scene from the film. William's Gansey (left); Tam o'Shanter and Sports Sweater (right). The gloves are from a private pattern. © Nick Loven

Repeat Rows 1 to 6 until 72 (82, 84, 104, 116, 126, 128, 148, 160) sts remain.

Work 30 rows straight. *Adjust length to waist here.*

Keeping patt correct, increase:

Row 1: K2, m1, patt to last 2 sts, m1, k2.

Rows 2 to 8: In patt.

Repeat Rows 1 to 8 until there are 82 (94, 104, 116, 126, 138, 148, 160, 170) sts on the needle.

Work straight until piece measures 20 (22, 22, 22, 23, 23, 23, 23, 24)", noting number of rows worked. *Adjust length here.*

Shape armholes

Row 1: Cast off 2 (3, 3, 4, 5, 6, 7, 8, 9), patt to end of row.

Row 2: As Row 1.

Row 3: K1, ssk, knit to last 3 sts, k2tog, k1.

Row 4: In patt.

Repeat Rows 3 and 4 until 74 (84, 92, 100, 106, 114, 120, 128, 134) sts remain.

Work straight until armhole measures 8 (8, 9, 9, 9, 10, 10, 11, 11)", ending after a WS row.

Next Row: Patt 23 (28, 31, 33, 36, 40, 42, 45, 48)

and place on holder, cast off 28 (28, 30, 34, 34, 34, 36, 38, 38) for neck, patt 23 (28, 31, 33, 36, 40, 42, 45, 48) and place on holder.

FRONT

Work as for back until armhole measures 6 (6, 6.5, 6.5, 6.5, 7.5, 7, 8, 8)".

Shape neck:
Next Row: Patt 23 (28, 31, 33, 36, 40, 42, 45, 48) and place on stitch holder, cast off 10 (10, 10, 12, 12, 12, 12, 12, 12), patt to end of row.

On these sts, continue with Left Shoulder:
Row 1 (WS): In patt.

Row 2: Cast off 2, patt to end of row.

Rows 3 and 4: As Rows 1 and 2.

Row 5: In patt.

Row 6: Ssk, patt to end of row.

Repeat Rows 5 and 6 until 23 (28, 31, 33, 36, 40, 42, 45, 48) sts remain.

Work straight until armhole measures the same as the back, ending after a WS row.

Leave sts on a stitch holder.

Right shoulder
Return to held sts. Rejoin yarn to neck edge.

Row 1 (WS): Cast off 2, patt to end of row.

Row 2: In patt.

Rows 3 and 4: As Rows 1 and 2.

Row 5: In patt.

Row 6: Patt to last 2 sts, k2tog.

Repeat Rows 5 and 6 until 23 (28, 31, 33, 36, 40, 42, 45, 48) sts remain.

Work straight until armhole measures the same as left, ending after a WS row.

Mary Lou specialises in accessible projects simple enough for less-experienced knitters but which also give experienced knitters a chance to relax and knit. Based in St. Paul, Minnesota, she's taught knitting locally and nationally. Mary Lou is the author of Wear-withall: Knits for Your Life. Her designs have appeared in Knitty, Craft Activism, and Shear Spirit. Her line of self-published patterns are sold at yarn stores nation-wide, as well as on Ravelry and Patternfish. She blogs sporadically at Yarnerinas (http://mle-gan.wordpress.com/)

Leave sts on a stitch holder.

SLEEVES

With smaller needle, cast on 36 (36, 44, 44, 48, 48, 48, 56, 56) sts.

Rows 1 to 9: K1, p1 rib.

Row 10 (WS): K.

Rows 11 to 20: Repeat Rows 1 to 10.

Change to larger needles and, beginning with a knit row, work in patt for 4 rows.

Keeping patt correct, shape sleeve:

Row 1: K2, m1, patt to last 2 sts, m1, k2.

Row 2: In patt.

Repeat Rows 1 and 2 until there are 72 (72, 82, 82, 84, 92, 92, 104, 104) sts on the needle.

Next Row: K2, m1, k to last 2 sts, m1, k2.

Next three Rows: In patt.

Repeat these 4 rows until there are 88 (90, 100, 100, 102, 114, 114, 126, 128) sts on the needle.

Work straight until sleeve measures 16 (17, 17, 18, 18, 18, 19, 19, 19)". **Adjust length here.**

Shape sleeve cap:
Row 1: Cast off 2 (3, 3, 4, 5, 6, 7, 8, 9), patt to end of row.

Row 2: As Row 1.

Row 3: K1, ssk, patt to last 3 sts, k2tog, k1.

Row 4: In patt.

Repeat Rows 3 and 4 until 80 (80, 88, 84, 82, 90, 86, 94, 92) sts remain. Cast off.

COLLAR

Join front to back at shoulders using three-needle bind off.

Using circular needle, attach yarn to left shoulder. Pick up and knit 13 (13, 14, 15, 15, 15, 16, 17, 17) sts down the left front neck, 10 (10, 10, 12, 12, 12, 12, 12, 12) sts from the centre front neck, 22 sts up the right front neck, and 28 (28, 30, 34, 34, 34, 36, 38, 38) from the back neck. Work in the round as follows:

Rnds 1 to 9: In k1, p1 rib.

Rnd 10: P.

Repeat these ten rounds once more then Rnds 1 and 2 again.

Cast off in rib.

FINISHING

Sew side and sleeve seams. Set in sleeves. Weave in all ends. Wash and dry flat.

William's Gansey

DESIGNED AND KNITTED BY ELIZABETH LOVICK

INSPIRATION

Versions of this gansey appeared in knitting pattern books in the 1890s, and continued to be published into the 1930s. Unlike the 'traditional' seaman's gansey it is knitted to and fro in pieces and then seamed. This version uses the traditional 5 ply wool yarn, but it can also be knitted in DK.

MATERIALS

550 (600, 700, 800, 900, 1000, 1100, 1200, 1350, 1600) g 5 ply yarn

Pairs 3 and 3.5 mm (US 2 and 4) needles or size to achieve tension

3 mm (US2) circular needle, or size to achieve tension

Stitch holders or lengths of thread

Row counter

SIZE

To Fit Chest 32 (36, 40, 44, 48, 52, 56, 60, 64, 68)"

Actual Chest 34 (38, 42, 46, 50, 54, 58, 62, 66, 70)"

Length 26 (27, 28, 29, 30, 30, 30.5, 31, 31.5, 32)"

Sleeve * 23 (23.5, 24, 24.5, 25, 25.5, 26, 26.5, 27, 27.5)"

Length and sleeve length are easily adjustable.

*Measured on the OUTSIDE of the arm from the point of the shoulder.

TENSION

24 sts and 32 rows to 4" over stocking stitch

ABBREVIATIONS

C8B - place the next 4 sts onto the cable needle and hold at the back of the work, k4, k4 from the cable needle

CONSTRUCTION

The back and front are knitted flat separately. The shoulder seams are sewn and the neck is knitted in the round. The two sleeves are knitted from the top down, the seams are sewn, and the sleeves are then inserted into the armholes.

PATTERN

BACK

With smaller needles, cast on 102 (114, 126, 138, 150, 162, 174, 186, 198, 210) sts. Work in rib for 3 (3, 3, 3, 3, 3.5, 3.5, 3.5, 3.5, 3.5)".

Change to larger needles. Starting with a knit row, work in stocking stitch until the piece measures 18 (18, 18, 18, 18, 17, 17, 17, 17, 17)" from the start, finishing after a purl row. *Adjust length here.*

Next Row: K10 (12, 14, 16, 18, 19, 20, 21, 27, 28), p5 (6, 7, 8, 9, 9, 10, 11, 15, 16), *k1, kfb, k2, kfb, k1, p5 (6, 7, 8, 9, 9, 10, 11, 15, 16). Repeat from * to last 10 (12, 14, 16, 18, 19, 20, 21, 27, 28) sts, k to end of row. 116 (128, 140, 152, 164, 180, 192, 204, 216, 228) sts

Next Row: P10 (12, 14, 16, 18, 19, 20, 21, 27, 28), k5 (6, 7, 8, 9, 9, 10, 11, 15, 16), *p8, k5 (6, 7, 8, 9, 9, 10, 11, 15, 16). Repeat from * to last 10 (12, 14, 16, 18, 19, 20, 21, 27, 28) sts, p to end of row.

YOKE

Row 1: K10 (12, 14, 16, 18, 19, 20, 21, 27, 28), p5 (6, 7, 8, 7, 8, 9, 9, 10), *k8, p5 (6, 7, 8, 9, 7, 8, 9, 9, 10). Repeat from * to last 10 (12, 14, 16, 18, 19, 20, 21, 27, 28) sts, k to end of row.

Row 2: P10 (12, 14, 16, 18, 19, 20, 21, 27, 28), k5 (6, 7, 8, 7, 8, 9, 9, 10), *p8, k5 (6, 7, 8, 9, 7, 8, 9, 9, 10). Repeat from * to last 10 (12, 14, 16, 18, 19, 20, 21, 27, 28) sts, p to end of row.

Row 3: K10 (12, 14, 16, 18, 19, 20, 21, 27, 28), p5 (6, 7, 8, 7, 8, 9, 9, 10), *C8B, p5 (6, 7, 8, 9, 7, 8, 9, 9, 10). Repeat from * to last 10 (12, 14, 16, 18, 19, 20, 21, 27, 28) sts, k to end of row.

Row 4: As Row 2.

Rows 5 to 10: Repeat Rows 1 and 2 three times.

These 10 rows form the pattern. Repeat them for the rest of the yoke.

ARMHOLES

Row 1: Cast off 2 (4, 6, 8, 10, 9, 10, 11, 15, 16) sts, patt to end of row.

Row 2: As Row 1.

Row 3: K2tog, patt to last 2 sts, ssk.

Row 4: P2tog, patt to last 2 sts, p2tog.

Rows 5 to 8: Repeat Rows 3 and 4 2 (2, 2, 2, 2, 3, 3, 4, 4) times more. 100 (108, 116, 124, 132, 146, 156, 166, 166, 176) sts

Work straight in patt until the yoke measures 9 (9.5, 10, 11, 12, 13, 13.5, 14, 14.5, 15)".

Shape shoulders:
Row 1: Cast off 8 (9, 10, 10, 11, 10, 11, 12, 11, 12) sts, patt to end of row.

Row 2: As Row 1.

Repeat Rows 1 and 2 2 (2, 2, 2, 2, 3, 3, 3, 3, 3) times more.

Next Row: Cast off 9 (9, 9, 11, 11, 10, 10, 10, 13, 13) sts, pattern to end of row.

Repeat this row once more.

Leave remaining 34 (36, 38, 42, 44, 46, 48, 50, 52, 54) sts on a stitch holder for the neck.

FRONT

Work as for the back until the armhole shaping has been completed.

Work straight for 7 (7.5, 8, 9, 10, 10, 10.5, 11, 11.5, 12)", ending after an even numbered row.

Shape neck:
Row 1: Patt 41 (44, 47, 49, 52, 60, 64, 68, 69, 73), ssk. Put remaining sts on a stitch holder.

Row 2: P2tog, patt to end of row.

Row 3: Patt to last 2 sts, ssk.

Row 4: P2tog, patt to end of row.

Repeat Rows 3 and 4 until 33 (36, 39, 41, 44, 50, 54, 58, 57, 61) sts remain.

Now work straight until the same number of rows as the back have been worked to the shoulder.

Shape shoulder:
Row 1: Cast off 8 (9, 10, 10, 11, 10, 11, 12, 11, 12) sts, patt to end of row.

Row 2: In patt.

Repeat Rows 1 and 2 2 (2, 2, 2, 2, 3, 3, 3, 3, 3) times more.

Next Row: Cast off remaining sts.

Return to the held sts. With RSF, place the first 14 (16, 18, 22, 24, 22, 24, 26, 24, 26) sts on a stitch holder for the front neck. Place the remaining 43 (46, 49, 51, 54, 62, 66, 70, 71, 75) sts on the needle and proceed as follows:

Row 1 (RS): K2tog, patt to end of row.

Row 2: Patt to the last 2 sts, p2tog.

Repeat Rows 1 and 2 until 33 (36, 39, 41, 44, 50, 54, 58, 57, 61) sts remain.

Now work straight until the same number of rows as the back have been worked to the shoulder.

Shape shoulder:
Row 1: In patt.

Row 2: Cast off 8 (9, 10, 10, 11, 10, 11, 12, 11, 12) sts, patt to end of row.

Repeat Rows 1 and 2 2 (2, 2, 2, 2, 3, 3, 3, 3, 3) times more.

Next Row: Cast off remaining sts.

NECK

Join both shoulder seams. With the smaller circular needle and starting at the neck end of the left shoulder, pick up and knit 18 (18, 18, 18, 18, 24, 24, 24, 24, 24) sts from the left side neck, knit the 14 (16, 18, 22, 24, 22, 24, 26, 24, 26) sts left for the front neck, pick up and knit 18 (18, 18, 18, 18, 24, 24, 24, 24, 24) sts from the right side neck, knit the 34 (36, 38, 42, 44, 46, 48, 50, 52, 54) sts left for the back neck. 84 (88, 92, 100, 104, 116, 120, 124, 124, 128) sts

Work in rib for 3 (3, 3, 3, 3, 3.5, 3.5, 3.5, 3.5, 3.5)", then change to the larger circular needle and work a further 3.5 (3.5, 3.5, 3.5, 3.5, 4, 4, 4, 4, 4)" in rib.

Cast off very loosely.

SLEEVES

With larger needles, cast on 74 (72, 70, 68, 66, 64, 66, 68, 70, 72) sts.

Row 1: K1, m1, k to last st, m1, k1.

Row 2: P1, m1, p to last st, m1, p1.

Repeat Rows 1 and 2 until there are 86 (96, 106, 116, 126, 136, 146, 156, 166, 176) sts on the needle.

Continuing in stocking stitch, work 8 rows straight. Mark the ends of the last row with loops of yarn.

Shape the sleeve:
Row 1: K2tog, k to last 2 sts, ssk.

Work 5 (5, 5, 5, 5, 3, 3, 3, 3, 3) rows in stocking stitch.

Repeat these 6 (6, 6, 6, 6, 4, 4, 4, 4, 4) rows until 56 (64, 70, 78, 84, 84, 92, 98, 106, 112) sts remain.

Work straight until the piece measures 20 (20.5, 21, 21.5, 22, 22, 22.5, 23, 23.5, 24)" from the start, noting the number of rows worked, and finishing after a knit row. *Adjust length here.*

Next Row: P to last 0 (2, 0, 2, 0, 0, 2, 0, 2, 0) sts, p2tog. 56 (63, 70, 77, 84, 84, 91, 98, 105, 112) sts

Next Row: *K2tog, k5. Repeat from * to end of row. 48 (54, 60, 66, 72, 72, 78, 84, 90, 96) sts

Change to smaller needles. Work in k1, p1 rib for 3 (3, 3, 3, 3, 3.5, 3.5, 3.5, 3.5, 3.5)", then change to larger needles and work a further 3.5 (3.5, 3.5, 3.5, 3.5, 4, 4, 4, 4, 4)" in rib.

Cast off loosely.

FINISHING

With right sides together, join side seams. Join sleeve seams from the cuff to the yarn markers at the end of the sleeve cap shaping. Turn the sleeves right side out and, with right sides together, sew the sleeves into the body, matching the centre of the cast on edge of the sleeve to the shoulder seam.

Weave in all ends. Wash and dry flat.

Above: Grace (Victoria Rigby) in the Tam o'Shanter and the Stocking Stitch Jacket. © Nick Loven

Stocking Stitch Jacket (left) and Tuxedo Cardigan

Stocking Stitch Jacket

TRANSLATED BY MARY LOU EGAN AND ELLY DOYLE • KNITTED BY MARY LOU EGAN

INSPIRATION

In one photo, Grace Crowder is leading a horse. She is wearing a sort of smoking jacket, with a handkerchief peeking out of one pocket. I ride a sweet Norwegian Fjord mare, and so was immediately committed to making the jacket Grace is wearing! — Mary Lou

MATERIALS

500 (500, 600, 700, 900, 1000, 1100, 1300, 1400) g MC and 300 (300, 400, 400, 500, 500, 600, 600, 700) g CC aran weight yarn

Pairs 3.5 and 4.5 mm (US 5 and 7) needles, or size to achieve tension

Circular 3.5 and 4.5 mm (US 5 and 7) needles

4.5 mm dpns

Row counter

Stitch holders

Mary Lou used Swans Island Worsted; 100% organic merino; 250 yds per 100 g skein; MC Seasmoke Grey, CC Tarragon

SIZE

To Fit Bust: 26 (30, 34, 38, 42, 46, 50, 54, 58)"

Actual Bust: 30 (34, 38, 42, 46, 50, 54, 58, 62)"

Length: 29 (30, 31, 33, 34, 34, 35, 36, 36)"

Sleeve Length: 17 (18.5, 18.5, 20, 20.5, 20.5, 21.5, 22, 22)"

TENSION

20 sts and 28 rows to 4" over stocking stitch

NOTES

The pattern is written for sewing the hems after the knitting is complete. If preferred, the hems can be closed by knitting the first row of the main piece together with the cast on stitches.

CONSTRUCTION

The jacket is worked flat in pieces, then sewn together.

PATTERN

BACK

Hem Facing
With larger needles, and CC, cast on 76 (86, 96, 106, 116, 126, 136, 146, 156) sts. Change to smaller needle, and starting with a knit row, work 11 rows in stocking stitch.

Row 12: K.

Body
Change to larger needles.

Rows 13 to 21: In stocking stitch, starting with a knit row.

Change to MC. Work straight in stocking stitch until piece measures 20 (20, 20, 21, 21, 21, 22, 22, 22)" from the hem row, finishing after a WS row, and noting number of rows worked. **Adjust length here.**

Armhole Shaping
Row 1: Cast off 6 (8, 8, 10, 12, 12, 12, 14, 14), patt to end of row.

Row 2: As Row 1. 64 (70, 80, 86, 92, 102, 112, 118, 128) sts

Work straight until armhole measures 9 (10, 11, 12, 13, 13, 13, 14, 14)" finishing after a WS row.

Next Row: K19 (22, 26, 28, 31, 36, 40, 42, 47), cast off 26 (26, 28, 30, 30, 30, 32, 34, 34) for back neck, k to end of row. Place shoulder sts on stitch holders.

RIGHT FRONT

Hem Facing
With larger needles, and CC, cast on 34 (40, 44, 50, 54, 60, 64, 70, 74) sts. Change to smaller needle, and starting with a knit row, work 11 rows in stocking stitch.

Row 12: K.

Body
Change to larger needles.

Rows 13 to 21: In stocking stitch, starting with a knit row.

Change to MC. Work straight in stocking stitch until piece measures 18" from the hem row, finishing after a WS row, and noting number of rows worked.

Neck Shaping
Row 1: K2, k2tog, knit to end of row.

Rows 2 to 6: In patt.

Repeat these 6 rows 8 (9, 10, 11, 10, 11, 11, 13, 12) times more.

AT THE SAME TIME when the same number of rows have been worked from the hem as on the back, work the armhole shaping.

Next Row: Cast off 6 (8, 8, 10, 12, 12, 12, 14, 14), patt to end of row.

Continue the armhole edge straight until it measures 9 (10, 11, 12, 13, 13, 13, 14, 14)". 34 (40, 44, 50, 54, 60, 64, 70, 74) sts remain after armhole and neck shaping is complete.

Place sts on holder.

LEFT FRONT

Hem Facing
With larger needles, and CC, cast on 34 (40, 44, 50, 54, 60, 64, 70, 74) sts. Change to smaller needle, and starting with a knit row, work 11 rows in stocking stitch.

Row 12: K.

Body
Change to larger needles.

Rows 13 to 21: In stocking stitch, starting with a knit row.

Change to MC. Work straight in stocking stitch until piece measures 18" from the hem row, finishing after a WS row, and noting number of rows worked.

Neck Shaping

She cannot wait another moment! She must have Swans Island yarn today! These Beautiful Yarns are spun and hand-dyed in Maine. Certified Organic Wool, All-Natural Dyes and Traditional hand-dyeing techniques produce incredibly Soft Yarns with Rich Colours and Uniquely Beautiful Variegation. You haven't a Moment to Lose! Run to Swans Island!

SWANS ISLAND COMPANY
www.swansislandcompany.com

Row 1:   K to last 4 sts, ssk, k2.

Rows 2 to 6:   In patt

Repeat these 6 rows 8 (9, 10, 11, 10, 11, 11, 13, 12) times more.

AT THE SAME TIME when the same number of rows have been worked from the hem as on the back, work the armhole shaping.

Next Row: K.

Next Row: Cast off 6 (8, 8, 10, 12, 12, 12, 14, 14), p to end of row.

Continue the armhole edge straight until it measures 9 (10, 11, 12, 13, 13, 13, 14, 14)". 34 (40, 44, 50, 54, 60, 64, 70, 74) sts remain after armhole and neck shaping is complete.

Place sts on holder.

SLEEVE

Hem Facing
With larger needles, and CC, cast on 44 (44, 44, 50, 50, 50, 56, 56, 56) sts. Change to smaller needle, and starting with a knit row, work 9 rows in stocking stitch.

Row 10:   K.

Change to larger needles.

Rows 11 to 17:   In stocking stitch, starting with a knit row.

Change to MC and purl 1 row.

Sleeve Shaping
Row 1:   K1, m1, k to last st, m1, k1.

Rows 2 to 4:   In patt.

Repeat these 4 rows until there are 90 (100, 110, 120, 130, 130, 130, 140, 140) sts on the needle.

Work straight until sleeve measures 17 (18.5, 18.5, 20, 20.5, 20.5, 21.5, 22, 22)". ***Adjust length here.***

Cast off.

FRONT BANDS

Joint fronts to back at shoulders using three needle bind-off.

With larger circular needle and RS facing, beginning at the hem, pick up and knit 3 sts for every 4 rows up the centre front and neck edge of the Right Front, pick up and knit 26 (26, 28, 30, 30, 30, 32, 34, 34) sts from the Back neck, pick up and

knit 3 sts for every 4 rows down the neck edge and the centre front of the Left Front down to the hem.

Starting with a purl row, work 8 rows in stocking stitch.

Next Row (WS):   K.

Change to smaller needles and, staring with a knit row, work 9 rows in stocking stitch.

Cast off.

POCKETS — MAKE 2
With larger needles and MC, cast on 24 sts. Work in stocking stitch for 4", ending after a WS row. Change to CC and work a further 7 rows.

Next Row (WS):   K.

Change to smaller needles and, starting with a knit row, work 6 rows in stocking stitch. Cast off.

BELT
With dpns and CC, cast on 10 sts. Join into a circle.

Rnd 1:   K.

Rnd 2:   [K1, m1] to end of rnd.

Rnd 3 and 4:   K.

Rnd 5:   [K2, m1] to end of rnd. 30 sts

Knit straight for 66 (72, 78, 84, 90, 94, 98, 102, 106)". Adjust length here.

Shape tip of belt:
Rnd 1:   *K1, k2tog, rep from * to end.

Rnd 2 and 3:   Knit.

Rnd 4:   *K2tog, rep. from * to end. 10 sts.

Break yarn, draw through all sts.

FINISHING

Sew sleeve and side seams. Matching sleeve and side seams, insert sleeves. Fold hem and cuff facings at the row of purl bumps, and slip stitch in place. Fold front band facing at the row of purl bumps and slip stitch in place.

Fold the pocket facing along the row of purl bumps and sew in place. Place the pockets on the fronts, about 1" in from the border and with the bottom 4" up from the hem. Pin, then sew in place.

Make 2 tassels. Attach to each end of belt.

Wash, then dry flat.

Ann's Tuxedo Jacket

TRANSLATED BY JUDITH BRODNICKI • KNITTED BY LIZ ROGERS

MATERIALS

500 (600, 650, 700, 750, 800, 900, 1000, 1100) g MC and 100 (100, 150, 150, 200, 200, 250, 300, 350) g CC DK yarn.

Pairs 3.5 mm and 4.5 mm (US 4 and 7) needles, or size to achieve tension

4 mm (US J) crochet hook

Row counter

Stitch holder

3 Small buttons, about 0.5" diameter

Liz used Rowan Pure Wool DK; 100% wool, 142 yds / 130 m per 50 g ball; MC Hyacinth 026, CC Port 037

SIZE

Size: XXS (XS, S, M, L, 1X, 2X, 3X, 4X)

Actual Bust: 28 (31, 34.5, 38.5, 41.5, 44.5, 48, 52, 55)"

Length: 25.5 (26.5, 28.5, 29, 30 30.5, 30.5, 31.5, 31.5)"

NOTE: Jacket does NOT close in front. It is specifically made to have a 2" gap.

TENSION

20 sts and 36 rows to 4" over garter stitch

CONSTRUCTION

This garment is worked flat starting at the lower back and then up and over the shoulders where each front is worked separately from the top down. Patch pockets and the front bands and collar are worked separately.

PATTERN

BACK

With larger needles and MC, cast on 70 (78, 86, 96, 104, 112, 120, 130, 138) sts. Work in garter st until piece measures 18 (18.5, 19.5, 20, 20, 20, 20, 20.5, 20.5)" from the cast-on edge, ending after a WS row, and noting the number of rows worked. *Adjust length here.*

Shape Back Armholes

Row 1: Cast off 0 (0, 0, 4, 4, 5, 5, 7, 8) sts, k to end of row.

Row 2: As Row 1.

Row 3: K2, k2tog, k to 4 sts before the end of the row, ssk, k2.

Row 4: K.

Repeat Rows 3 and 4 until there are 66 (74, 80, 86, 92, 98, 104, 110, 116) sts on the needle.

Continue straight until piece measures 7.5 (8, 9, 9, 10, 10.5, 10.5, 11, 11)" from start of armhole shaping, ending after working a WS row.

Divide at shoulders:
K16 (16, 18, 19, 19, 20, 23, 22, 24), place on a holder; cast off 34 (42, 44, 48, 54, 58, 58, 66, 68) sts for back neck; k16 (16, 18, 19, 19, 20, 23, 22, 24) sts.

LEFT FRONT
On remaining sts, knit 53 (53, 57, 57, 63, 63, 61, 57, 55) rows.

Shape armhole:
Row 1 (RS): K to last 2 sts, m1, k2.

Row 2: K.

Repeat Rows 1 and 2 until there are 16 (18, 22, 23, 23, 26, 30, 33, 36) sts on the needle.

Increase at armhole and neck:
Row 1: K2, m1, k to last 2 sts, m1, k2.

Row 2: K.

Repeat Rows 1 and 2 until there are 30 (34, 38, 39, 43, 46, 50, 53, 56) sts on the needle.

Next Row: K.

Next Row (WS): Cast on 0 (0, 0, 4, 4, 5, 5, 7, 8) sts, k to end of row. 30 (34, 38, 43, 47, 51, 55, 60, 64) sts

Work straight for the same number of rows as the Back. Cast off.

RIGHT FRONT
Return to held sts. With WS facing, join yarn at neck edge and knit 53 (53, 57, 57, 63, 63, 61, 57, 55) rows.

Shape armhole:
Row 1 (RS): K2, m1, knit to end.

Row 2: K.

Repeat Rows 1 and 2 until there are 16 (18, 22, 23, 23, 26, 30, 33, 36) sts on the needle.

Increase at armhole:
Row 1: K2, m1, k to last 2 sts, m1, k2.

Row 2: K.

Repeat Rows 1 and 2 until there are 30 (34, 38, 39, 43, 46, 50, 53, 56) sts on the needle.

Next Row (RS): Cast on 0 (0, 0, 4, 4, 5, 5, 7, 8) sts, k to end of row. 30 (34, 38, 43, 47, 51, 55, 60, 64) sts

Work straight for the same number of rows as the Back. Cast off.

SLEEVES
With smaller needles and MC, cast on 42 (42, 42, 42, 46, 46, 46, 46, 50) sts and work in k2, p2 rib for 4".

Change to larger needles and work 16 (18, 22, 22, 30, 30, 36, 40, 40) rows in garter st.

Sleeve Increase:
*Row 1: K2, m1, k to 2 sts before the end of the row, m1, k2.

Knit 8 (8, 6, 6, 4, 4, 3, 3, 3) rows.

Repeat from * until there are 64 (68, 72, 78, 86, 96, 104, 112, 118) sts, then work straight until sleeve measures 18.5 (19, 19, 19.5, 19.5, 20, 20, 20.5, 20.5)". *Adjust length here.*

Shape Cap:
Row 1: Cast off 1 (2, 1, 1, 1, 1, 1, 1, 2), k to end of row.

Repeat this row until 32 (60, 56, 58, 84, 40, 64, 52, 60) sts remain.

Next Row: Cast off 2 (1, 1, 1, 1, 1, 2, 4, 1), k to last 2 sts, k2tog.

Repeat this row until 8 (8, 8, 8, 16, 16, 16, 16, 16) sts remain.

Cast off.

POCKETS — MAKE 2
With larger needles and MC, cast on 28 (28, 28, 32, 32, 32, 32, 36, 36, 36) sts and work in garter stitch until pocket measures 3.5". Change to CC and knit 15 rows. Cast off sts.

COLLAR AND FRONT BANDS
With larger needles and CC, cast on 18 (20, 22, 24, 24, 24, 24, 28, 28) sts and work in garter st until the piece is long enough to reach up the edge of the Right Front, round the neck and down the Left Front. Leave sts on a stitch holder.

BELT
With larger needles and CC, cast on 16 sts and work in garter st until belt measures 25 (30, 33, 38, 42, 46, 50, 54, 58)". Cast off and transfer the last st to the crochet hook.

To make the button loops, slip stitch 2 sts on the short edge of the belt, then [ch 4, skip 3 sts, slip 2 sts] 3 times. Slip the last 2 sts, pull yarn through and fasten off.

FINISHING
Sew the side seams. Sew the sleeve seams, reversing the seam for the cuff turn back. Sew sleeves into armholes. Sew the Front Band and Collar to the front and neck edges, leaving a 3" gap for the belt on each side. Adjust the length of the band as needed and cast off the stitches. Turn this band back so that it rests against the jacket. Place one pocket on each Front, centered between the side seam and the turned-back Front Bands. Sew in place. Sew buttons onto belt. Wash and dry flat.

Previous page: Lydia Staniaszek models the Skater Tam and the Scarf with Shaped Ends. (Knitted cardigan is from a private collection.)
© Nick Loven

Skater Scarf & Tam

TRANSLATED BY JUDITH BRODNICKI • KNITTED BY LORRAINE BURNETT & KICKI FRISCH

Tam o'Shanter worked in the same yarn as the Skater Scarf. Also shown with Grace's Jacket.

MATERIALS

Scarf: 350 g aran weight yarn

Tam: 200 g aran weight yarn

Pairs 4 and 5 mm (US 6 and 8) needles, or size to achieve tension

Crochet hook about 4 mm for finishing

Row counter

7 buttons about half an inch diameter

Lorraine used Rowan Creative Focus Worsted; 75% wool, 25% alpaca; 200 m per 100 g ball; shade Lavender Heather

Kicki used Blacker Llyen and BFL DK; 100% wool; undyed (this yarn is a heavy DK)

SIZE

Scarf: 11" wide by 66" long

Tam: To fit an adult woman

TENSION

20 sts and 36 rows to 4" over garter stitch

CONSTRUCTION

A rectangular scarf, worked in garter stitch and moss stitch, which buttons up at one end to make a pocket for the hands; the other end is finished with a fringe. It features a large hole about midway for pulling one end of the scarf through. The tam is worked in moss stitch, and is shaped using short rows. The band is then picked up along the long edge.

The crown of the tam is worked sideways in short row sections. The band is then knitted from stitches picked up along the longer edge of the crown.

PATTERN

SCARF

With larger needles, cast on 55 sts. Work 4 rows in garter stitch.

Row 5: K2, [cast off 3 sts, k5] 6 times, cast off 3 sts, k2.

Row 6: K2, [cast on 3 sts, k5] 6

INSPIRATION

This Skater Scarf and Tam from Minerva Yarns has a pouch on the end of the scarf for keeping your hands warm, and a hole part way along for threading the end through. Both features are equally useful today as a hundred years ago! The Scarf with Shaped Ends was in the same book as the Skater's Tam, and for the film the set was knitted in shades of purple. The little balls at the ends of the points are optional, but fun! — Liz

times, cast on 3 sts, k2.

Work in garter st for 100 more rows, then work 15" in moss stitch.

Keeping the moss stitch correct, work the opening as follows:

Row 1:   Patt 15, cast off 25 sts, patt 15.

Row 2:   Patt 15, cast on 25 sts, patt 15.

Work 25" more in moss stitch, then work 60 rows in garter stitch.

Cast off.

Finishing

Weave in ends. Sew buttons to the junction between the garter stitch and moss stitch sections at the beginning of the scarf. For the fringe, cut strands of yarn 17" long and make into a fringe, in groups of 5 strands, along the cast off edge. If desired, crochet 1 round of dc around the opening in the scarf.

In wear, button the end to form the pouch, and thread the fringed end through the hole in the middle of the scarf

TAM

Crown

With larger needles, cast on 47 sts. Work 1 row in moss stitch.

Continuing with moss stitch throughout, work the short-row sections as follows:

Row 1:   Patt 44, turn.

Row 2 and all alternate rows: In patt.

Row 3:   Patt 41, turn.

Row 5:   Patt 38, turn.

Row 7:   Patt 35, turn.

Row 9:   Patt 32, turn.

Row 11:   Patt 29, turn.

Row 13:   Patt 26, turn.

Row 15:   Patt 23, turn.

Row 17:   Patt 20, turn.

Row 19:   In patt.

Row 20:   In patt.

Repeat these 20 rows 17 times more.

Cast off.

Band

With smaller needles, pick up 96 sts along the longer edge of the crown. Work in k4, p4 rib for 2.5", then change to larger needles and work 24 rows in garter stitch.

Cast off.

Finishing

Sew up back seam. Weave in all ends. If desired, make 2 tassels and join them to the top of the tam with a crocheted chain.

Scarf with Shaped Ends

TRANSLATED BY JUDITH BRODNICKI • KNITTED BY MANDY LYNE

MATERIALS

300 g MC and 50 g CC DK yarn

Pair 4 mm (US 6) needles

Crochet hook, 2 mm (US A) (optional)

Row counter

Small amount of stuffing

Mandy used Rowan Pure Wool DK; 100% wool; 142 yds/130 m per 50 g ball; MC shade 030 Damson and CC shade 010 Indigo

SIZE

11" wide and 66" long

TENSION

23 sts and 40 rows to 4" over garter stitch

CONSTRUCTION

The two triangular ends are worked separately at the start then joined for the rest of the scarf. An opening is worked into the scarf so that one end can pull through when it is wrapped around the neck. Stripes and tassels are optional.

PATTERN

FIRST POINT

With MC, cast on 3 sts.

Row 1 (RS):   S1p, kfbf, k1. 5 sts

Row 2:   S1p, k4.

Row 3:   S1p, kfb, k to last 2 sts, kfb, k1.

Row 4:   S1p, k to end of row.

Repeat Rows 3 and 4 until there are a total of 31 sts on the needle, ending after a 4th row. Break yarn, leaving a tail. Place sts on holder.

Pattern Trivia — There were three things we saw recurring in patterns from this period: (1) garter stitch, (2) belts or ties, and (3) little ornaments (such as the crocheted balls on this scarf) for the ties.

SECOND POINT

Work as for the First Point, but leave the sts on the needle and do not break yarn.

BODY OF SCARF

Row 1 (RS): S1p, knit the 30 sts of the Second Point. Place the 31 sts of the First Point on the needle and knit across. 62 sts

Row 2: S1p, k to end of row.

Continue in patt, changing colours as follows:

In CC, work 12 rows.

In MC, work 12 rows.

In CC, work 12 rows.

Work in MC for 24".

OPENING

Next Row: S1p, k30. Place remaining sts on a stitch holder.

On these 31 sts only, work as set for 6", ending after a WS row, noting the number of rows worked. Break yarn and place sts on a holder.

Return to held sts. Place them on the needle and work the same number of rows as before. Do not break yarn.

Next Row (RS): S1p, k across both sets of sts. 62 sts.

Continue working in MC across all sts until the scarf measures 50" from the joining of the two points, ending after working a WS row.

Work the stripe sequence as follows:

In CC work 12 rows.

In MC work 12 rows.

In CC work 12 rows.

In MC work 1 row.

Next Row: S1p, k30. Place remaining 31 sts on a stitch holder.

THIRD POINT

Work on the first set of 31 sts as follows:

Row 1 (RS): S1p, k2tog, k to last 3 sts, ssk, k1.

Row 2: S1p, k to end of row.

Repeat Rows 1 and 2 until 3 sts remain. Cast off sts. Break yarn.

FOURTH POINT

Return to held sts. Complete as for the Third Point.

FINISHING

Weave in ends. If desired, make 4 crochet balls, or tassels or pom-poms, and sew one to the tip of each point.

CROCHET BALLS:

With MC, 3 ch. Work in the round as follows:

Rnd 1: 7 dc in second ch from hook. 7 sts

Rnd 2: 2 dc in each st. 14 sts

Rnd 3: *1 dc in next st, 2 dc in next st, repeat from * to end of rnd. 21 sts

Repeat Rnd 3 twice more or until desired circumference is reached.

Next Rnd: 1 dc in each st.

Repeat this rnd once more.

Decrease:
Rnd 1: *Skip 1 st, 1 dc in next st. Repeat from * to end of rnd.

Repeat this sequence until 7 st remain. Stuff the ball, then continue the sequence until 3 sts. Do not break yarn.

Attach to the scarf point as follows:

6 ch, 1 dc into end of point, 6 ch, sl st into ball.

Break yarn and finish off.

Repeat for the other three points.

Grace's Tam & Scarf

DESIGNED AND KNITTED BY ELIZABETH LOVICK

INSPIRATION

Pauline asked me to create a tam and scarf in the same stitch pattern as Grace's jacket. The original idea was them to be worn by another character, but Grace ended up wearing them herself in several scenes! — Liz

MATERIALS

Scarf

150 (200, 250, 300, 400) g DK yarn

Pairs 3.5 and 4 mm (US 4 and 6) needles, or size to achieve tension

Tam

100 (100, 150, 150, 200) g DK yarn

3.5 and 4 mm (US 4 and 6) circular needles, or size to achieve tension

8 stitch markers

Row counter

Liz used Rowan Pure Wool DK; 100% Superwash Merino Wool; 144 yds / 130 m per 50g ball; shade Cypress

SIZE

Tam To Fit: Toddler (Child, Teen, Woman, Plus)

Scarf: 5.5 (7, 9, 10.5, 12)" wide by 37 (49, 55, 61, 67)" long

TENSION

24 sts and 38 rows to 4" on 4 mm needle over pattern

NOTES

To achieve the given measurements, the row tension must be correct as well as the stitch tension.

PATTERN

SCARF

With smaller needles cast on 34 (44, 54, 64, 74) sts.

Grace (Victoria Rigby) being taught to drive by her brother Robert (Reece Ackermann). She is also wearing Grace's Jacket (page 38). © Nick Loven. Opposite: Photo © Thomas Hinckley

Row 1: S1p, k to end of row.

Repeat this row five times more.

Change to larger needles and pattern as follows:

Row 1: S1p, k3, *p3, k2. Repeat from * to last 5 sts, p1, k4.

Row 2: S1p, k3, *k1, p2, k2. Repeat from * to last 5 sts, k5.

Row 3: S1p, k3, *p1, k2, p2. Repeat from * to last 5 sts, p1, k4.

Row 4: S1p, k3, *k3, p2. Repeat from * to last 5 sts, k5.

These 4 rows form the pattern. Repeat them until the scarf measures 36 (48, 54, 60, 66)". *Adjust length here.*

Change to smaller needles.

Next Row: S1p, k to end of row.

Repeat this row five times more.

Cast off.

Finishing
Weave in ends. Wash and dry flat.

TAM
With smaller needle, cast on 80 (80, 100, 120, 160) sts. Join into a circle.

Work 8 (10, 12, 14, 14) rows in k1, p1 rib.

Change to larger needle.

Increase Row: *Kfb, k1 (0, 0, 0, 1). Repeat from * to end of row. 120 (160, 200, 240, 240) sts

Start pattern as follows:

Round 1: *P3, k2. Repeat from * to end of row.

Round 2: As Round 1.

Round 3: *P1, k2, p2. Repeat from * to end of row.

Round 4: As Round 3.

These 4 rounds form the pattern. Repeat them 7 (8, 9, 11, 12) times more, then Rounds 1 to 3 again.

Next Round: *Patt 15 (20, 25, 30, 30), PM. Repeat from * to end of round.

Decrease for the crown as follows, keeping the pattern correct where possible:

Round 1: *P2tog, patt to M, SM. Repeat from * to end of round.

Round 2: In patt.

Repeat these two rounds until 48 sts remain, ending after an even numbered round.

Next Round: P2tog across round. 24 sts

Next Round: P.

Next Round: P2tog across round. 12 sts

Break yarn, and run through the remaining sts and draw up. Fasten securely.

Finishing
Weave in all ends. If desired, make a pompom and attach to the centre of the crown.

Winter Shawl

TRANSLATED AND KNITTED BY JUNIPER ASKEW

INSPIRATION

This pattern is in one of the Godey's Lady's Books, which were published during the second half of the Nineteenth Century. — Juniper

---

MATERIALS
150g MC and 60 g CC DK yarn

4 mm (US 6) circular needle, or size required to give the correct tension

4 mm crochet hook for fringe

Row counter

1 stitch marker

Juniper used MC - Debbie Bliss Cashmerino; 55% merino, 33% PA, 12% cashmere; 240 yds / 216 m per 100 g; colour Graphite. CC - Debbie Bliss Rialto DK Solids; 100% merino, 230 yds / 207 m per 200 g; colour Duck Egg

SIZE

32" deep by 64" across, excluding fringe

TENSION

22 sts and 30 rows to 4" over garter stitch

NOTES

The shawl can be made any size, and can be knitted in one or more colours.

CONSTRUCTION

The shawl is worked from the centre back neck down, increasing on the centre back and the edges of the shawl.

PATTERN

THE PLAIN CENTRE

With MC, cast on 6 sts and knit 1 row.

Row 1: S1p, kfb, k to end of row. 7 sts

Row 2: S1p, kfb, k1, PM, k4. 8 sts

Continue:

Row 1: S1p, kfb, k to 1 st before M, kfb, SM, kfb, k to end of row.

Row 2: S1p, kfb, k to end of row.

Repeat these two rows until the edge of the work measures about 24". Adjust size here.

THE STRIPED BORDER

Repeat Rows 1 and 2, working stripe sequence:

4 rows CC, 6 rows MC, 4 rows CC, 6 rows MC, 10 rows CC, 6 rows MC, 4 rows CC, 6 rows MC, 4 rows CC, 6 rows MC.

Cast off in MC.

FINISHING

Weave in all ends. For the fringe, cut wool to 6-inch lengths and use two lengths in each cast off stitch.

I have been knitting since I was 14, in the last few years I have really come to enjoy and appreciate knitting. I suffer from a condition called Ehlers-Danlos syndrome (EDS) this lead me to take up my needles more, adapt things to suit my needs, I don't have to give up knitting, I have a blog where I write about life, EDS and knitting! www. thebendyknitter.co.uk/ I chose to be called 'The Bendy Knitter' (TBK) because my EDS means I am bendy and I love my bendy needles so this seemed fitting! — Juniper

Two Colour Wrap & Tam

TRANSLATED BY ELIZABETH LOVICK • WRAP KNITTED BY LINDA FULLER • TAM KNITTED BY ELLY DOYLE

INSPIRATION

This simple but effective wrap was originally called the Princess Maxixe Wrap and worked in wool and cotton. I changed it to two shades of wool, and added a tam to make the set.
— Liz

MATERIALS

Wrap

    100 (100, 100, 150, 200) g MC 4 ply / fingering

    50 (50, 50, 100, 100) g CC 4 ply / fingering

    Pair 6 mm needles, or size to achieve tension

    Row counter

Tam

    50 (60, 75, 90, 110) g 4 ply yarn in MC

    20 (25, 30, 30, 35) g 4 ply yarn in CC

    Pair 3 mm needles, or size to achieve tension

    6 stitch markers

    Row counter

    Linda and Elly used Orkney Wool 4 ply; 100% Orkney wool as MC and ColourMart 3/14; 100% cashmere as CC.

SIZE

Wrap: 29 (38, 48, 59, 66)" long and 11 (12, 13, 15.5, 18)" wide

Tam: To Fit toddler (child, teen, adult, plus)

TENSION

Wrap: 18 sts and 44 rows to 4"

Tam: 24 rows and 42 sts to 4"

CONSTRUCTION

The wrap is knitted from end to end. The band of the tam is knitted first, then stitches for the crown are picked up along one long edge.

PATTERN

WRAP

With MC, cast on 50 (55, 60, 70, 80) sts and knit 26 (32, 40, 50, 56) rows.

Now start the strip sequence. Knit as follows, without breaking the yarn each time.

Rows 1 and 2: K in CC.

Rows 3 and 4: K in MC.

Repeat Rows 1 to 4 until the striped section measures 24 (28, 32, 36, 40)". Break CC.

Knit 26 (32, 40, 50, 56) rows in MC. Cast off.

The Two Colour Garter Stitch Wrap works nicely as a scarf, too.

No. 9. - SLIPPER.

MATERIALS.—Paton's 4-ply Super Fingering, in 2 colours, mixed with a light and dark twist, 1 oz. each; 2 needles, No. 14; a pair of fleecy soles; ½ yard of pale blue quilted silk; ¼ yard sarsnet ribbon to match the wool, for binding.

Cast on with the darker wool 20 stitches.

Knit a row.

Increase at the commencement of each row in the 2nd stitch, and always knit the two 1st stitches in the dark wool.

I give the pattern now *without* any increasings.

1st Row.—Purl a row with dark wool.

2nd Row.—Knit a row with dark wool. Have 2 balls of dark wool and do not knit tightly.

3rd Row.—Take the light wool, knit 2 with dark wool *, knit the 2 next with light, slip the 2 following without knitting. Repeat from *, knit the last with dark.

4th Row.—Knit the edge stitch in dark, * purl the 2 light stitches, slip the 2 dark stitches. Repeat from *, knit the last with dark.

5th Row.—Purl all the stitches with dark wool.

6th Row.—Knit with dark.

Repeat these last 4 rows, always making the light stitches over the light colour in the preceding row.

Knit 32 rows in this manner, increasing in commencing each row. There will be 54 stitches on the needle.

33rd Row.—Knit 20 stitches in the pattern, cast off 14, knit the last 20 stitches in the pattern for 52 rows, then 2 rows of the dark wool, and cast off.

Knit the same on the 1st 20 stitches, and cast off.

Sew these 2 ends neatly together, line with the quilted silk, bind the inside of the shoe with ribbon, bind the soles and sew the shoe to the sole on the inside very neatly.

Finishing

Weave in all ends. Make two large tassels about 4 (5, 6, 6, 6)" long. Gather the cast on end and the cast off end, and sew one tassel on each. Wash, and dry flat.

TAM

Band

With MC, cast on 18 (22, 26, 30, 34) sts and work in garter stitch until the strip measures 12 (13, 14, 16, 17)" unstretched. Cast off.

Crown

With MC, pick up and knit 72 (80, 92, 100, 112) sts along one long edge of the band.

Foundation Row (WS): *K1, kfb. Repeat from * to end of row. 108 (120, 138, 150, 168) sts

Work in the garter stitch stripe pattern as follows:

Rows 1 to 4: Knit in MC.

Rows 5 and 6: Knit in CC.

Repeat these 6 rows until the Crown measures 6 (7, 8, 10, 11)", finishing after an odd numbered row.

Next Row (WS): *K18 (20, 23, 25, 28), PM. Repeat from * to end of row.

Continuing with the stripe sequence, shape the top of the crown as follows:

Row 1 (RS): *K2tog, k to M, SM. Repeat from * to end of row.

Row 2: Knit.

Repeat these two rows until 48 (66, 72, 84, 84) sts remain. Break CC and continue in MC only.

Continue repeating Rows 1 and 2 until 36 sts remain.

Next Row: K2tog along row.

Next Row: K2tog along row.

Break yarn and thread through remaining stitches.

Finishing

Sew the band and crown seam. Make a tassel or pair of bobbles on strings and attach to the centre of the crown. Wash and dry as flat as possible.

In wear, fold the band up in half.

Diced Bag Hat

TRANSLATED BY ELIZABETH LOVICK • KNITTED BY JULIA LUPA

MATERIALS

75 (100, 125, 150, 175) g 4 ply yarn

Pair 3.25 mm (US 3) needles, or size required to achieve tension

Row counter

2 stitch markers

2 buttons, size not critical

Julia used Texere Jura; 90% wool, 10% nylon; 3556 yds / 320 m per 100g; shade Eau de Nil

INSPIRATION

The original pattern says: This cap is knitted in a "bag-shape" which is at present the most fashionable wear for ladies and children. It is very easy to make, being simply a piece of knitting .... sewn in the shape of a bag. — Liz

SIZE

To Fit Toddler (Child, Teen, Adult, Large Adult)

Actual Circumference 16 (18, 20, 22, 24)"

TENSION

32 sts and 38 rows to 4" over dice pattern

CONSTRUCTION

The hat is worked in one piece from side to side.

PATTERN

Cast on 100 (108, 116, 124, 132) sts.

Foundation Row: K18 (18, 22, 26, 26), PM, k64 (72, 72, 72, 80), PM, k to end of row.

Row 1: S1p, k to M, SM, *k4, p4. Repeat from * to M, SM, k to end of row.

Row 2: S1p, k to M, SM, *p4, k4. Repeat from * to M, SM, k to end of row.

Rows 3 and 4: Repeat Rows 1 and 2.

Row 5: S1p, k to M, SM, * p4, k4. Repeat from * to M, SM, k to end of row.

Row 6: S1p, k to M, SM, * k4, p4. Repeat from * to M, SM, k to end of row.

Rows 7 to 8: Repeat Rows 5 and 6.

Repeat these 8 rows until the piece measures about 8 (9, 10, 11, 12)", finishing after a 4th or 8th row. Cast off.

FINISHING

Fold the piece in half so that the two garter stitch edges lie on top of each other. Sew the cast on and cast off edges to form the side seams. Weave in all ends. Fold the top corners of the hat into a point and bring down to the garter stitch brim (see photo). Sew in place with a button. Repeat for the other corner. Fold brim up.

Turban & Fingerless Mitts

TRANSLATED AND KNITTED BY ELIZABETH LOVICK

MATERIALS

50 (75, 100, 125, 160) g MC and 25 (25, 50, 50, 50) g CC DK yarn for set

Pairs 3 and 3.5 mm (US 2/3 and 4) needles, or size to achieve correct tension

One smaller sized needle for picking up stitches

Row counter

6 buttons about 1" diameter

Stitch holders or lengths of thread

2 stitch markers

Liz used Jamison's DK; 100% Shetland wool; 83 yds / 75 m per 25 g ball, shades 750 Petrol and 764 Cloud

SIZE

To Fit Child (Teen, Small Woman, Average Woman, Large Woman)

The construction of the turban means it can be adjusted easily. The length of the wrist ribbing and the palm are easily adjustable.

TENSION

24 sts and 32 rows to 4" over stocking stitch

NOTES

If there is only one figure it applies to all sizes.

CONSTRUCTION

The crown of the turban is knitted first, then the cast on stitches are picked up and the brim is knitted on. Note that it is not advisable to use a provisional cast on for the turban as the cast on edge gives stability to the hat. The mitts are knitted from the wrist down.

PATTERN

TURBAN

CROWN

With MC and larger needles, cast on 84 (92, 100, 108, 116) sts.

Row 1: K.

Row 2: K3, p to last 3 sts, k3.

Repeat these two rows until the piece measures 6 (6.5, 7, 7.5, 8)", finishing after an even numbered row.

Next Row: K.

INSPIRATION

I found the turban in the Priscilla Sweater Book, published by The Priscilla Publishing Company, Boston, Mass, in 1917, and loved both the look of it, and the idea of a turban into which you could pile your long hair without having to spend the time dressing it! There is still the need for such a hat today. The original was in a yarn of about a 4 ply/fingering thickness, but I felt that it would look good in DK. Several books have instructions for mittens tipped with a different colour to the main parts. The ones here make use of yarn left over from the turban. — Liz

Next Row: K3, p36 (40, 44, 48, 52), k6, p36 (40, 44, 48, 52), k3.

Repeat these two rows twice more.

Next Row: K42 (46, 50, 54, 58), turn. Place remaining sts on a stitch holder or length of thread.

Next Row: K3, p to last 3 sts, k3.

On these 42 (46, 50, 54, 58) sts, work another 6.5 (7, 7.5, 8, 8.5)" in pattern, noting the number of rows worked. Cast off.

Return to the held sts. Place on the needle with RSF, and knit to the end of the row.

Next Row: K3, p to last 3 sts, k3.

On these 42 (46, 50, 54, 58) sts, work the same number of rows as the first piece. Cast off.

BRIM

Return to the cast on edge of the crown, and with the smallest needle, pick up 84 (92, 100, 108, 116) loops.

Foundation row: With MC, k2tog along row. 42 (46, 50, 54, 58) sts

Row 1: K21 (23, 25, 27, 29), turn. Leave remaining 21 (23, 25, 27, 29) sts on a stitch holder.

On the remaining sts, knit 17 (19, 21, 23, 25) rows. Leave these sts on a stitch holder.

Return to the held sts, and knit 18 (20, 22, 24, 26) rows. Break yarn but leave these sts on the needle.

BRIM BORDERS

With CC, pick up and knit 9 (10, 11, 12, 13) sts from the row ends of the brim nearest the needle tip; yo, PM, k1, yo, k21 (23, 25, 27, 29), yo, k1, PM, yo, pick up and knit 9 (10, 11, 12, 13) sts from the rows ends of the brim.

Row 1: K.

Row 2: K to M, yo, SM, k1, yo, k to 1 st before M, yo, k1, SM, yo, k to end of row.

Repeat Rows 1 and 2 one (two, two, three, three) times more. Cast off.

Repeat for the other brim.

Finishing

Weave in all ends. Make three pleats in the ends of the crown as shown in the photo and stitch the pleats together. Make a buttonhole loop on the top of each end. Sew on buttons - one on the top pleat of each side of the crown and two on the each side of the brim as shown in the photos.

To wear, cross the ends of the crown, fasten the loop over one of the buttons of the brim, and pile the hair into the 'pouches' so made.

MITTENS

LEFT MITTEN

With MC and larger needles, cast on 32 (36, 40, 44,

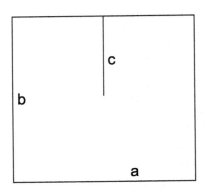

Width (a): 14 (15, 16.5, 18, 19)"

Length (b): 13 (14, 15, 16, 17)"

Length (c): 6.5 (7, 7.5, 8, 8.5)"

48) sts. Knit 3 (3, 3, 5, 5) rows.

Change to CC and smaller needles, and k1, p1 rib for 16 (18, 20, 22, 24) rows.

Change to larger needles and stocking stitch and work the thumb gusset as follows:

Row 1: K17 (19, 21, 23, 25), PM, m1, k2, m1, PM, k to end of row.

Row 2: P.

Row 3: K to M, SM, m1, k to M, m1, SM, k to end of row.

Row 4: P.

Row 5: K.

Row 6: P.

Repeat Rows 3 to 6 until there are 12 (12, 14, 16, 18) sts between the markers, finishing after a 6th row.

Next Row: K to M, SM, k to M, RM, turn.

Next Row: P to M, RM, turn.

On these 12 (12, 14, 16, 18) sts, work 2 (4, 4, 6, 8) rows on stocking stitch.

Change to MC and knit 3 (3, 3, 5, 5) rows. Cast off.

With RSF, rejoin CC to base of thumb. Pick up and knit 2 sts from the base of the thumb, then knit across the rest of the row. 32 (36, 40, 44, 48) sts

Starting with a purl row, work in stocking stitch for 7 (9, 11, 13, 15) rows.

Change to MC and knit 3 (3, 3, 5, 5) rows. Cast off.

RIGHT MITTEN

Work as for the Left Mitten to the start of the thumb gusset.

Row 1: K13 (15, 17, 19, 21), PM, m1, k2, m1, PM, k to end of row.

Complete as for the Left Mitten.

Finishing

Sew side seams. Weave in ends. Wash and dry flat.

CosyCoat

TRANSLATED BY ALISON CASSERLY AND ELLY DOYLE • CROCHETED BY ALISON CASSERLY

INSPIRATION

The CosyCoat was originally from Fleisher's Knitting & Crocheting Manual No 16 c1918, and the original was quite tiny. Alison adapted it to fit the 5' 10" actress playing the teacher, and Elly wrote the other sizes. — Liz

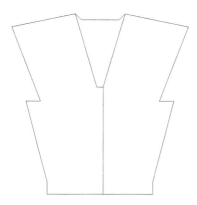

MATERIALS

300 (350, 400, 450, 550, 650, 800, 900) g aran weight yarn

4.5 mm hook, or size to achieve tension

8 buttons about 1" diameter

Alison used Rowan Creative Focus; 75% wool, 25% alpaca; 200 m/220 yds per 100 g ball; shade Lavender Heather

SIZE

To Fit Bust: 28 (32, 36, 40, 44, 48, 52, 56, 60)"

Actual Bust: 30.5 (34.5, 38.5, 42.5, 46.5, 50.5, 54.5, 58.5, 62.5)"

Length: 17 (17, 17, 17, 17, 17, 18, 18, 18)"

TENSION

20 sts and 16 rows to 4" over pattern stitch

I have always been passionate about knitting and crochet since learning at an early age, and taught myself to use a knitting machine 33 years ago. I live in rural Lincolnshire with my husband and elderly dog, Sox, and have a small studio at The Ropewalk, Barton Upon Humber, where I hold classes, knit to commission, design and help with pattern work. I Naturally dye my own British yarns with locally gathered dye-stuffs. While studying knitwear at Nottingham Trent University I did a work placement with hand-knit designer Di Gilpin, based in Fife. My website is www.alisoncasserly.co.uk and I am Naturally Yarns and Knitwear on Facebook. — Alison

ABBREVIATIONS

Pattern stitch: Bring yarn forward, make a DC, keeping yarn under the hook.

Inc: Work 2 pattern sts into one.

CONSTRUCTION

The back and fronts are worked separately, flat. Side seams are sewn and all edges finished with pretty scalloped trim.

PATTERN

BACK

Chain 58 (62, 70, 80, 90, 100, 110, 114, 122).

Row 1: Miss 1 st, dc to end.

Work in pattern stitch for 2".

Continuing in patt, shape the body as follows:

Row 1: Inc, patt to last st, inc.

Row 2: In patt.

Repeat these 2 rows 10 (10, 9, 8, 5, 1, 3, 1, 2) times IN TOTAL. 76 (86, 96, 106, 116, 126, 136, 146, 156) sts

Work patt until work measures 11 (11, 11, 9, 9, 9, 9, 9, 9)" finishing

after a WS row. *Adjust length here.*

Shape underarm:

Row 1: Patt to last 8 (12, 12, 14, 14, 14, 16, 16, 16) sts remain, turn.

Row 2: As Row 1. 60 (62, 72, 78, 88, 98, 104, 114, 124) sts

Row 3: Inc, patt to last st, inc.

Row 4: In patt.

Repeat these 2 rows until there are 80 (82, 90, 94, 98, 100, 110, 116, 128) sts.

Work straight to 6 (6, 6, 8, 8, 8, 10, 10, 10)" from the start of the armhole.

Shoulder shaping:

Rows 1 to 4: Patt to last 7 (7, 8, 9, 9, 9, 10, 11, 12) sts, turn.

Rows 5 and 6: Patt to last 8 (8, 9, 8, 9, 9, 10, 10, 11) sts, turn. 36 (38, 40, 42, 44, 46, 50, 52, 58) sts

Fasten off.

LEFT FRONT

Chain 33 (35, 39, 44, 49, 54, 59, 61, 65).

Row 1: Miss 1 st, dc to end.

Row 2: 8 dc, patt to end of row.

Row 3: Patt to last 8 sts, 8 dc.

Repeat Rows 2 and 3 for 2", ending after a 3rd Row.

Continuing in patt with the 8 dc button border, shape the body as follows:

Row 1: Patt to last st, inc.

Row 2: In patt.

Repeat these 2 rows until there are 42 (47, 52, 57, 62, 67, 72, 77, 82) sts, finishing after a 2nd row.

Work patt until work measures the same as the back to the underarm, finishing at the front edge. *Adjust length here.*

Shape underarm:

Row 1: Patt to last 8 (12, 12, 14, 14, 14, 16, 16, 16) sts remain, turn.

Row 2: In patt.

Row 3: Patt to last st, inc.

Row 4: In patt.

Repeat Rows 3 and 4 until work measures 12 (12, 12, 12, 12, 12, 12.5, 12.5, 12.5)" finishing after a 3rd row.

Next Row: Patt to last 8 sts, turn. This finishes the button band.

Next Row: Patt 2, miss 1 st, patt to last st, inc.

Next Row: In patt.

Repeat the last two rows 10 (10, 9, 8, 5, 1, 3, 1, 2) times, then work the armhole straight while continuing to decrease at the neckline as set until 22 (22, 25, 56, 27, 27, 30, 32, 35) sts remain.

Work straight until underarm measures 7.5 (7.5, 7.5, 9.5, 9.5, 9.5, 11.5, 11.5, 11.5)", finishing at the neckline edge.

Shoulder shaping:

Row 1: Patt to last 7 (7, 8, 9, 9, 9, 10, 11, 12) sts, turn.

Row 2: In patt.

Rows 3 and 4: As Rows 1 and 2. 8 (8, 9, 8, 9, 9, 10, 10, 11) sts remain.

Fasten off.

RIGHT FRONT

Place Left Front flat, and mark the positions of the buttons. The first one about 1" up from the hem, the last about 1" below the end of the button band and the others evenly spaced between.

On the Right Front work buttonholes in the front band in place of the 8 dc as follows:

Row 1: 3 dc, miss 3 sts, 3 ch, 2 dc.

Row 2: 2 dc, 3 dc into 3 ch space, 3 dc.

Buttonholes will not be mentioned below.

Chain 33 (35, 39, 44, 49, 54, 59, 61, 65).

Row 1: Miss 1 st, dc to end.

Row 2: Patt to last 8 sts, 8 dc.

Row 3: 8 dc, patt to end of row.

Repeat Rows 2 and 3 for 2", ending after a 3rd Row.

Continuing in patt with the 8 dc button border, shape the body as follows:

Row 1: Inc, patt to end of row.

Row 2: In patt.

Repeat these 2 rows until there are 42 (47, 52, 57, 62, 67, 72, 77, 82)

sts, finishing after Row 2.

Work patt until work measures the same as the back to the underarm, finishing at the side edge. **Adjust length here.**

Shape underarm:
Row 1: In patt.

Row 2: Patt to last 8 (12, 12, 14, 14, 14, 16, 16, 16) sts remain, turn.

Row 3: In patt.

Row 4: Patt to last st, inc.

Repeat Rows 3 and 4 until work measures 12 (12, 12, 12, 12, 12, 12.5, 12.5, 12.5)" finishing after a 4th row.

Next Row: Patt to last 8 sts, turn. This finishes the button band.

Next Row: Patt 2, miss 1 st, patt to last st, inc.

Next Row: In patt.

Repeat the last two rows 10 (10, 9, 8, 5, 1, 3, 1, 2) times, then work the armhole straight while continuing to decrease at the neckline as set until 22 (22, 25, 56, 27, 27, 30, 32, 35) sts remain.

Work straight until underarm measures 7.5 (7.5, 7.5, 9.5, 9.5, 9.5, 11.5, 11.5, 11.5)", finishing at the neckline edge.

Shoulder shaping:
Row 1: Patt to last 7 (7, 8, 9, 9, 9, 10, 11, 12) sts, turn.

Row 2: In patt.

Rows 3 and 4: As Rows 1 and 2. 8 (8, 9, 8, 9, 9, 10, 10, 11) sts remain.

Fasten off.

FINISHING

Join the shoulders & side seams.

Scallop Edging: Join yarn at one of the side seams and work [1 dc, 2 ch, 2 tr] in every 3rd st. Repeat all around the waistcoat and the armhole edges.

Weave in ends. Wash and dry flat.

Straight & Striped Ties

TRANSLATED BY ELIZABETH LOVICK
CROCHETED BY ALISON CASSIDY AND GAIL LEE

MATERIALS

For each tie: 40 (50) g 4 ply crochet cotton

3 mm Tunisian crochet hook

SIZE

To Fit "a Lady and Gentleman"

Four in Hand Tie: 2.5 (3)" wide and 32 (38)" long

Straight Tie: 2 (2.5)" wide and 36 (42)" long

TENSION

36 sts to 4"

NOTES

The ties are worked in the basic Tunisian crochet stitch.

PATTERN

For a striped tie, work 6 double row stripes throughout the tie, finishing after a full stripe.

STRIPED TIE

Chain 24 (28).

Work straight for 9 (11)"

Decrease 1 st each side of the next and every alternate pair of rows until 14 (18) sts remain.

Work straight for 12 (14)".

Increase 1 st each side of the next and every alternate pair of rows until you have 20 (24) sts.

Work straight for 9 (11)". **Adjust length here.**

Fasten off.

Finishing
Weave in all ends. Wash and dry flat.

STRAIGHT TIE

Chain 20 (24).

Work straight for 36" for a lady and 42" for a gentleman.

Fasten off.

Finishing
Weave in all ends. Wash and dry flat.

Rough and Ready Cardigan

TRANSLATED BY JUDITH BRODNICKI • KNITTED BY JANE LAWRENCE

INSPIRATION

Another pattern from one of the Bear brand books, and another which is as useful today as it was when first published. The original was for a 6 year old, but Judith has resized it for adults and children. — Liz

MATERIALS

Adult sizes: 600 (650, 700, 800, 900, 1050, 1200, 1300, 1500) g aran weight yarn

Child sizes: 400 (450, 500, 550) g aran weight yarn

Pairs 3.75 mm and 4.5 mm (US 5 and 7) needles, or size to achieve tension

Buttons: 5 for Child sizes and 7 for Adult sizes; 1/2" to 3/4" in diameter

Row counter

SIZE

Adult Sizes: XXS (XS, S, M, L, 1X, 2X, 3X, 4X)

Actual Chest: 32 (36, 40, 43, 47, 51, 56, 60, 65)"

Length: 23 (23.5, 24, 24.5, 25, 25.5, 26, 27, 28)"

Sleeve Length*: 18.5 (21.5, 21.5, 22, 22, 24, 26, 26.5, 26.5)"

* including the long turn-back cuff

Child Sizes: C1 (C2, C3, C4)
Actual Chest: 24 (26.5, 28, 29.5)"
Length: 14.5 (15.5, 16.5, 18.5)"
Sleeve Length: 7.5 (9.5, 10.5, 11.5)"

TENSION

18 sts and 32 rows to 4" over garter stitch

ABBREVIATIONS

R&R Pattern
Row 1 (RS): *K1, p1, k1* repeat.
Row 2: K.

CONSTRUCTION

This shawl-collar cardigan is worked flat starting at the lower back and then up and over the shoulders where each front is worked separately from the top down. Sleeves are worked from the top down. The front bands and collar and the patch pockets are worked separately.

PATTERN

PATTERN FOR ADULT SIZES

BACK

With larger needles, cast on 60 (69, 84, 84, 93, 99, 108, 114, 126) sts and knit 8 rows.

Change to R&R pattern and work until piece measures 15.5 (15.5, 15.5, 15.5, 14, 14, 15, 15, 15)" from cast on edge, ending after a WS row and noting the number of rows worked. **Adjust length here.**

Shape Back Armholes
Row 1: Cast off 2 (2, 2, 2, 3, 3, 4, 5, 7), patt to end of row.

Row 2: As Row 1.

Row 3: Patt 2, k2tog, patt to last 4 sts, ssk, patt 2.

Row 4: In patt.

Repeat Rows 3 and 4 until 54 (63, 66, 72, 75, 81, 84, 84, 84) sts remain.

Continue in patt until upper back measures 6.5 (7, 7.5, 8, 10, 10.5, 10, 11, 12)" from the start of the armhole, ending after a WS row.

Knit 8 rows.

Divide Back and Front at Shoulders
Next Row: K18 (22, 24, 27, 29, 31, 30, 30, 30) sts, and place on holder; cast off the next 18 (19, 18, 18, 17, 19, 24, 24, 24) sts for back neck; k to end of row. These 18 (22, 24, 27, 29, 31, 30, 30, 30) sts will be the Left Front.

LEFT FRONT

Knit 7 rows.

Left Front Neck Shaping
Row 1 (RS): In R&R pattern.

Row 2: Patt to last st, m1, k1.

Repeat these 2 rows until there are 39 (45, 39, 45, 51, 54, 60, 63, 69) sts on the needle, ending after a WS row.

Work 0 (6, 12, 10, 18, 14, 8, 10, 8) more rows in patt.

Left Front Armhole Shaping
Row 1 (RS): In patt.

Row 2 (WS): K1, M1, patt to end of row.

Repeat Rows 1 and 2 until there are 42 (46, 45, 51, 57, 62, 64, 67, 72) sts on the needle, finishing after a WS row.

Patt 1 row.

Next Row (RS): Cast on 0 (2, 3, 3, 3, 4, 8, 11, 12), patt to end of row. 42 (48, 48, 54, 60, 66, 72, 78, 84) sts

Work in patt for the same number of rows as the back.

Knit 8 rows. Cast off.

RIGHT FRONT

Return to the held sts. With WSF, join yarn and knit 7 rows.

Right Front Neck Shaping
Row 1 (RS): In R&R pattern.

Row 2: K1, m1, patt to end of row.

Repeat these 2 rows until there are 39 (45, 39, 45, 51, 54, 60, 63, 69) sts on the needle, ending after a WS row.

Work 0 (6, 12, 10, 18, 14, 8, 10, 8) more rows in patt.

Right Front Armhole Shaping
Row 1 (RS): In patt.

Row 2 (WS): Patt to last st, m1, k1.

Repeat Rows 1 and 2 until there are 42 (46, 45, 51, 57, 62, 64, 67, 72)

sts on the needle, finishing after a WS row.

Next Row (RS): Cast on 0 (2, 3, 3, 3, 4, 8, 11, 12), patt to end of row. 42 (48, 48, 54, 60, 66, 72, 78, 84) sts

Next Row: In patt.

Now work in patt for the same number of rows as the back.

Knit 8 rows. Cast off.

SLEEVES

Sleeve cap
With larger needles, cast on 24 sts.

Row 1 (RS): In R&R patt.

Row 2: Cast on 3 sts, patt to end of row.

Repeat Row 2 until there are 60 (60, 66, 72, 78, 84, 90, 102, 108) sts on the needle.

Patt 8 rows.

Sleeve Decrease
*Row 1 (WS): K1, k2tog, patt to last 3 sts, ssk, k1.

Work 5 (7, 5, 5, 5, 3, 3, 3, 3) rows in patt.

Repeat from * until 30 (36, 36, 36, 42, 42, 48, 48, 54) sts remain.

Work straight until the sleeve measures 13.5 (14.5, 14.5, 15, 15, 15, 17, 17.5, 17.5)" from the cast on edge. *Adjust length here.*

Cuff
Change to smaller needles and knit 8 rows, then work 4 (6, 6, 6, 6, 8, 8, 8, 8)" in k1, p1 rib.

Cast off.

FRONT BANDS AND COLLAR

Before working front bands and collar, place Right Front flat, and mark the positions of the buttons with pins. Place the first 1" from the hem and the last 1" down from the start of the neck shaping, with the other 3 even spaced between. Place a marker on both fronts where the neck shaping finishes.

To make buttonholes, work as follows:

Row 1 (RS): S1p, k2, cast off 2 sts, k3.

Row 2: K3, cast on 2 sts, k3.

Buttonholes will not be mentioned in the following instructions.

With larger needles, cast on 8 sts and knit until piece measures 1" less than the length from the hem to the start of the V-neck.

Collar Increases
Row 1 (RS): S1p, k2, kfb, k to end of row.

Row 2: K.

Repeat Rows 1 and 2 until there are 36 sts on the needles.

Place a row marker at this point.

Knit straight until the piece after the row marker is long enough to reach between the markers on the neck of the garment.

Collar Decreases
Row 1 (RS): S1p, k2, k2tog, k to end of row.

Row 2: K.

Repeat Rows 1 and 2 until 8 sts remain.

Knit until the band fits the front to the hem. Cast off.

POCKETS (MAKE 2)

With larger needles, cast on 30 sts and work in R&R patt for 5". Knit 8 rows. Cast off.

FINISHING

Sew side and sleeve seams, reversing the seam for the lower half of the cuff. Sew sleeves to armholes. Sew the front bands and collar in place. Sew on pockets and buttons. In wear, turn back cuffs.

Weave in all ends. Wash and dry flat.

PATTERN FOR CHILDREN'S SIZES

BACK

With larger needles, cast on 48 (48, 54, 60) sts and knit 8 rows.

Change to R&R pattern, until work measure 10.5 (11, 11.5, 14)" from cast on edge, ending after a WS row and noting the number of rows worked. *Adjust length here.*

Shape Back Armholes
Cast off 2 (0, 0, 0) sts at the beginning of the next 2 rows.

Row 1: Patt 2, k2tog, patt to last 4 sts, ssk, patt 2.

Row 2: In patt.

Repeat Rows 1 and 2 until 42 (42, 48, 48) sts remain.

Continue in patt until upper back measures 5 (5.5, 6, 6.5)" from the start of the armhole, ending after a WS row.

Knit 6 rows.

Divide Back and Front at Shoulders
Next Row: K16 (15, 17, 16), and place on holder; cast off the next 10 (12, 14, 16) for back neck; k to end of row. These 16 (15, 17, 16) sts will be the Left Front.

LEFT FRONT

Knit 5 rows.

Left Front Neck Shaping
Row 1 (RS): In R&R pattern.

Row 2: Patt to last st, m1, k1.

Repeat these 2 rows until there are 27 (33, 33, 30) sts on the needle, ending after a WS row.

Work 14 (5, 12, 18) more rows in patt.

Left Front Armhole Shaping
Row 1 (RS): In patt.

Row 2: K1, m1, patt to end of row.

Repeat Rows 1 and 2 until there are 28 (34, 34, 32) sts on the needle, finishing after a WS row.

Patt 1 row.

Next Row (RS): Cast on 2 (2, 2, 4) sts, patt to end of row. 30 (36, 36, 36) sts

Work in patt for the same number of rows as the back.

Knit 8 rows. Cast off.

RIGHT FRONT

Return to the held sts. With WSF, join yarn and knit 5 rows.

Right Front Neck Shaping
Row 1 (RS): In R&R pattern.

Row 2: K1, m1, patt to end of row.

Repeat these 2 rows until there are 27 (33, 33, 30) sts on the needle, ending after a WS row.

Work 14 (6, 12, 18) more rows in patt.

Left Front Armhole Shaping
Row 1 (RS): In patt.

Row 2: Patt to last st, m1, k1.

Repeat Rows 1 and 2 until there are 28 (34, 34, 32) sts on the needle, finishing after a WS row.

Next Row (RS): Cast on 2 (2, 2, 4) sts, patt to end of row. 30 (36, 36, 36) sts

Next Row: In patt.

Now work in patt for the same number of rows as the back.

Knit 8 rows. Cast off.

SLEEVES

Sleeve cap
With larger needles, cast on 30 (30, 30, 24) sts.

Row 1 (RS): In R&R patt.

Row 2: Cast on 3, patt to end of row.

Repeat Row 2 until there are 54 (60, 60, 66) sts on the needle.

Patt 8 (0, 0, 8) rows.

Sleeve Decrease
*Row 1 (WS): K1, k2tog, patt to last 3 sts, ssk, k1.

Work 1 (2, 2, 2) rows in patt.

Repeat from * until 30 (36, 36, 42) sts remain.

Work straight until the sleeve measures 7.5 (8.5, 9.5, 10.5)" from end of sleeve cap shaping. *Adjust length here.*

Cuff
Change to smaller needles and knit 8 rows, then work 4" in k1, p1 rib.

Cast off.

FRONT BANDS AND COLLAR

Before working front bands and collar, place Right Front flat, and mark the positions of the buttons with pins. Place the first 1" from the hem and the last 1" down from the start of the neck shaping, with the other 3 even spaced between. Place a marker on both fronts where the neck shaping finishes.

To make buttonholes, work as follows:

Row 1 (RS): S1p, k2, cast off 2 sts, k3.

Row 2: K3, cast on 2 sts, k3.

Buttonholes will not be mentioned in the following instructions.

With larger needles, cast on 6 sts and knit until piece measures 1" less than the length from the hem to the start of the V-neck.

Collar Increases
Row 1 (RS): S1p, k2, kfb, k to end of row.

Row 2: K.

Repeat Rows 1 and 2 until there are 30 sts on the needles.

Place row marker at this point.

Knit straight until the piece after the row marker is long enough to reach between the markers on the neck of the garment.

Collar Decreases
Row 1 (RS): S1p, k2, k2tog, k to end of row.

Sailor Sweater. Photo © Stewart Wall

Row 2: K.

Repeat Rows 1 and 2 until 6 sts remain.

Knit until the band fits the front to the hem. Cast off.

POCKETS (MAKE 2)

With larger needles, cast on 24 sts and work in R&R patt for 4". Knit 6 rows. Cast off.

FINISHING

Sew side and sleeve seams, reversing the seam for the lower half of the cuff. Sew sleeves to armholes. Sew the front bands and collar in place. Sew on pockets and buttons. In wear, turn back cuffs.

Weave in all ends. Wash and dry flat.

Note that the fronts will appear to overlap before the button band is attached; this is because of the narrow back construction. Sleeves are worked from the top down.

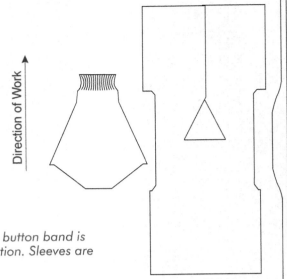

Sailor Sweater for Adults and Children

TRANSLATED BY JUDITH BRODNICKI • KNITTED BY GILL HOLLISTER

MATERIALS

Adult sizes: 400 (450, 500, 600, 700, 850, 1000, 1200, 1400) g DK weight yarn

Child sizes: 300 (350, 400, 450) g DK weight yarn

Pairs 3.75 mm and 4 mm (US 5 and 6) needles, or size to archive tension

Row counter

Stitch holders

Gill used Drops Karisma; 100% wool; 111 yds / 100 m per 50 g ball; shade 68, light sky blue

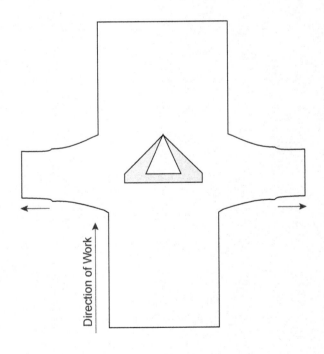

SIZE

Adult Sizes: XXS (XS, S, M, L, 1X, 2X, 3X, 4X)

Actual Bust: 32 (36, 40, 44, 48, 52, 56, 60, 64)"

Length: 22.5 (23, 23, 23.5, 24, 24, 24, 24.5, 24.5)"

Sleeve Length: 16 (16, 16, 17, 17, 17, 18, 18)" plus 3" turn back

Child Sizes: C1 (C2, C3, C4)

Actual Chest: 28.5 (31, 33.5, 36)"

Length: 14.5 (15.5, 16.5, 18.5)"

Sleeve Length: 11 (14, 15.5, 17)" plus 2" turn back

TENSION

24 sts and 30 rows to 4" over garter stitch

CONSTRUCTION

This garment is worked flat starting at the lower back and then up and over the shoulders and down the front. The main part of the sleeves are worked with the body, and the cuffs are added after. The sailor collar is worked last.

PATTERN

PATTERN FOR ADULTS

BACK

With larger needles, cast on 85 (97, 109, 121, 133, 145, 157, 169, 181) sts. Work in k3, p3 rib as follows:

Row 1: K2, p3, *k3, p3. Repeat from * to last 2 sts, k2.

Row 2: P2, k3, *p3, k3. Repeat from * to last 2 sts, p2.

Continue in patt for 16.5 (16.5, 16.5, 16, 15.5, 15, 14, 14, 13)" from hem, ending after a WS row and noting the number of rows worked. *Adjust length here.*

UPPER BACK AND SLEEVES

Row 1 (RS): K1, kfb, k to end of row.

Rows 2 to 6: As Row 1. 91 (103, 115, 127, 139, 151, 163, 175, 187) sts

Row 7: Cast on 26 (26, 26, 28, 28, 28, 28, 30, 30) sts, k to end of row.

Rows 8 to 12: As Row 7. 247 (259, 271, 295, 307, 319, 331, 355, 367) sts

Work straight for 52 (56, 58, 64, 74, 82, 88, 96, 102) rows.

Next Row: K 104 (109, 115, 126, 132, 136, 141, 153, 158) sts and place on stitch holder; cast off 39 (41, 41, 43, 43, 47, 49, 49, 51) sts for the back neck. The remaining 104 (109, 115, 126, 132, 136, 141, 153, 158) sts are worked as the Upper Left Front.

UPPER LEFT FRONT

Knit 3 rows.

Next Row (RS): Cast on 19 (20, 20, 21, 21, 23, 24, 24, 25) sts, k to end of row. 123 (129, 135, 147, 153, 159, 165, 177, 183) sts

Knit 48 (52, 54, 60, 70, 78, 84, 92, 98) rows.

Decrease sleeve:
Row 1 (WS): Cast off 26 (26, 26, 28, 28, 28, 28, 30, 30) sts, k to end of row.

Row 2: K.

Rows 3 to 6: Repeat Rows 1 and 2 twice.

Row 7: K1, k2tog, k to end of row.

Row 8: K.

Rows 9 to 12: Repeat Rows 7 and 8 twice.

Place remaining 54 (60, 66, 72, 78, 84, 90, 96, 102) sts on a stitch holder.

UPPER RIGHT FRONT

With WS facing, join new yarn at neck edge. Knit 4 rows.

Next Row (WS): Cast on 19 (20, 20, 21, 21, 23, 24, 24, 25) sts, k to end of row. 123 (129, 135, 147, 153, 159, 165, 177, 183) sts

Knit 48 (52, 54, 60, 70, 78, 84, 92, 98) rows.

Decrease sleeve:

Row 1 (RS): Cast off 26 (26, 26, 28, 28, 28, 28, 30, 30) sts, k to end of row.

Row 2: K.

Rows 3 to 6: Repeat Rows 1 and 2 twice.

Row 7: K1, k2tog, k to end of row.

Row 8: K.

Rows 9 and 10: Repeat Rows 1 and 2 twice.

Row 11: As Row 7.

Row 12: K to last 2 sts, kfb, k1; place the sts held from the Upper Left Front on to the needle and knit across. 99 (121, 133, 145, 157, 169, 181, 193, 205) sts

Work in rib as for the back, for the same number of rows as the Back.

Cast off.

COLLAR

With WS facing and using larger needles pick up 77 (81, 81, 85, 85, 93, 97, 97, 101) sts along the neckline starting with the Upper Right Front neck edge. Work in garter stitch for 4". Cast off.

CUFFS

With smaller needles, pick up 55 (61, 61, 67, 79, 85, 91, 97, 103) sts around the sleeve edge.

Work in rib as for the back for 6". Cast off.

FINISHING

Sew side and sleeve seams. If desired, crochet a cord 36" long and trim each end with a 2" tassel. Place under the collar and tie at the centre front.

PATTERN FOR CHILDREN

BACK

With larger needles, cast on 67 (73, 79, 85) sts. Work in k3, p3 rib as follows:

Row 1: K2, p3, *k3, p3. Repeat from * to last 2 sts, k2.

Row 2: P2, k3, *p3, k3. Repeat from * to last 2 sts, p2.

Continue in pattern for 10 (10.5, 11, 13)" from hem, ending after a WS row and noting the number of rows worked. *Adjust length here.*

UPPER BACK AND SLEEVES

Row 1 (RS): K1, kfb, k to end of row.

Rows 2 to 6: As Row 1. 73 (79, 85, 91) sts

Row 7: Cast on 18 (24, 27, 30) sts, k to end of row.

Rows 8 to 10: As Row 7. 145 (175,

Motor Cap for a Youth and Aran Gansey. Each of the children who sang in the choir at the film premiere was given one of the ganseys.

193, 211) sts

Work straight for 36 (40, 44, 48) rows.

Next Row: K57 (70, 78, 87) sts and place on stitch holder; cast off 31 (35, 37, 37) sts for the back neck. The rem 57 (70, 78, 87) sts are worked as the Upper Left Front.

UPPER LEFT FRONT

Knit 3 rows.

Next Row (RS): Cast on 21 (23, 24, 24) sts, k to end of row. 78 (93, 102, 111) sts

Knit 20 (20, 24, 28) more rows.

Decrease sleeve:

Row 1 (WS): Cast off 18 (24, 27, 30) sts, k to end of row.

Row 2: K.

Rows 3 and 4: As Rows 1 and 2.

Row 5: K1, k2tog, k to end of row.

Row 6: K.

Rows 7 to 10: As Rows 5 and 6.

Place remaining 39 (42, 45, 48) sts on a stitch holder.

UPPER RIGHT FRONT

With WS facing, join new yarn at neck edge. Knit 4 rows.

Next Row (WS): Cast on 21 (23, 24, 24) sts, k to end of row. 78 (93, 102, 111) sts

Knit 20 (20, 24, 28) more rows.

Decrease sleeve:
Row 1 (RS): Cast off 18 (24, 27, 30) sts, k to end of row.

Row 2: K.

Rows 3 and 4: As Rows 1 and 2.

Row 5: K1, k2tog, k to end of row.

Row 6: K.

Rows 7 and 8: As Rows 5 and 6.

Row 9: As Row 5.

Row 10: K to last 2 sts, kfb, k1; place the sts held from the Upper Left Front on to the needle and knit across. 79 (85, 91, 97) sts

Change to k3, p3 rib, and work the same number of row as the Back.

Cast off.

COLLAR

With WS facing and using larger needles pick up 72 (81, 85, 85) sts along the neckline starting with the Upper Right Front neck edge. Work in garter stitch for 2 (2, 3, 3)". Cast off.

CUFFS

With smaller needles, pick up 36 (42, 48, 48) sts around the sleeve edge.

Work in k3, p3 rib for 4". Cast off.

FINISHING

Sew side and sleeve seams. If desired, crochet a cord 24 (24, 30, 36)" long and trim each end with a 2" tassel. Place under the collar and tie at the centre front.

INSPIRATION

The Motor Cap pattern is from The Book of Hows, 7th edition, 1911 or earlier, Published by Needlecraft, Manchester.

Motor Cap for a Youth

TRANSLATED AND CROCHETED BY MELANIE SMITH

MATERIALS

Teen size:

150 g Sport weight or 5 ply yarn

3.5 mm crochet hook, or size to achieve tension

Adult size:

200 g DK yarn

4 mm crochet hook, or size to achieve tension

2 small gold buttons

Melanie used Knit Picks Comfy Sport; 75% Pima cotton, 25% Acrylic; 136 yds/123 m per 50 g ball; shade Bison.

SIZE

To fit: Teen (Adult)

TENSION

19 sts and 22 rows to 4" for the Teen size

16 sts and 19 rows to 4" for the Adult size

CONSTRUCTION

This cap is constructed from the centre of the crown out. It is worked in the round, back and forth, by closing each round with a slip-stitch, and working a turning chain. The brim and peak are worked separately.

PATTERN

CROWN TOP

Chain 4, sl-st into first ch to form a ring.

Rnd 1: 1 ch, 8 dc in ring, sl-st ring closed, turn.

Rnd 2: 1 ch, dc in each stitch round, ss in the middle of the first dc in round to close, ch 1, turn work.

Rnd 3: Dc across rnd, sl-st closed. 1 ch, turn.

Rnd 4: Inc across rnd, sl-st closed. 1 ch, turn. 16 sts

Rnd 5: Dc across rnd, sl-st closed. 1 ch, turn.

Rnd 6: As Rnd 3. 32 sts

Rnd 7: As Rnd 4.

Rnd 8: [2 dc, inc] 10 times, dc into each rem st, sl-st closed. 1 ch, turn. 42 sts

Rnd 9: [3 dc, inc] 10 times, dc into each rem st, sl-st closed. 1 ch, turn. 52 sts

Rnd 10: [9 dc, inc] 5 times, dc into each rem st, sl-st closed. 1 ch, turn. 57 sts

Rnd 11: As Rnd 4.

Rnd 12: [3 dc, inc] 14 times, dc into each rem st, sl-st closed. 1 ch, turn. 71 sts

Rnd 13 and 14: As Rnd 4.

Rnd 15: [5 dc, inc] 11 times, dc into each rem st, sl-st closed. 1 ch, turn. 82 sts

Rnds 16 and 17: As Rnd 4.

Rnds 18: [4 dc, inc] 16 times, dc into each rem st, sl-st closed. 1 ch, turn. 98 sts

Rnds 19 and 20: As Rnd 4.

Rnd 21: [9 dc, inc] 9 times, dc into each rem st, sl-st closed. 1 ch, turn. 107 sts

Rnd 22: As Rnd 4.

Rnd 23: [14 dc, inc] 7 times, dc into each rem st, sl-st closed. 1 ch, turn. 114 sts

Rnds 24: As Rnd 4.

Rnds 25: 2 dc, [inc, 11 dc] 9 times, dc into each rem st, sl-st closed. 1 ch, turn. 123 sts

Rnds 26 to 28: As Rnd 4.

UNDERCROWN

Chain 14.

Row 1: Skip first ch, 13 dc, 1 ch, turn.

Row 2 to 6: 13 dc, 1 ch, turn.

Row 7: 5 dc, sl-st in next st, turn.

Row 8: Dc to end of row, 1 ch, turn.

Row 9: 9 dc, 1 ch, turn.

Row 10: As Row 8.

Row 11: 11 dc, 1 ch, turn.

Row 12: As Row 8.

Row 13 to 16: As Row 8.

Row 17: As Row 7.

Row 18: As Row 8.

Rows 19 to 24: As Row 2.

Repeat Rows 7 to 24 until the widest part is long enough to fit around the crown.

HAT BAND
Chain 9.

Row 1: Skip first ch, dc in next 8 chs, ch 1, turn work.

Row 2: Dc in each st across, 1 ch, turn work.

Repeat Row 2 until the band fits round the cap.

PEAK
Chain 59.

Row 1: Miss first ch, dc in each st across.

Row 2: Sl-st in first 4 sts, dc to last 4 sts, sl-st in remaining sts, turn.

Row 3: Sl-st in first 5, sts, dc to last 6 sts, sl-st in next 2 sts, turn.

Row 4: Sl-st in next two sts, dc to last 6 sts, turn.

Row 5 to 15: Sl-st in next 2 sts, dc to last unworked dc in previous row.

Row 16: Dc around all sides of peak, finish off.

Make a second piece, but do not finish off. Holding both pieces together, join them with sl-st around. Finish off.

STRAP
Chain 5.

Row 1: Skip first ch, dc in next 4 sts, ch 1, turn.

Repeat Row 1 until the strap fits the inner edge of the peak.

Finish off.

FINISHING
Seam both crown pieces together. Seam the first row of the hat band to the last, then seam to under crown. Pin, then sew, the peak into place at front of hat. Sew the strap over the seam, and attach the buttons.

Aran Ganseys for Children & Teens

DESIGNED BY ELIZABETH LOVICK • KNITTED BY MANY VOLUNTEERS

MATERIALS
300 (350, 400, 500, 600, 700) g aran weight yarn

Pairs 4 mm and 5 mm (US 6 and 8) needles, or size to achieve tension

Row counter

Crochet hook, about 4 mm, for the two smallest sizes

3 Small buttons for the two smallest sizes

SIZE
To Fit Age: 3/4 (5/6, 7/8, 9/10, 11/12, 13/14) years

Actual Chest: 26 (28, 30, 32, 34, 36)"

Body Length: 14 (16, 18, 20, 22, 24)"

Yoke Depth: 5 (5.5, 6, 6.5, 7, 7.5)"

Sleeve Length: 10 (11, 12, 14, 16, 18)"

Sleeve and body length are easily adjustable.

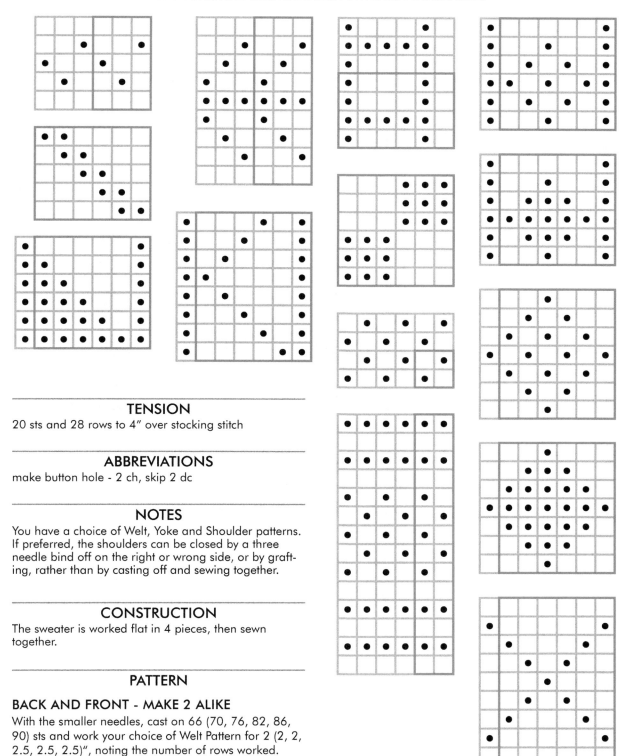

TENSION

20 sts and 28 rows to 4" over stocking stitch

ABBREVIATIONS

make button hole - 2 ch, skip 2 dc

NOTES

You have a choice of Welt, Yoke and Shoulder patterns. If preferred, the shoulders can be closed by a three needle bind off on the right or wrong side, or by grafting, rather than by casting off and sewing together.

CONSTRUCTION

The sweater is worked flat in 4 pieces, then sewn together.

PATTERN

BACK AND FRONT - MAKE 2 ALIKE

With the smaller needles, cast on 66 (70, 76, 82, 86, 90) sts and work your choice of Welt Pattern for 2 (2, 2, 2.5, 2.5, 2.5)", noting the number of rows worked.

Change to larger needles and stocking stitch.

Work straight until the piece measures 9 (10.5 12, 13.5, 15, 16.5)" from the cast on, noting the number of rows worked. *Adjust length here.*

Now work your choice of Yoke Pattern until the piece measures 13 (15, 17, 19, 21, 23)" from the cast on, ending after an even numbered row and noting the number of rows worked.

Split for the shoulders and neck:
Row 1: K22 (22, 26, 26, 28, 30); place remaining sts on a stitch holder or length of yarn.

Working on the stitches left on the needle only, knit 1 row.

Now work your choice of Shoulder Pattern for 1", noting the number of rows worked. Cast off.

Return to the sts on the thread. With RSF, place the first 22 (26, 24, 30, 30, 30) sts on a length of thread for the Neck. Place the remaining 22 (22, 26, 26, 28, 30) sts on the needle for the other shoulder, and knit 2 rows.

Now work the same pattern as the first shoulder for the same number of rows. Cast off.

SLEEVES

With the smaller needles, cast on 26 (30, 32, 38, 42, 42) sts. Work the Welt exactly as for the Back.

Change to the larger needles and stocking stitch, increasing as follows:

Row 1: K1, m1, k to last st, m1, k1.

Rows 2 to 4: In stocking stitch.

Repeat these four rows until there are 50 (56, 60, 66, 70, 76) sts on the needle.

Work straight in stocking stitch until the piece measures 10 (11, 12, 14, 16, 18)" from the cast on. Cast off.

NECKBAND

Join the front and back together at the right shoulder seam.

With the smaller needles, pick up and knit 5 sts from the left front shoulder extension; knit the 22 (26, 24, 30, 30, 30) sts from the thread for the front neck; pick up and knit 10 sts from the right shoulder extensions; knit the 22 (26, 24, 30, 30, 30) sts from the thread for the back neck; pick up and knit 5 sts from the left back shoulder extension.

Now work in the Welt Pattern for 1 (1, 1.5, 1.5, 2, 2)".

Cast off loosely using one of the

larger needles.

FINISHING

For the smallest two sizes: join the outer half of the left shoulder seam. Starting at the cast off edge of the neckband, work 1 row of dc down the neckband, round the rest of the seam, and up the other edge of the neckband. Mark the position of 3 buttons with pins. Now work a second row of dc, working 1 dc into each dc, and making three button holes to correspond with the pins.

For the larger four sizes, sew the left shoulder and neck band seam.

For all sizes, mark the centre of the cast off edge of the sleeves. With right sides facing, pin the sleeve to the front and back, matching the centre of the sleeve with the shoulder seam. Pin, then sew, the sleeve to the front and back. Note that the sleeve will come approximately to the start of the yoke, but this is not critical.

With right sides facing, sew the body and sleeve seams.

Weave in all ends. Wash roughly (to take the newness out!) and dry. If needed, sew on buttons to match the button holes.

Service Cardigan

TRANSLATED AND KNITTED BY JUDITH A. BRODNICKI

INSPIRATION

I was between projects when another cardigan was needed, so I volunteered to knit something. I suggested several from the Bear Brand Blue Book, Vol. 20. Pauline liked The Service Sweater (which is really a cardigan) and I was quite pleased because I'd not worked a garment that was all in ribbing. I learned a lot about the way the shaping was worked (often in paired rows), something I will bring into my own designs at a future date. — Judith

MATERIALS

700 (700, 800, 900, 900, 1000) g aran weight yarn

Pairs 3.5 mm and 4.5 mm (US 4 and 7) needles or size to achieve tension

5 (5, 5, 6, 6, 6) buttons about 3/4" in diameter

Stitch holders or lengths of waste yarn

Judith used Cascade 220; 100% Peruvian wool; 220 yds / 200 m per 100 g), shade 9449 Midnight Heather

SIZE

Men's Size: S (M, L, 1X, 2X, 3X)

Actual Chest: 37.5 (42.5, 46, 50, 54, 58)"

Length: 26 (27.5, 28, 29, 29, 30)"

TENSION

28 sts and 25 rows to 4" in k1, p1 rib on larger needles, blocked but not stretched. When stretched in wear, 24 sts and 25 rows to 4".

Note that because of the construction, row tension is important as well as stitch tension.

CONSTRUCTION

The cardigan is worked flat starting at the lower back and then up and over the shoulders where each front is worked separately from the top down. Sleeves are worked flat from the cuff to the top. Patch pockets, the front bands and the collar are worked separately, then sewn on. The main pieces are worked in k1, p1 rib and edged in k2, p2 rib.

PATTERN

BACK

With larger needles, cast on 96 (108, 116, 128, 136, 148) sts. Work 16 rows of k2, p2 rib.

Next Row: K1, m1, *k1, p1. Repeat from * to last st, k1. 97 (109, 117, 129, 137, 149) sts

Work in k1, p1 rib as set until piece measures 17 (18, 18, 18, 18, 18)" from the cast on edge, ending after

working a WS row, noting the number of rows worked. *Adjust length here.*

Back Armholes
Row 1 (RS): Cast off 4 (4, 6, 8, 10, 12) sts, patt to end of row.

Row 2: As Row 1.

Row 3: K1, p1, ssk, patt to last 5 sts, p1, k2tog, p1, k1.

Row 4: P1, ssk, patt to last 4 sts, p1, k2tog, p1.

Rows 5 and 6: In patt.

Repeat Rows 3 to 6 0 (1, 1, 2, 2, 3) times more. 85 (93, 97, 101, 105, 109) sts

Work straight until the armhole measures 9 (9.5, 10, 10.5, 11, 11.5)" from the beginning of Back Armhole shaping, ending after working a WS row.

Shoulders
Work 27 (31, 33, 33, 35, 37) sts; place these sts on a stitch holder. Cast off the next 31 (31, 31, 35, 35, 35) sts for the back neck. The remaining 27 (31, 33, 33, 35, 37) sts will be worked as the Left Front.

LEFT FRONT

Neck Increase
Row 1 (RS): In patt.

Row 2: In patt.

Row 3: K1, p1, m1, patt to last st, k1.

Row 4: Patt to last 4 sts, p1, m1, p1, k1, p1.

Repeat Rows 1 to 4 9 (11, 9, 9, 7, 9) times more. 47 (55, 53, 53, 51, 57) sts

Armhole Increase
Rows 1 and 2: In patt.

Row 3: Patt to last 2 sts, m1, p1, k1.

Row 4: P1, k1, m1, patt to end of row.

Repeat Rows 1 to 4 3 (2, 5, 5, 8, 7) times more. 55 (61, 65, 65, 69, 73) sts

Next Row: In patt.

Next Row: Cast on 10 (12, 14, 20, 24, 26) sts for the underarm, patt to end of row. 65 (73, 79, 85, 93, 99) sts

Work in k1, p1 rib for the same number of rows as the

back, decreasing 1 st at the side edge of the last row. Work 16 rows in k2, p2 rib.

Cast off loosely.

RIGHT FRONT

With WS facing, join yarn at neck edge and work 1 row in patt.

Neck Increase
Row 1 (RS): Patt to last 3 sts, k1, m1, p1, k1.

Row 2: P1, k1, p1, m1, patt to end of row.

Rows 3 and 4: In patt.

Row 5: Patt to last 3 sts, k1, m1, p1, k1.

Row 6: P1, k1, p1, m1, patt to end of row.

Repeat Rows 3 to 6 8 (10, 8, 8, 6, 8) times more. 47 (55, 53, 53, 51, 57) sts

Rib 2 (0, 0, 2, 2, 0) rows.

Armhole Increase
Rows 1 and 2: In patt.

Row 3: K1, p1, m1, patt to end of row.

Row 4: Patt to last 4 sts, p1, m1, p1, k1, p1.

Repeat Rows 1 to 4 3 (2, 5, 5, 8, 7) times more. 55 (61, 65, 65, 69, 73) sts

Next Row: Cast on 10 (12, 14, 20, 24, 26) sts for the underarm, rib to end of row. 65 (73, 77, 83, 93, 99) sts

Complete to match the Left Front.

SLEEVES

With smaller needles, cast on 52 (52, 56, 56, 60, 60) sts and work in k2, p2 rib for 26 rows.

Change to larger needles and k1, p1 rib.

Row 1: *Work 1, m1, work 2 (2, 2, 2, 3, 3). Repeat from * to last 1 (1, 5, 5, 0, 0) sts, work to end of row. 69 (69, 73, 73, 75, 75) sts

Shape sleeve:
*Row 1 (RS): Patt 2, m1, rib to last 2 sts, m1, patt 2.

Rows 2 to 4: In patt.

Repeat from * until there are 97 (103, 115, 121, 127, 133) sts on the needle.

Work in pattern until the sleeve measures 18 (18, 20, 20, 21, 21)" from cast on edge, ending after a WS row. *Adjust sleeve length here.*

Shape Sleeve Cap
Row 1: Cast off 7 (9, 11, 15, 17, 20) sts, patt to end of row.

Row 2: As Row 1. 83 (85, 93, 91, 93, 93) sts.

*Row 3 (RS): Cast off 3 sts, patt to last 2 sts, k2tog.

Row 4: Cast off 3 sts, patt, to last 2 sts, k2tog.

Work 4 (4, 4, 4, 6, 6) rows in patt.

Repeat from * until 59 (61, 61, 51, 85, 61) sts remain.

**Next Row: Cast off 3 sts, patt to last 2 sts, k2tog.

Next Row: Cast off 3 sts, patt to last 2 sts, k2tog.

Work 2 (2, 2, 2, 4, 4) rows in pattern.

Repeat from ** until 27 (21, 29, 27, 29, 29) sts remain.

Extension Strap
Cast off 9 (6, 10, 9, 10, 10) sts in patt at the beginning of the next 2 rows. 9 sts remain. Change to smaller needles and work in stocking stitch until, when slightly stretched, it reaches along the shoulder to the neck. Cast off.

FRONT BANDS AND COLLAR

Lay the fronts flat. On the Left Front place pins to indicate the positions of the buttons, placing the first 1" up from the hem, the last 1" below the end of the V neck shaping and the other equally spaced between.
With larger needles, cast on 12 sts.

Row 1 (RS): S1p, k11.

Row 2: Slp, k11.

Repeat Rows 1 and 2 until piece measures 15 (16, 16, 16, 16, 16)", or length of the left front to the start of the neck shaping.

Increase for the Collar:
Row 1: S1p, k10, kfb.

Row 2: S1p, knit to the end of the row.

Repeat Rows 1 and 2 until there are 36 sts, ending after a WS row.

If necessary, work a few rows straight in garter stitch so that the strip reaches from to the shoulder when slightly stretched. Note number of rows worked.

Short-Row Transition (Front to Back)
Row 1 and all odd numbered rows: S1p, knit to the end of the row.

Row 2 (WS): S1p, k2, W&T.

Row 4: S1p, k5, W&T.

Row 6: S1p, k8, W&T.

Row 8: S1p, k11, W&T.

Row 10: S1p, k14, W&T.

Row 12: S1p, k17, W&T.

Row 14: S1p, k20, W&T.

Row 16: S1p, k23, W&T.

Row 18: S1p, k26, W&T.

Row 20: S1p, k29, W&T.

Row 22: S1p, k32, W&T.

Work 32 (32, 32, 34, 34, 34) rows in garter stitch.

Short-Row Transition (Back to Front)
Row 1 and all odd numbered rows: S1p, knit to the end of the row.

Row 2 (WS): S1p, k32, W&T.

Row 4: S1p, k29, W&T.

Row 6: S1p, k26, W&T.

Molly Marie Buckley and Thomas Hinckley get their feet wet in a photo of the Service Cardigan.

Row 8: S1p, k23, W&T.
Row 10: S1p, k20, W&T.
Row 12: S1p, k17, W&T.
Row 14: S1p, k14, W&T.
Row 16: S1p, k11, W&T.
Row 18: S1p, k8, W&T.
Row 20: S1p, k5, W&T.
Row 22: S1p, k2, W&T.

Decrease the collar:
If necessary, work the same number of rows in garter stitch as for the other side.

Row 1 (RS): S1p, to 2 sts before the end of the row, k2tog.

Row 2: S1p, knit to the end of the row.

Repeat Rows 1 and 2 until there are 12 sts, ending after a WS row.

RIGHT FRONT BAND

Work in garter stitch until Right Front Band is the same length as the Left Front Band. AT THE SAME TIME, work button holes to correspond with the button placements as follows:

RS: S1p, k3, cast off 4 sts, k to end of row.

WS: S1p, k3, cast on 4 sts, k4.

Cast off.

POCKETS (optional, make 1 or 2)

With larger needles, cast on 33 (33, 33, 37, 37, 37) sts and work in k1, p1 rib until piece measures 5". Change to smaller needles and work in garter stitch for 7 rows. Cast off.

FINISHING

Block all pieces.

Sew side seams. Sew sleeve seams, then set each sleeve into the armhole with the underarm seam slightly forward of the side seam and with the extension strap tucked to the inside of the garment at the top.

Place the short-row section at the point where the fronts and back meet at the shoulders. Pin, then sew, the front bands and collar into place. Tack the ends of the extension straps to the neck edge along the shoulder. (These help the shoulders retain their shape.) Sew on buttons. Place the patch pockets on the fronts, and pin. Now sew in place using a flat seam.

Servicemen's Socks

Translated by Elizabeth Lovick • Knitted by Alison Davies

MATERIALS

150g (200) DK yarn

Set 3.25 mm (US 3) dpns, or size to achieve tension

One 4 mm (US 6) dpn

stitch markers

Row counter

Alison used Artesano Superwash Merino; 100% wool; 112 m per 50 g ball; Shade Grey and Regia 6 ply sock yarn; 75% wool, 25% nylon; 137 yds / 125 m per 50g ball; shade 44 Grey Mix

SIZE

To Fit a male (large male)

Foot: 10.5 (11)"

TENSION

20 sts and 28 rows to 4" over stocking stitch

CONSTRUCTION

The socks are knitted in the round from the top down.

PATTERN

Cast 56 (60) sts on to the larger needle. Knit one round on to the smaller dpns, arranging them equally over the 3 needles.

Welt
Work in k2, p2 rib for 4.5".

Leg
Change to stocking stitch and work for a further 6.5".

Heel Flap
Knit 28 (30), turn. Place remaining sts on one needle.

Next Row (WS): S1p, p to end of row.

Next Row: S1p, k to end of row.

Repeat these two rows 13 (14) times more.

Heel Gusset
Row 1 (WS): P16 (17), p2tog, p1, turn.

Row 2: S1p, k5, ssk, k1, turn.

Row 3: S1p, p6, p2tog, p1, turn.

Row 4: S1p, k7, ssk, k1, turn.

Continue in this way until 17 (18) sts remain.

Purl 1 row.

Ankle Gussets
Go back to knitting in the round.

Rnd 1: K across heel sts; pick up and knit 14 (15) sts up the Heel Flap; on to a second needle knit the 28 (30) held sts; on to a third needle pick up and knit 14 (15) sts down the Heel Flap, then onto the same needle, knit the first 8 (9) sts from the heel gusset. The end of rounds is now under the foot.

Rnds 2 and 3: K.

Rnd 4: K to 3 sts before end of first needle, k2tog, k1; k the second needle; k1, ssk, k to end of third needle.

Repeat Rnds 2 to 4 until 56 (60) sts remain, with 28 (30) sts on the second needle for the top of the foot.

Foot
Continue in stocking stitch until the foot (from the point of the heel) measures 6.5 (7)".

Toe
Rnd 1: K to last 4 sts of first needle, k2tog, k2; k2, ssk, k to last 4 sts of second needle, k2tog, k2; k2, ssk, k to end of third needle.

Rnds 2 to 4: K.

Repeat Rnds 1 to 4 once more.

Rnd 9: As Rnd 1.

Rnds 10 and 11: K.

Repeat Rnds 9 to 11 twice more.

Rnd 18: As Rnd 1.

Rnd 19: K.

Repeat Rnds 18 and 19 until 20 (24) sts remain.

Finishing
Graft toe. Weave in all ends. Wash and dry flat.

DIRECTIONS FOR STANDARD SOCKS FOR OUR MEN ON ACTIVE SERVICE

Word-for-word from one of the Red Cross knitting booklets.

GENERAL DIRECTIONS

To prevent disappointment in results, use only the correct kind of wool and exact size of needles. If you knit loosely, choose the finer needles; if tightly then the coarser ones. Never knot the wool, join either by beginning to knit with the fresh ball a few inches before the end of the last, and after several stitches thus with double wool, cut off the tag of the old ball; or else thin out the two ends, and with a darning needle run first one end then the other into the opposite wool, thus making a 'splice'.

The names of parts of a sock used in knitting instructions are:- (1) Welt or Ribbing. (2) Leg. (3) Instep. (4) Heel Flap. (5) Heel Gusset. (6) Ankle. (7) Foot. (8) Toe.

WELT OR RIBBING

Cast on very loosely the number of stitches chosen (56 or 60); knit 1 round plain, and very loosely, then two plain, two purl for 4.5".

LEG

Now knit plain till you have from the top of the welt 11".

HEEL FLAP

Now put half the stitches on one needle and equally divide the remainder (required for instep) on the second and third needles, which are left until the heel is finished.

On the single needle knit alternate rows of plain and purl until a good oblong is formed, measuring over 2", and having 26 or 32 rows in it according to your needles and style of knitting. The first stitch in each row is always slipped.

N.B. By knitting a strand of mending-wool or silk into the heel-flap and gusset, the life of the sock will be lengthened.

HEEL GUSSET

Find and mark the centre of the heel stitches, and with inside of heel towards you *purl to centre of heel, and 2 sts beyond, then purl two together, purl one and turn over to the plain side. Slip one, knit on to centre and two beyond. Knit two together (by slipping one, knitting one and pulling slipped stitch over), and knit one more. Now turn and proceed from *, always taking one stitch further away from the centre, till all the stitches are used up and a neat gusset thus formed. Finish on the knitting side, not the purling side.

ANKLE GUSSETS

With your free needle pick up stitches down one side of heel flap (one for every pair of lines), about 13, 14 or 15. Knit these on to the same needle as the heel gusset stitches. Now knit on to a second needle all the stitches left for the instep when beginning the heel flap.

Now pick up with your third needle 13, 14, or 15 stitches up the other side of the heel flap, and transfer half the heel gusset stitches also on to this needle, and knit all these stitches. Your three needles are now a sort of triangle. Beginning now from centre of heel the needles are numbered I., II., and III. Knit two rounds plain, taking care to avoid a hole at the ankle by drawing your wool very tightly when changing from one needle to another. Then knit needle I. to within 3 sts of the end; knit two together, knit last stitch. Needle II. plain, Needle III. knit one slip one, knit one and pull slipped stitch over, knit plain to end of needle. This reducing to be done every alternate row till there are the same number of stitches as were on the leg.

FOOT

Knit plain, same as the leg, till within 2.25" of the full length required from back of heel to tip of toe. i.e. if 10.5" then foot = 8.25" if 11" then foot + 8.75". (10.5 preferred.)

TOE

Begin on needle II. Knit two, knit two together, knit to four from end, slip one, knit one, and pull slipped stitch over and knit remaining two. Needle III., knit two, knit two together. Needle 1., knit to four from end, slip one, knit one, pull over slipped stitch, and knit remaining two stitches. You have now knitted one full round, and have taken in four times. Now knit three rounds without taking in. Now knit a round and decrease four times as above; then three rounds plain, and a decrease as before on the next round. Then two more plain rounds, and decrease round; two more plain rounds, and decrease again; two more plain, then decrease. Now only one plain row between each decrease until there are 20 or 24 left. Transfer stitches from needle III. to I. to get an equal number on front and back needles. Break off your wool, leaving 9", and thread it into a darning needle or bodkin. *Begin with stitches next to you, and use the bodkin as if to knit and take off the first stitch, pulling the wool well through. Put bodkin through 2nd stitch as if purling, draw wool closely through, but leave the stitch on. Now pass wool round (not over knitting needle) to back needle, and purl the first stitch and take it off. Knit the 2nd stitch (with the darner), but leave it on the needle. Repeat from * till the toe is grafted together. Draw wool closely up, and secure it by neatly running it down the side of toe.

MEASUREMENTS

When finished, tops must not measure less than 14" round when stretched (7" across) from under heel to top of welt = 14", 15" or 16". From back of heel to tip of toe = 10.5" or 11". (10.5" preferred.)

Knitters should provide themselves with a tape measure for frequent reference.

REMEMBER!

That a single thread of 4-ply fingering on needles coarser than No. 13 makes a sock too thin for active service.

That socks should be washed, or at least pressed under a damp cloth.

That a safety pin is a good way of fastening socks together.

That our men like to find some written message inside their socks, as evidence that the socks are gifts.

Riflemen's Gloves

TRANSLATED BY ELIZABETH LOVICK • KNITTED BY KATY-JAYNE LINTOTT

INSPIRATION

Many publications had versions of these gloves for the troops, which were supposed to make firing guns easier. In the patterns only the right hand glove was explained. It was assumed you would be able to work out the differences for the left hand for yourself! — Kay-Jayne

MATERIALS

100 g DK yarn

Set 5 2.75 mm (US 2) dpns, or size to achieve tension

Waste yarn

Katy-Jayne used ColourMart DK; 100% lambswool; 330 yds / 300 m per 100 g; shade Nettle

SIZE

To Fit an average man's hand

10" round palm

TENSION

28 sts and 38 rows to 4" over stocking stitch

NOTES

Exact numbers for each needle are only mentioned where it is important. At other times distribute the stitches evenly.

PATTERN

RIGHT HAND GLOVE

Cuff
Cast on 56 sts, 16 on each of 2 needles and 12 on each of 2 needles.

K2, p2 for 6".

Hand
Knit for 2.5".

Thumb opening
With waste yarn k11. Break waste yarn. Slip these 11 sts back onto the needle they were knitted from. Now,

with the working yarn, knit over the waste yarn, and finish the rnd.

Palm
K 14 rnds. Adjust length here.

Index Finger
K8 onto one needle; slip next 37 sts onto a thread. Cast on 3 sts, k7 onto the second needle, k4 onto the third. 22 sts

Knit for 1.5".

Work 5 rnds in k1, p1 rib.

Cast off.

Three Fingers
Place the 37 held sts on the needles, pick up 3 sts from those cast on for the Index Finger. 40 sts

Rejoin yarn and knit 22 rnds.

Decrease for the top as follows:

Rnd 1: K15, k2tog, k3, ssk, k to end of rnd.

Rnd 2: K.

Repeat Rnds 1 and 2 3 times more. 32 sts

Rnd 9: *Ssk, k12, k2tog. Repeat from * once more.

Rnd 10: *Ssk, k10, k2tog. Repeat from * once more.

Rnd 11: *Ssk, k8, k2tog. Repeat from * once more.

Rnd 12: *Ssk, k6, k2tog. Repeat from * once more.

Rnd 13: *Ssk, k4, k2tog. Repeat from * once more.

Rnd 14: *Ssk, k2, k2tog. Repeat from * once more. 8 sts

Put the first 4 sts of the rnd on one needle and the other 4 sts on a second. Graft together.

Thumb
Return to the waste yarn. Pick up 11 sts from above the waste yarn and put on one needle; pick up 11 sts from below the waste yarn and put on another needle.

Remove waste yarn.

Rejoin yarn to the palm side of the Thumb.

Rnd 1: M1, k11, m1, k11. 24 sts

K 15 rnds.

Work 5 rnds in k1, p1 rib.

Cast off.

LEFT HAND GLOVE

Cuff and Hand
Work as for Right Hand Glove.

Thumb opening
K45. With waste yarn k11. Break waste yarn. Slip these 11 sts back onto the needle they were knitted from. Now, with the working yarn, knit over the waste yarn, and finish the round.

Palm
As Right Hand Glove

Index Finger
K11 onto one needle; slip next 37 sts onto a thread. Cast on 3 sts, k4 onto the second needle, k4 onto the third. 22 sts

Complete as for the Right Hand Glove.

Three Fingers and Thumb
As Right Hand Glove

FINISHING
Weave in all ends. Wash and dry flat.

Riflemens's Gloves. Keeping the thumb and forefinger free made it possible to fire a rifle. In the modern era, these could be just the thing for sending text messages while waiting for a communter train.

Service Gloves

TRANSLATED BY ELIZABETH LOVICK • KNITTED BY SANDY COWAN

INSPIRATION
This pattern comes from a Red Cross leaflet of things to knit for men on active service.

MATERIALS
100 g DK yarn

Set of 4 3.5 mm (US 4) dpns, or size to achieve tension

Lengths of waste yarn to keep held stitches on

Row counter

2 Stitch markers

SIZE
To Fit an average man's hand.

Hand circumference 10", length 10.5"

TENSION
24 sts and 32 rows to 4" over stocking stitch

PATTERN

RIGHT GLOVE

Cuff
Cast on 58 sts (20 sts each on first two needles, 16 on third). Join to work in the round. Work in k2, p2 rib for 3".

Next Rnd: Patt 1, m1, patt to last st, m1, patt 1.

Thumb gusset
Rnd 1: P1, k5, PM, p1, knit to end of rnd.

Rnd 2: P1, k to M, SM, p1, k to end of rnd.

Rnd 3: As Rnd 2.

Rnd 4: P1, m1, k to M, m1, SM, p1, k to end of rnd.

Rnds 5 to 9: As Rnd 2.

Repeat Rnds 4 to 9 until there are 13 sts between purl sts. 51 sts

Next Rnd: As Rnd 2, removing markers as you go.

Slip first 15 sts on to thread for the thumb.

EW Carter (Ben Atkinson) (left) and Robert Crowder (Reece Ackerman) in the bunker. Robert wears Service Gloves. Notice the leg wrappings, too. © Nick Loven

Palm

Next Rnd: Cast on 3 sts, k to end of rnd. 54 sts

Work 13 rnds.

First Finger

Rnd 1: K5, slip next 38 sts on to thread, cast on 2, k11 sts. 18 sts

Work 26 rnds.

Next round: [K2tog] to end of rnd.

Break yarn. Run end through remaining sts and draw up.

Second Finger

Rnd 1: K the first 7 sts from thread, cast on 2, knit last 7 from thread, pick up 2 sts from base of first finger. 18 sts

Work 30 rnds.

Next round: [K2tog] to end of rnd.

Break yarn. Run end through remaining sts and draw up.

Third Finger

Work as for Second Finger.

Fourth Finger

Rnd 1: K remaining 10 sts from thread, pick up 4 sts from base of third finger. 14 sts

Work 19 rnds.

Next round: [K2tog] to end of rnd.

Break yarn. Run end through remaining sts and draw up.

Thumb

Rnd 1: K15 sts held for thumb gusset; pick up and k 4 sts from side of first finger. 19 sts

Work 21 rnds.

Next round: [K2tog] to last st, k1.

Break yarn. Run end through remaining sts and draw up.

LEFT GLOVE

Cuff, Thumb Gusset and Palm: Work as for Right Glove.

First Finger

Rnd 1: K11, slip next 38 sts on to thread, cast on 2, k5 sts. 18 sts

Work 26 rnds.

Next round: [K2tog] to end of rnd.

Break yarn. Run end through remaining sts and draw up

Second Finger, Third Finger, Fourth Finger and Thumb

As for the Right Glove.

Helmet for a Serviceman

TRANSLATED AND KNITTED BY FREYALYN CLOSE HAINSWORTH

INSPIRATION

One of the many helmet or balaclava patterns published during WW1. This one is particularly practical as the flaps nestle inside the neck of a coat. — Freyalyn

MATERIALS

200 g DK yarn

Pair 4 mm (US 6) needles, or size to obtain tension

2.5 mm (US 2) circular needle

Freyalyn used ColourMart DK; 100% lambswool; 330 yds / 300 m per 100 g; shade Nettle

SIZE

To Fit an adult head. The fabric is very stretchy.

TENSION

24 sts and 30 rows to 4" over pattern for flaps

NOTES

The helmet needs to be knitted in an elastic yarn, such as wool, so it retains its shape and snugness.

PATTERN

BACK FLAP

Using larger needles, cast on 68 sts.

Rows 1 to 4: K1, p1 rib

Rows 5 and 6: Knit.

These 6 rows form the pattern. Continue in pattern until the flap measures 5".

Break yarn and place sts on the circular needle.

FRONT FLAP

Work as for the Back Flap, but do not break yarn.

NECK

Knit the 68 sts of the Front Flap on to the circular needle, then knit across the sts from the Back Flap. 136 sts

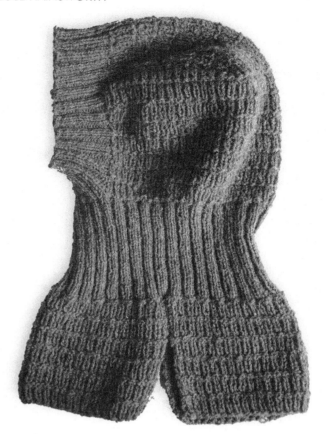

Working in the round on all sts, work in k2, p2 rib for 4". Break yarn.

HEAD

Slip the last 18 sts of the previous round back on to the needle. Rejoin yarn and knit 104 sts. Place the remaining 32 sts on a stitch holder for the centre front.

Change to the larger needles and work in flap patt for 12.5".

Next Row: Cast off 30 sts, patt to end of row.

Repeat this row once. 44 sts remain.

Continue in pattern for 5". Do not break yarn.

OPENING FOR FACE

Using the circular needle, work in k2, p2 rib across the live stitches of the top of the head, pick up and knit 60 sts down the side of the face, work in k2, p2 rib across the 32 sts from the centre front, pick up and knit 60 sts up the side of the face. 196 sts

Work in the round in k2, p2 rib for 2". Cast off.

FINISHING

Sew the head seams. Weave in all ends. Wash and dry flat, without pinning, to allow the ribbing to contract.

I have knitted for as long as I can remember, and I think I'm largely self-taught. Ten years ago I started to spin too, and now have added dyeing and weaving to the skill set. Although there is a day job to pay the bills, I have a 'hobby' that's taken over my life in dyeing yarns and British wools to sell at wool shows in the summer, and online in the winter. I also teach, and run workshops on various techniques in spinning, dyeing, and knitting. www.freyalyn.blogspot.co.uk/ is where I describe all my dyeing adventures and www.etsy.com/uk/shop/Freyalyn is where I sell my yarns and fibres when they are not packed up for a wool festival. — Freyalyn

William's Muffler & Fingerless Gloves

TRANSLATED BY ELIZABETH LOVICK • KNITTED BY JACKIE SOANES

MATERIALS

For the Muffler:

250 g 4 ply yarn

Pair 3.25 mm (US 3) needles, or size to achieve tension

For the Mitts:

50 g 4 ply yarn

Pair 3.75 mm (US 5) needles, or size to achieve tension

Jackie used Jamison's Spindrift; 100% wool; 105 yds / 117 m per 25 g ball; shade Thyme

SIZE

To fit: Child (Teen, Woman, Man, Large Man)

Muffler 7 (8, 9, 10, 11)" wide by 48 (54, 60, 66, 72)" long

Mitts: 8 (9, 10, 11, 12)" long

Mitts are very stretchy and will fit a wide variety of hands.

TENSION

Muffler: 32 sts and 32 rows to 4" over broken rib pattern unstretched

Mitts: 22 sts and 24 rows to 4" over ribbing slightly stretched

PATTERN

MUFFLER

Cast on 59 (67, 75, 83, 91) sts.

Row 1: *K2, p2. Repeat from * to last st, k1.

Repeat Row 1 until the muffler measures 48 (54, 60, 66, 72)".

Cast off.

Finishing
Weave in ends. Wash and dry flat.

MITTS

Use the yarn double throughout.

Cast on 38 (42, 46, 50, 54) sts.

Row 1: K2, *p2, k2. Repeat from * to end of row.

Row 2: P2, *k2, p2. Repeat from * to end of row.

Repeat these two rows for 8 (9, 10, 11, 12)". Cast off.

Finishing
Sew up the top 0.5 (0,5, 1, 1, 1.5)" of the side seam, and the bottom 6.5 (7.5, 7.5, 8.5, 8.5)", leaving a gap for the thumb. Weave in all ends. Wash and dry flat.

Above: William (Adam Fox) sports his muffler and gloves. Building in the background is Baumber House Bed & Breakfast, which was used as the exteriors of the Crowder family home. © Nick Loven

Cushion for a Soldier

TRANSLATED BY ELIZABETH LOVICK
KNITTED BY ANNIE LAWRENCE BROWN & SANDRA GIBBON

INSPIRATION

These simple cushions were valued by soldiers in the trenches. They were small enough to stuff in a kit bag, but were big enough to give a bit of comfort to weary men. Nowadays, they are perfect for children, and can be knitted in all sorts of colours with oddments of yarn. If you use polyester wadding as stuffing they can be easily washed. — Liz

MATERIALS

200 g 5 ply or DK yarn

Pair 3.5 mm (US 4) needles, or size required to give the correct tension

Stuffing - polyester stuffing or wadding if the cushion is to be washed often

Annie used Frangipani 5 ply; 100% wool, 240 yds / 219 m per 100 g; shade Bottle.

Sandra used a ColourMart DK

SIZE

About 10″ by 15″

TENSION

24 sts and 32 rows to 4″ over stocking stitch

CONSTRUCTION

The cushion is worked in one piece from end to end, then folded and sewn.

PATTERN

Cast on 120 sts. Work in stocking stitch for about 15″ (or until you run out of yarn!).

Cast off.

FINISHING

Wash the piece and dry flat. When dry, fold in half with right sides together and sew up two sides, plus half of the third. Turn to right side. Insert stuffing. Sew up the remainder of the seam.

No. 3.—TAM O' SHANTER FOR A MAN.

MATERIALS.—1 skein Paton's 3-Ply Alloa Wheeling, No. 31, or other colour ; 1 skein Paton's Alloa Wheeling, No. 123, or other mixture ; hook, No. 6.

With the variegated wool make a chain of 3, and unite. In this work a round of D.C., working 5 D.C. in the ring.

2nd and 3 following Rounds.—D.C., taking up both edges of the loop, and increasing in each round to keep it flat.

6th Round.—Join the red wool, draw it through the last D.C. stitch of last round, so that there is no break. 4 chain; take up each chain on the needle, both edges of the D.C. in which you joined the wool, and the following 1, * wool on the needle, draw through all the loops on the needle; 1 chain, take up the thread before the chain, the last loop next the round, the *last* D.C. used, and the next D.C., always taking up both edges of the loop. Repeat from * without increasing the stitches; at the end of the round take up the 1st D.C., and join to the 3rd chain, bringing the other wool through the stitch.

7th Round.—This is in purl D.C. Bring the wool to the front of the needle, take up the 1st chain; hold the wool with the thumb of the left hand, draw the wool through behind that in front of the needle, then through the 2 loops on the needle. Work a purl D.C. in this manner over the long loop and over the chain of last round.

No increasings are necessary.

8th Round.—D.C., taking up the back of the stitch only.

Repeat the 6th, 7th and 8th rounds until there are 5 rounds like the 6th round, and 5 rounds or stripes of D.C., always increasing to keep the work flat.

Then work 3 stripes like the 6th round, with red, and 3 between them with speckled wool, decreasing about every 6th stitch by missing 1 on the previous row to keep the work the same shape and size.

After that, work with speckled wool 6 rounds of D.C., no decreasings, and 1 of red. This finishes the cap. Make a tuft over a card and place it on the top.

Ironing the work with a cool iron, and a damp cloth laid over the crochet, greatly improves the appearance.

Garter Stitch Scarf & Beret

TRANSLATED BY ELIZABETH LOVICK • KNITTED BY CYNTHIA EASEMAN

MATERIALS

Scarf:

150 (200, 275, 325, 400) g 5 ply or Sport yarn.

Pair 3.75 mm (US 5) needles, or size to achieve tension

Beret:

80 (90, 100, 120, 150)g 5 ply or Sport yarn

Pair 3.5 mm needles or size to achieve tension

8 stitch markers

Cynthia used Frangipani 5 ply; 100% wool; 240 yds / 219 m per 100 g; MC natural; CC1 Dark Navy, CC2 Claret, CC3 Bottle, CC4 Falmouth Navy.

SIZE

To Fit Toddler (Child, Teen, Woman, Man)

Scarf: 6 (8, 10, 11, 12)" wide by 42 (48, 60, 66, 72)" long

Beret: 16 (18, 20, 22, 24)" circumference head

All sizes are very stretchy and will fit a variety of head sizes.

TENSION

Scarf: 22 sts and 40 rows to 4" over garter stitch

Beret: 24 sts and 44 rows to 4" over garter stitch

NOTES

If you are using stripes, change colour after an odd numbered row.

PATTERN

SCARF:

Using MC, cast on 33 (44, 55, 61, 66) sts. Knit for 2".

Change to CC1 and knit 12 rows, then 20 rows in MC. Repeat the stripe sequence with CC2, CC3 and CC4.

Continue in MC until the work measures 30 (36, 48, 54, 60)". Now work the stripe sequence in reverse, to match the first end.

Cast off.

Finishing
Weave in all ends. Wash and dry flat.

BERET:

Cast on 96 (112, 120, 136, 144) sts.

Work in k3, p3 rib for 3 (3.5, 4, 4.5, 5)".

Change to garter stitch and work for a further 3 (3.5, 4, 4.5, 5)".

Shape crown as follows:

Row 1: *K2tog, k10 (12, 13, 15, 16), PM. Repeat from * to end of row.

Row 2: K.

Row 3: *K2tog, k to M, SM. Repeat from * to end of row.

Row 4: K.

Repeat Rows 3 and 4 until 8 sts remain. Break yarn and thread through the remaining sts.

Finishing
Sew back seam. Weave in all ends. Make a tassel or pompom and sew to the centre of the crown. Wash and dry flat.

My name is Cynthia Easeman and I live on the cliff top by the Lighthouse at Hunstanton, in some 1902 Coastguard Cottages, what is probably unusual about me is that I am visually impaired and I have a guide dog called Olivia.

I have been knitting 61 years and crocheting for 35, my grandmother taught me to knit whilst we listened to the radio.

I heard about the project through Elizabeth Lovick, who i met (so to speak) via an audio book club forum on the internet, started by Calibre Audio Books. I looked at Elizabeth's web site and saw that she was involved with WWI knitting. I searched on facebook and came across their account.

Elizabeth was asking for some knitting to be done, so I said was there anything simple I could do, so she said yes, a comforter scarf. I had nearly finished that when i saw Pauline Loven asked was there any unemployed knitters who could help with a Tammy, I said I would try and she sent me the pattern. It was a great challenge to interpret the old pattern, yet i enjoyed it, having to decide what was meant by the scant instructions. I was fascinated by the term "roll" and found out it was actually stocking stitch, garter stitch being the norm for the era.

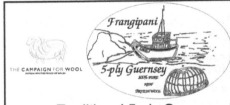

Traditional 5-ply Guernsey Wool

Jan & Russ at Frangipani
are delighted and flattered to have been
asked to contribute our yarn to "Tell Them of Us"

Just as it was then (oiled), it still is today (un-oiled),
but with many more shades.

Frangipani has been proudly supplying its own traditional
5-ply Guernsey Wool for more than 20 years.

Starting off with 6 shades and gradually expanding to
the current 26 glorious colours.

Will there be even more shades in the future??

Proud recipient of the British Wool Marketing Board
"Platinum Logo" and a trading partner of the
'Campaign for Wool'

We also stock patterns, needles, books and tutorial DVDs,
everything you need to knit your own beautiful gansey

For one of our Colour Cards which are sent <u>free</u> Worldwide,
please e-mail: jan@guernseywool.co.uk,
'phone +44 (0) 1736 366339 or write to:
Frangipani, 15 Clarence Street, Penzance, Cornwall TR18 2NU

www.guernseywool.co.uk

Cheerful Muff & Hat

Designed by Elizabeth Lovick • Knitted by Sandy Cowan

MATERIALS

75 (100, 125, 175, 200) g MC, angora yarn or other 4 ply/fingering

25 (50, 50, 75, 75) g CC, angora or other 4 ply/fingering

Pairs 2.5 and 3 mm (US 1 and 2) needles, or size to achieve tension

Row Counter

Polyester wadding about 6.5, (7.5, 9, 11, 13)" by 10 (12, 14,16, 18)"

2 (2, 2.5, 3, 3) yds 1" ribbon

3 buttons about 1" in diameter

Sandy used Rowan Angora Haze; 69% Angora, 20% nylon, 11% wool; 150 yds /137 m per 25g ball; MC shade 527 Cherry, CC shade 520 Cuddle

SIZE

To fit Toddler (Child, Teen, Adult, Plus)

Hat: 12 (14, 16, 18, 20)" brim unstretched

TENSION

28 sts and 40 rows to 4" over garter stitch

CONSTRUCTION

The crown of the hat and the band are knitted separately and then sewn together. The outside is worked in one piece from end to end, with the lining being worked separately.

PATTERN

HAT

CROWN
With MC, cast on 120 (135, 150, 165, 190) sts.

Work in garter stitch for 8 (9, 10, 11, 12)".

Next Row: K2tog across row.

Repeat this row twice more.

Break yarn and draw through remaining sts.

BAND
With CC, cast on 28 (28, 32, 36, 40) sts.

Work in garter stitch until the piece measures 12 (14, 16, 18, 20)" unstretched.

MUFF

With CC, cast on 72 (84, 96, 108, 120) sts and knit 10 rows.

Change to MC and knit 5 rows.

Next Row: *K2tog, k1. Repeat from * to end of row. 48 (56, 64, 72, 80) sts

Next Row: *K2, p2. Repeat from * to end of row.

Repeat this row 17 (19, 21, 23, 25) times more.

Next Row: *K1, m1, k1. Repeat from * to end of row. 72 (84, 96, 108, 120) sts

Work straight in garter stitch for 7 (8, 10, 12, 14)", ending with RSF for next row.

Next Row: *K2tog, k1. Repeat from * to end of row. 48 (56, 64, 72, 80) sts

Next Row: *K2, p2. Repeat from * to end of row.

Repeat this row 17 (19, 21, 23, 25) times more.

Next Row: *K1, m1, k1. Repeat from * to end of row. 72 (84, 96, 108, 120) sts

Knit 5 rows.

Change to CC and knit 10 rows.

Cast off.

Above: Another charming model from among the children.

Previous page: The model on the right is wearing the Garter Stitch Scarf & Beret; the model on the left is wearing items worked from private patterns.

Page 138: Back view of the Garter Stitch Beret; coat is from a private pattern.

Muff is shown from the inside out.

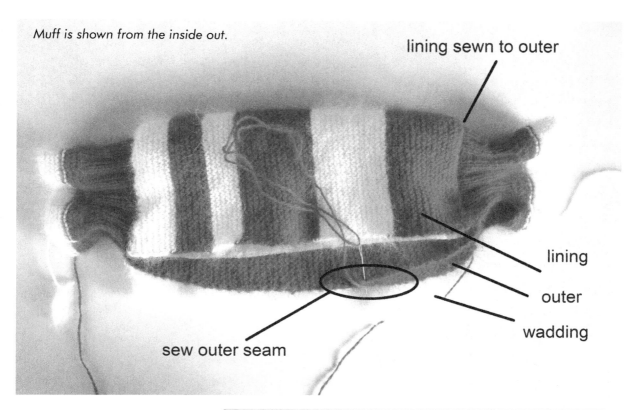

lining sewn to outer

lining

outer

wadding

sew outer seam

Lining
With CC cast on 72 (84, 96, 108, 120) sts. Knit 6.5 (7.5, 9, 11, 13)" in stripes to use up yarn. (The lining will not be seen.) Cast off.

FINISHING
Cut the ribbon into 4 equal parts.

HAT
Sew the back seam of the crown. Sew the ends of the band together. Matching the seams, sew one edge of the band on to the cast on edge of the crown, stretching to fit.

Weave in ends. Fold the band up. Make a ribbon cockade and attach to the side of the hat with a button. If desired, brush the surface with a wire brush.

MUFF
Cut a piece of polyester wadding the same size as the lining. Lay muff flat, with wrong side up, then lay the wadding on the centre section, with the lining on top. Sew the short edges of the lining to the central garter stitch section of the muff, enclosing the wadding. Fold in half, with wrong sides facing, and sew the outer seam of the muff from end to end. Now sew the seam of the lining. Turn right side out.

Weave in ends. Attach ribbon to each end of the muff at the start of the centre section as in the photograph. Make two rosettes and attach over the ends of the ribbon.

COMFORT YOUR BOYS WITH COLOURMART
You spend time knitting comforts for your Boys and you want them to enojy the warm of your gifts in the midst of battle. So choose ColourMart yarns to keep them warm for longer. Perfect for mufflers, hats and cushions. And also perfect for YOUR shawls and jumpers

www.colourmart.com

ColourMart Cashmere
wool silk cashmere and more

Pompom Scarf & Hat

DESIGNED AND KNITTED BY ELIZABETH LOVICK

MATERIALS

Hat: 60 (80, 100, 150, 200) g DK yarn

Scarf: 90 (120, 175, 250, 300) g DK yarn

Pair 4 mm (US 6) needles, or size to achieve tension

Row counter

1 stitch marker for the hat

Tapestry needle for sewing up

2 buttons for the hat, about ¾" diameter

Liz used Blacker Yarns British Classic DK Dyed Yarn in Blue and Blacker Breeds Pure Jacob in natural; both 100% British wool; 110 m/119 yds per 50 g ball.

TENSION

20 sts and 31 rows to 4" over pattern stitch after washing and drying

SIZE

To fit Toddler (Child, Teen, Woman, Man)

Hat:

Circumference: 15 (17, 19, 21, 23)"

Height (with brim folded): 8 (9.5, 11, 12.5, 14)"

Scarf:

Width: 6 (7.5, 9, 10.5, 12)"

Length: 32 (38, 48, 60, 66)"

The hats are stretchy and the length of the scarves can be easily adjusted.

PATTERN

HAT

Cast on 47 (54, 63, 72, 81) sts.

Continue as follows, working the brim in garter stitch and the crown from the Hat Chart.

Row 1: K18 (18, 20, 22, 24), PM, pattern 29 (36, 43, 50, 57).

Row 2: Pattern to M, SM, k to end of row.

Row 3: K to M, SM, pattern to end of row.

Repeat Rows 2 and 3 until the work measures 15 (17, 19, 21, 23)" along the crown edge without stretching.

Cast off in pattern.

Finishing

Sew the cast on edge to the cast off edge. Fold the hat so that the seam is at the back, then sew the top edge. If desired, crochet two chains 2" long and attach them to the corners of the crown. Sew buttons to match just above the garter stitch border as in the photo. Alternatively, to keep the hat in period, make two small pompoms for the corners of the crown, or make tassels.

SCARF

Cast on 31 (38, 45, 52, 59) sts and knit 5 rows.

Work from the chart until the work measures 31 (37, 47, 59, 65)" or desired length.

Knit 6 rows.

Cast off.

Finishing

Weave in all ends. Wash and dry flat, pulling into shape. If using a pompom on the hat, consider making 4 pompoms and sew on the corners of the scarf. If desired, the scarf can be fringed along the short edges.

Blacker Yarn Keeps Me Warm!

BLACKER YARNS

Blacker Pure Yarns have a Softer and Smoother finish, so they can be Worn Next to the Skin by more people.

www.blackeryarns.co.uk

SCARF CHART

Row 1: K3, p1, *p3, k1, p1, k1, p1. Repeat from * to last 6 sts, p3, k3.

Row 2: K6, *k2, p1, k4. Repeat from * to last 4 sts, k4.

Row 3: K3, p1, *k2, [p1, k1] twice, p1. Repeat from * to last 6 sts, k2, p1, k3.

Row 4: K4, p2, *k2, p1, k2, p2. Repeat from * to last 4 sts, k4.

HAT CHART

Row 1: P1, *[k1, p1] twice, k2, p1. Repeat from * to end of section.

Row 2: *K1, p2, k2, p1, k2. Repeat from * to last st, k1.

Row 3: P1, *k1, p1, k1, p4. Repeat from * to end of section.

Row 4: *K5, p1, k1. Repeat from * to last st, k1.

Bib for an Infant

TRANSLATED AND KNITTED BY MELANIE SMITH

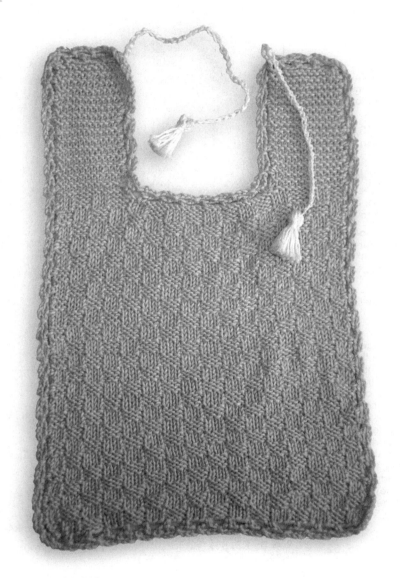

INSPIRATION

This bib, perfect for special occasions, was from the original pattern in Fancy and Practical Knitting, published by The Butterick Publishing Company Ltd, London and New York, in 1902.

MATERIALS

65 g DK yarn

Pair 3.25 mm (US 3) needles, or size to achieve tension

3 mm Crochet hook

Stitch holder

Row counter

Melanie used Paton's Bamboo Silk; 70% bamboo, 30% silk; 102 yds/93 m per 65 g ball; shade pink

SIZE

9" wide by 14" for the knitted part

TENSION

21 sts and 22 rows to 4" over dice pattern

PATTERN

Cast on 48 sts.

Rows 1 to 3: *K3, p3. Repeat from * to end of row.

Rows 4 to 6: *P3, k3. Repeat from * to end of row.

These 6 rows make up the dice pattern. Repeat them 11 times more. 72 rows worked.

Divide for the neck:
K12, and place on a holder, cast off 24, k last 12 sts.

RIGHT STRAP

Rows 1 to 38: K.

Row 39: Cast off all sts. Place the remaining loop on a crochet hook and ch 35. Fasten off.

LEFT STRAP

Return to held sts and attached yarn to neck edge.

Work as for Right Strap.

EDGING

With crochet hook, and starting at the bottom right corner of bib, attach yarn with a sl st, *Ch 3, skip next st or row, sl st in next st. Repeat from * all around piece. Fasten off.

FINISHING

Weave in all ends.

Make 2 small tassels and stitch firmly to the ends of the ties.

Reins

TRANSLATED BY ELIZABETH LOVICK • KNITTED BY MELANIE SMITH

INSPIRATION

As a child my friends and I used a skipping rope for reins as we cantered round the playground. I would have loved a pair of these. — Liz

MATERIALS

100 (100, 125, 150) g 4 ply cotton yarn

Pair 2.75 (US 2) needles, or size to achieve tension.

Embroidery thread and bells (optional)

SIZE

To fit 2 (4, 6, 8) years

Chest 22 (24, 26, 28)"

TENSION

24 sts and 40 rows to 4" over garter stitch

NOTES

These can also be worked in Tunisian crochet. This will produce a firmer fabric which can also be used for keeping a toddler from running away when out for a walk.

PATTERN

HARNESS

Chest Piece
Cast on 12 (12, 14, 14) sts, and work 6 (8, 10, 12)" in garter stitch.

Cast off.

Back Strap
Cast on 10 (10, 12, 12) sts and work 6 (8, 10, 12)" in garter stitch.

Cast off.

Arm Strap (make 2)
Cast on 10 (10, 12, 12) sts and

work 12 (13, 14, 16)" in garter stitch.

Cast off.

REINS

Cast on 12 sts and work 90 (90, 108, 108)" in garter stitch.

Cast off.

FINISHING

Note that all finishing must be done very securely. I suggest the use of a sewing machine if available.

Sew the ends of each Arm Strap together into a circle. Sew to ends of the Back Strap to each of the Arm Straps, just above the join. Now sew the Chest Piece to the Arm Straps opposite the Back Strap. Sew the reins to the outer edge of the Arm Straps by the Back Strap.

Embroider the name of the child or the horse on the Chest Piece. For older children, sew bells to the Chest Piece and Back Strap.

Weave in all ends. Wash and dry flat.

From the original pattern:

There is no amusement that little children are so fond of as that of "playing horse", and for this purpose they are always asking mothers, sisters, etc, to buy or make reins for them.

We give, above, a design for some reins in plain knitting. They are knitted with coarse yarn. No. 12 needles are required.

Cast on 14 sts, and in plain knitting, knit a length of 3 yards for the reins, and 4 pieces of half-a-yard for each arm and cross pieces. Work the name of the child, or of a favourite horse, on the front, in cross stitch, with white wool, and add little bells, front and back, to complete it. Or, if preferred, make the reins plain as seen in the engraving.

Wash Mitt for Bathing an Infant

TRANSLATED AND KNITTED BY ELIZABETH LOVICK

INSPIRATION

This bath mitt, from The Art of Knitting, is another item which is useful today. Use it when showering yourself as well as bathing your children! — Liz

MATERIALS

50 g DK cotton

4 mm needles

Waste yarn

Row counter

2 Stitch markers

Liz used Chiltern Craft Cotton; 100% cotton; unbleached

SIZE

To fit an adult hand; circumference 8"

TENSION

18 sts and 36 rows to 4" over garter stitch

PATTERN

CUFF

Cast on 36 sts and work 14 rows in k3, p3 rib.

K 3 rows.

Next Row: K17, PM, k2, PM, k17.

THUMB

Row 1: K to M, SM, yo, k2, yo, SM, k to end of row.

Row 2: *K to M, knit into the back of the yo. Repeat from * once, k to end of row.

Repeat Rows 1 and 2 until there are 16 sts between the markers.

K 4 rows.

Next Row: K to second M, RM, turn.

Next Row: K to M, RM, turn.

On these 16 sts, k 12 rows.

Next Row: Ssk, k to end of row.

Repeat this row 5 times more. 10 sts remain.

Break yarn, and thread through remaining sts. Sew the thumb seam.

With RS facing, rejoin yarn to base of thumb, and knit across to finish the row. 34 sts

PALM

K 32 rows.

TOP

Row 1: Ssk, [k14, k2tog] twice.

Row 2 and all alternate rows: K.

Row 3: Ssk, k12, k2tog, k13, k2tog.

Row 5: Ssk, [k11, k2tog] twice.

Row 7: Ssk, k9, k2tog, k10, k2tog.

Row 9: Ssk, [k8, k2tog] twice.

Row 10: Ktog to last st, k1.

Break yarn, and thread through remaining sts.

FINISHING

Sew side seam. Make a button hole stitch loop on the seam side of the mitt. Weave in all ends.

Washcloth for a Child

DESIGNED AND KNITTED BY ELIZABETH LOVICK

MATERIALS
60 g DK cotton

4 mm needles

4 mm crochet hook

Waste yarn

Row counter

2 Stitch markers

Liz used Chiltern Craft Cotton; 100% cotton; unbleached

SIZE

11" square

TENSION

18 sts and 36 rows to 4" over garter stitch

PATTERN

Cast on 46 sts.

Row 1: S1p, k to end of row.

Rows 2 to 7: As Row 1.

Row 8: S1p, k5, *yo, k2tog to last 10 sts, k6.

Repeat Rows 2 to 8 7 times more.

K 8 rows. Cast off

FINISHING

Starting at one corner, work round the cloth as follows:

*Dc into next st, miss 1, 5 tr into next st, miss 1. Repeat round all four sides. End by working a sl-st into first dc.

Weave in all ends.

Opposite: Period dolls posed with the Wash Mitt and Washcloth.

Ball for a Child

TRANSLATED AND KNITTED BY ELIZABETH LOVICK

INSPIRATION

This is a translation of a pattern in one of the Weldon leaflets from about 1900. The pattern says, "This ball is worked throughout in simple plain knitting; it is quickly and easily made, and much appreciated by children, who always take delight in possessing a pretty ball... Make up the foundation of the ball with wadding, flock, or scraps of wool knotted together, and wound up, pressing it into a nicely rounded shape, or use an india-rubber ball of the right size." — Liz

MATERIALS

50 g DK yarn in up to 8 colours

Pair 3.5 mm (US 4) needles, or size required to achieve the correct tension

Polyester wadding or oddments of other stuffing, or a ball to fit

1 yd 1" ribbon if required

Liz used Jamison's Jamieson's DK; 100% Shetland wool; 83 yds / 75 m per 25 g ball, in 555 Blossom and 530 Fuchsia

SIZE

About 5" diameter, 16" circumference

TENSION

16 sts and 32 rows to 4" over garter stitch

NOTES

When you slip the first stitch (s1) of the short rows, pull the yarn tightly.

CONSTRUCTION

Each section is worked using short rows. You can either use two colours worked alternately, or use four or eight different ones.

PATTERN

Cast on 32 sts and knit 1 row.

Row 1: K18, turn.

Row 2: S1, k3, turn.

Row 3: S1, k4, turn.

Row 4: S1, k5, turn.

Continue in this way until you have worked the row s1, k31, and all the sts are on the same needle.

Break yarn. This completes one section. Join a second colour. Repeat from Row 1.

Continue in this way until you have completed 8 sections. Cast off.

FINISHING

Sew the cast on and cast off edges together, inserting the filling as you go. Weave in all ends. If desired, add a crocheted chain loop and bow to one end for hanging up over a baby's pram etc.

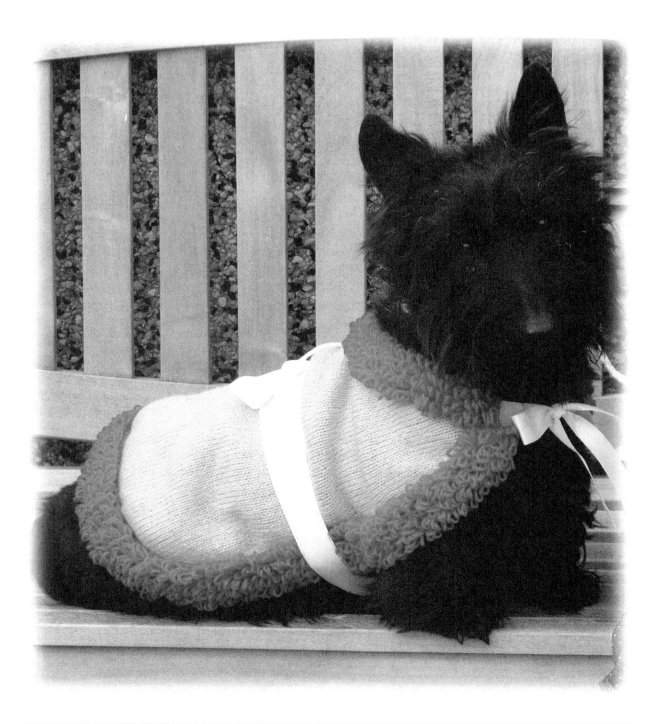

Coat for a Little Dog

TRANSLATED AND KNITTED BY ELIZABETH LOVICK

INSPIRATION

When I saw this coat in an old book I knew I had to make one! Finding a dog to wear it came second. However, one of my new rescue Scotties, Isla, fitted the coat to perfection! — Liz

MATERIALS

100 g MC and 50 g CC DK yarn

Pair 3.5 mm (US 4) needles, or size required to achieve tension

Row counter

3 yds 1" ribbon

Sewing thread and needle to match the ribbon

Liz used Jamieson's DK; 100% Shetland wool; 83 yds / 75 m per 25 g ball; shades 555 Blossom and 530 Fuschia

SIZE

Back length from nape of neck: 12"

Overall length to centre of chest: 21"

Width across body: 16"

Neck edge: 16"

TENSION

24 sts and 32 rows to 4" over stocking stitch

CONSTRUCTION

The coat is started at the back and worked towards the neck. The loopy edge is worked separately, in two pieces, and sewn on.

PATTERN

BODY

Cast on 60 sts and knit 7 rows.

Shape back as follows:

Row 1: K5, m1, k to last 5 sts, m1, k5.

Row 2: K5, m1, p to last 5 sts, m1, k5.

Repeat Rows 1 and 2 until there are 72 sts on the needle.

Next Row: As Row 1.

Next Row: K5, p to last 5 sts, k5.

Repeat these two rows until there are 100 sts on the needle.

Now work straight until the piece measures 12" finishing after an even numbered row.

Shape Neck:

Row 1 and all odd numbered rows: K.

Row 2: K5, p38, k14, p38, k5.

Row 4: K5, p34, k22, p34, k5.

Row 6: K5, p30, k30, p30, k5.

Row 8: K5, p30, k5, place these sts on a thread; cast off 20, k5, p30, k5.

Continue on remaining sts only:

Row 1: K to last 7 sts, k2tog, k5.

Row 2: K5, p to last 5 sts, k5.

Repeat Rows 1 and 2 until 34 sts remain, finishing after a second row.

Next Row: K5, ssk, k to end of row.

Next Row: K5, p to last 5 sts, k5.

Repeat these two rows until 13 sts remain.

Knit 9 rows. Cast off.

Return to held sts:

Row 1: K5, ssk, k to end of row.

Row 2: K5, p to last 5 sts, k5.

Repeat these two rows until 34 sts remain, finishing after a second row.

Next Row: K to last 7 sts, k2tog, k5.

Next Row: K5, p to last 5 sts, k5.

Repeat these rows until 13 sts remain.

Knit 9 rows. Cast off.

NECK BORDER

Cast on 6 sts and knit 1 row.

Row 1: K1, loop st four times, k1.

Row 2: K.

Repeat these two rows until the piece is long enough to fit round the neck edge of the coat. Cast off.

COAT BORDER

Work as for the neck border until the piece is long enough to fit round the edge of the coat from one front edge to the other. Cast off.

FINISHING

Wash the coat and dry flat. Pin, then sew, the neck border over the garter stitch of the neck of the coat. Pin, then sew, the coat border to the edge of the coat, starting at one front and finishing at the other. Weave in all ends.

Cut two 12" pieces of ribbon and attach to the front edges of the coat. Cut two 30" pieces of ribbon and attach to the coat under the border, positioning them as in the photo.

In wear, tie the front ribbons in a bow, then bring the body ribbons under the belly and tie in a bow over the back of the dog.

My Mistress likes me to have **THE BEST** so she always orders **Jamieson's of Shetland** for my coats. It comes in **BRIGHT COLOURS** which STAY Bright when LAUNDERED.

Jamieson's of Shetland
The Best Shetland Wool You Can Buy
www.jamiesonsofshetland.co.uk

Lead for a Dog

DESIGNED AND CROCHETED BY ELIZABETH LOVICK

INSPIRATION

I found patterns for collars and leads in several publications. Some were very fancy, with lots of beading. Others were more work-a-day! This one is typical. — Liz

MATERIALS

50 g cotton 4 ply/fingering yarn

3 mm crochet hook

Metal ring about 1" in diameter

Liz used Paton's Cotton 4 ply; 100% mercerised cotton; 361 yds / 330 m per 100 g; shade 1691 White

SIZE

1" wide and about 66" long

TENSION

32 sts to 4"

IMPORTANT NOTE

Please do not use this lead on a dog who pulls. The collar will tighten like a choke chain, but will not easily loosen.

CONSTRUCTION

The collar and lead are worked in a single piece.

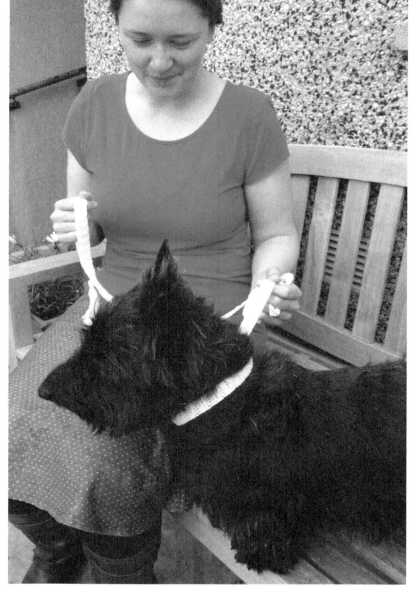

PATTERN

COLLAR AND LEAD

Work 6 dc into the metal ring, turn.

Row 1: 1 ch, miss 1 st, 1 dc into each st, turn. 6 sts

Row 2: As Row 1.

Row 3: 2 ch, miss 1 st, 1 tr into each st, turn. 6 sts

Repeat Row 3 until the work measures 72" long, or length required.

HANDLE

Fold the last 6" of the strip back on itself.

Work 1 dc round each of the 6 sts of the row below to form the loop.

Draw loop through and fasten off, leaving a 10" tail.

FINISHING

Use the tail to further secure the handle. Weave in ends. Make a 3" tassel and attach firmly to the bottom of the handle on a half inch length of yarn covered in buttonhole stitch. If desired, the collar and lead can be sewn to a length of grosgrain ribbon.

In use, pull a loop of the lead through the ring to form the collar.

Knitted Cloth for Polishing Floors

TRANSLATED AND KNITTED BY ELIZABETH LOVICK

MATERIALS

50 g DK cotton yarn

Pair 5 mm (US 8) needles, or size to achieve tension

SIZE

10" square

TENSION

16 sts and 28 rows to 4" over stocking stitch

PATTERN

Cast on 90 sts and knit 2 rows.

Next Row: Cast off 45 sts, knit to end of row.

Knit until the piece is square. Cast off.

FINISHING

Sew the end of the narrow strip across the diagonal of the square. Now bring these diagonal corners together and catch, so that the narrow strip forms a loop for the wrist. Weave in all ends.

IRON HOLDERS AND POLISHING CLOTHS

In the days when irons had metal handles and were heated on the stove, pads were needed to hold them. This pad might not be needed for today's irons, but it works equally well as a pot holder.

Another of the many household items found in one of my old books. The pattern tells the knitter to 'use needles 2 sizes bigger than usual'. No mention of the yarn thickness! This pattern makes a useful cloth for cleaning many things, and the wrist strap does actually stop you dropping it. — Liz

Iron Holder

TRANSLATED AND CROCHETED BY ELIZABETH LOVICK

MATERIALS

60 g DK cotton yarn

4 mm hook, or size to achieve tension

Piece of wadding 8" x 12"

Liz used Chiltern Craft Cotton; 100% cotton; unbleached

SIZE

6.5" x 8.5"

TENSION

20 sts and 8 rows to 4" over pattern

PATTERN

Chain 27.

Row 1: Miss 3 ch, [2 tr, 2 ch, 1 dc] into next ch, *miss 2 ch, [3 tr, 2 ch, 1 dc into next ch. Repeat from * to end of row. 8 groups

Row 2: *[3 tr, 2 ch, 1 dc] into 2 ch space. Repeat to end of row.

Repeat Row 2 until the piece measures 6". Finish off.

Make a second piece the same, but do not finish off.

FINISHING

Cut 2 pieces of wadding the same size as the crochet pieces. With RS out, sandwich the wadding between the two crochet pieces. Join with dc all round. Finish with 12 ch. Fasten off. Sew end of chain to holder to make a hanging loop.

Sunflower Pincushion

TRANSLATED AND KNITTED BY ELIZABETH LOVICK

INSPIRATION

Pauline found this pincushion in an old Weldon's leaflet. The original suggested you attach three layers of black fabric at the back to use as a pen wiper. It says you can leave the pin cushion on the drawing room table, or attach a ribbon to hang it up. I think it would also be good on a stick, with several others in different colours! — Liz

MATERIALS

7 g MC and 32 g CC 4 ply/fingering yarn

Pair 3 mm needles

Small amount of wool ends for stuffing

Liz used J&S 2 ply Jumper Weight; 100% wool; 125 yds /115 m per 25 g ball; MC shade 5. CC shade 91.

SIZE

Centre 3" diameter; overall 9" diameter

TENSION

24 sts and 48 rows to 4" over garter stitch

NOTES

If desired, the two strips of petals can be worked in different colours, in which case 10 g yarn will be needed for the inner row and 22 g for the outer.

CONSTRUCTION

The centre and the two strips of petals are worked separately then sewn together.

PATTERN

CENTRE

Cast on 31 sts. Work in moss stitch until the piece is square. Cast off.

INNER PETALS

With CC, cast on 8 sts.

Row 1: K to last 2 sts, kfb, k1.

Row 2: Kfb, k to end of row.

Repeat Rows 1 and 2 3 times more. 16 sts.

Row 17: K to last 3 sts, k2tog, k1.

Row 18: K1, ssk, k to end of row.

Repeat Rows 17 and 19 3 times more. 8 sts.

This forms one petal. Repeat these rows until you have 13 petals in the strip. Cast off.

OUTER PETALS

With CC, cast on 12 sts.

Work as for the inner row of Petals, but increasing to 24 sts before decreasing back down to 12 sts.

Repeat until you have 13 petals in the strip. Cast off.

FINISHING

Press the two strips of petals, or wash them and pin to dry.

Work running stitches round the edges of the Centre, draw up then stuff lightly. Pull the running stitches tight over the stuffing and pull the centre into shape. Sew the gathers in place.

Join the cast on and cast off edge of the Inner Petals. Work running stitches along the straight edge. Pull up to fit round the Centre. Secure and sew to centre. Repeat for the Outer Petals.

If desired, sew a circle of felt over the back of the pincushion, and attach a ribbon to hang it by.

Techniques

CROCHET BUTTONS

With a 3 mm hook, chain 3. Sl-st into a ring.

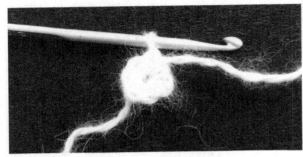

1. Round 1: 2 dc into each dc. Ss to close.

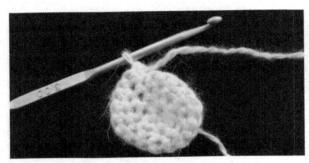

2. Now work in a spiral as follows:

   *2 dc into next dc, 1 dc into next dc. Repeat from *
   until the diameter of the button is as big as you want.

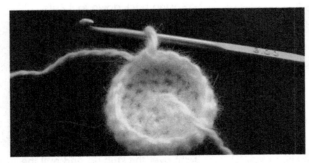

3. Now work 1 dc into each dc for 2 rounds.

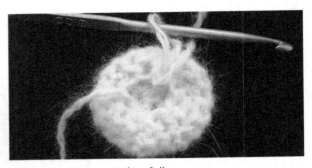

4. Decrease in a spiral as follows:

   *[1 dc into next dc] twice, miss 1 dc. Repeat from *
   until the hole is about 1 cm across.

5. Fill the button with a bit of stuffing or odds and end
   of the yarn.

6. Close the hole by continuing the spiral. Fasten off
   and cut yarn leaving a tail for sewing on to the garment.

7. Finish by weaving the first end of the yarn into the
   centre. Use the end of the yarn to sew the button on
   to the garment.

MAKING TASSELS

Tassel making is an art in itself. Feel free to substitute fancier tassels as preferred.

1. Cut a piece of card about 5 or 6" deep – or use a book. Wind the yarn round it, being careful not to wind too tightly. (This stretches the yarn and you end up with a shorter tassel.) Start and stop the yarn at the bottom of the card. Aim for a tassel about the thickness of your finger.

2. Cut a length of yarn about 24" long, and thread it into a blunt needle. Wind this round the yarn at the top of the card, leaving the free end about the same length as the card.

3. Pull the yarn tight and knot it.

4. Cut the wound yarn at the bottom of the card.

5. Then smooth the threads down.

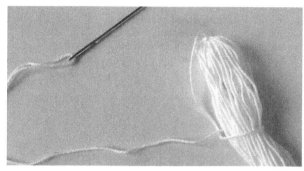

6. Now use the threaded yarn to wind tightly round the bundle about half an inch down from the knot.

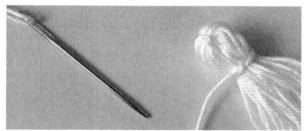

7. Wrap the yarn 3 times then tie tightly.

8. Thread the needle back up through to the top of the tassel and take a stitch round the knot.

9. Use your fingers to shape the tassel, then cut the threads evenly. Use the long thread at the top to attached the tassel to its final position.

MAKING A FRINGE

1. Cut lengths of yarn by wrapping round a suitably sized book and cutting along one edge. Find a suitable crochet hook - the exact size does not matter.

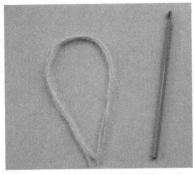

2. Fold one or two strands in half, forming a loop. You will hold the cut ends together.

3. Insert the crochet hook through the place where the fringe is to be. (Here it is in every other cast off stitch of a scarf, and two strands of yarn are used.)

4. Catch the yarn loop on the hook and pull a loop of yarn through.

5. Place the tails of yarn over the hook and draw them through the loop of yarn.

6. Remove the hook, and put the ends of the yarn through the loop.

7. Pull tight, using your fingers to guide the knot into the right place.

8. The finished knot.

9. Note that on one side you end up with a row of loops over the strands, and on the other just the strands are visible.

MAKING A BUTTON LOOP

1. Thread a length of yarn into a blunt needle and secure it at one end of the loop's position. Take a small stitch at the other end, then repeat to give two threads.

2. Put your finger in the loops and pull them to the correct size for your button.

3. Make the first stitch into the loop, and pull tight to secure.

156

4. Now start covering these strands with blanket stitch, keeping your finger in the loops.

5. Continue making blanket stitches into the loop, keeping them as even as possible.

6. Push the stitches close together after every few stitches.

7. Continue until the whole loop is covered. End by making a tight stitch on the loop, then fasten off on the inside.

8. The completed loop.

Size Charts

Children's Sizes	C1	C2	C3	C4	
Chest Circumference	21	23	25	26	ins
	53	58	63	67	cm
Sleeve Length	8.5	10.5	11.5	12.5	ins
	21	26	29	31	cm

Men's Sizes	XS	S	M	L	1X	2X	3X	
Chest Circumference	32	36	40	44	48	52	56	ins
	81	92	102	112	122	132	142	cm
Sleeve Length	17.5	18	18.5	19.5	20	20.5	21	ins
	44	46	47	49	51	52	53	cm

Women's Sizes	XXS	XS	S	M	L	1X	2X	3X	4X	
Bust Circumference	28	30	34	38	42	46	48	52	56	ins
	71	76	86	96	106	117	127	137	147	cm
Sleeve Length	13.5	16.5	17	17	17.5	17.5	18	18	18.5	ins
	34	42	43	43	44	44	45	45	47	cm

Abbreviations • Stitch Patterns • Notes

GENERAL ABBREVIATIONS

alt............alternate
approx.....approximately
beg..........beginning
CC...........contrasting colour
dec...........decrease
inc............increase/increasing
LH.............left hand
M..............marker
MC...........main colour
PM............place marker
rnd(s).......round(s)
RH............right hand
RS............right side
SM............slip marker
st(s).........stitch(es)
WS............wrong side

CROCHET ABBREVIATIONS
(UK TERMINOLOGY)

ch ....chain (crochet)
dc.............double crochet
dtr............double treble
sl-st ....slip stitch (crochet)
tr ....treble (crochet)
ss..............single crochet
inc ....work two sts in the next st

KNITTING ABBREVIATIONS

dpn(s) ......double pointed needle(s)
k...............knit
kfb...........knit into front and back
of stitch
kfbf..........knit into front, back and
front of stitch
k2tog.......knit the next two sts
together
k3tog.......knit the next three sts
together
m1...........make 1 by picking up
the strand before the
next st and knitting into
the back of it
m1p.........make 1 purlwise
p...............purl
p2tog.......purl 2 together
pfb...........purl into front and back
of stitch

psso.........pass slipped st over
s1.............slip 1 stitch
s1p..........slip 1 stitch purlwise
ssk...........slip 2 sts (one at a time),
knit 2 slipped stitches
together tbl
tbl............through back loop
W&T ....yarn to front, s1p; turn;
yarn to front, s1p (no
stitch worked)
yo............yarn over

STITCH PATTERNS

GARTER RIB
Row 1: K.
Row 2: [K1, p1] to end of row.

MOSS STITCH
Over an odd number of stitches
Every Row: K1, [p1, k1] to end of
row.

RIBBING
k1, p1 rib: *K1, p1. Repeat from *
to end of row.
k2, p2 rib: *K2, p2. Repeat from *
to end of row.
k3, p3 rib: *K3, p3. Repeat from *
to end of row.
k4, p4 rib: *K4, p4. Repeat from *
to end of row.

GARTER STITCH
Every Row: K.

REVERSE STOCKING STITCH
Row 1 (RS): P.
Row 2: K.

CABLE (C8B)
Place the next 4 sts onto the cable
needle and hold at the back of the
work, k4, k4 from the cable needle

LOOP STITCH
Insert the needle tip as if to knit.
Pass the yarn anticlockwise round
the needle tip and your finger twice,
then round the needle only. Complete the stitch as usual. There are
three loops on the needle for each
stitch knitted. On the return row all
three loops are knitted together.

GENERAL NOTES
for All Patterns

• If only one number is
mentioned it is for all sizes.

• Stitch markers are not
mentioned unless they are
important. When they are not
mentioned, slip markers as you
get to them.

• The stitch left after casting off is included in the stitch
count after the cast off.

• In crochet, any turning
chain(s) count as a stitch.

CHARTS
All charts were made in Stitch
Mastery.

Working from a Chart
Each square on the chart represents
one stitch or action. Charts are
read from the bottom up. Right
side rows are read from right to left.
Wrong side rows are read from left
to right.

KEY TO ALL CHARTS

☐ k - odd rows knit, even rows purl
● p - odd rows purl, even rows knit
▨ grey no stitch
V kfb - knit into front and back
O yo - yarn over
/ k2tog - k 2 together
\ ssk - or k2togtbl
Λ k3tog tbl
⌒ cast off
Ѵ s1p - slip 1 purlwise
Ø m1 - make 1 by picking up strand
⧖ C8B

With heartfelt thanks to . . .

Artesano Yarns, Blacker Yarns, ColourMart, Frangipani, Jamieson's of Shetland, Kraemer Yarns, Rowan, Swans Island Yarns and Texere for their kind donation of yarns for some of the designs.

Iva Rose publications for permission to use images from their pages.

Pauline Loven and Nick Loven for their photography; Robert Holland for sharing his family's story and photographs; Crow's Eye Costume Department for the costumes; Thimbleby village, Baumber Park B&B and Crowder's Nurseries for the locations.

The knitters and crocheters involved in the project were Jo Amsden, Sheila Anderson-Wray, Kelly Ashfield, Debra Ashkar, Juniper Askew, Ingrid Babbidge, Katie Ball, Gill Banks, Angela Bannister, Clare Bartlett, Sally Black, Joy Blackburn, Trish Blake, Su Bonnet, Linda Bowers, Sam Braid, Sandra Braithwaite, Jeanette Brodie, Judith Brodnicki, Tracy Bruce, Loraine Burnett, Louise Butt, Marianne Cant, Jessamy Carlson, Alison Casserly, Elizabeth Cassie, Annie Cholewa, Freyalyn Close-Hainsworth, Ellen Cook, Natasha Coombs, Jacky Cooper, Sandy Cowan, Jessica Crocker, Sheila Cunnea, Jane Daniels, Alison Davies, Linda Devaney, Cassy Dominic, Elly Doyle, Lesley Draper, Hayley Duke, Morag Duller, Cynthia Easeman, Alison Edward, Mary Lou Egan, Karen Evans, Hayley Fisher, Natalie Ford, Kicki Frisch, Linda Fuller, Andi Gallegos, Debbie Garriock, Nicky Gathergood Appleby, Joy Getha, Sandra Gibbons, Susan Glennie, Claire Greathead, Elaine Hacker, Jan Hatwell, Debbie Heeley, Margaret Hinchliffe, Felicity Hoare, Gill Hollister, Catherine Hopkins, Helen Hutchings, Jean Jackson, Linda Jacobs, Carrolle Jamieson, Kirsty Johnston, Diane Jones, Tracie Kilbey, Tina Kinnar, Jane Lawrence, Annie Lawrence Brown, Gail Belinda Lee, Pat Leggett, Katy-Jane Linott, Cheryl Litchfield, Pauline Loven, Elizabeth Lovick, Julie Lupa, Mandy Lyne, Louise McCullough, Shonnah McGeough, Patricia McLean, Joyce Meader, Mandy Monkman, Melanie Nabarro, Debbie Orr, Sarah Parsons, Pam Peake, Sally Pointer, Dorothy Potts, Becca Read, Jenny Roberts, Muriel Rogers, Liz Rogers, Clare Salters, Susan Sanders, Carrie Schutrick, Nicky Smith, Melanie Smith, Jackie Soanes, Julie Speed, Suzanne Stallard, Rita Taylor, Lesley Taylor, Nicola Taylor, Genevieve Tocci, Clare Tucker, Wendy Wall, Gladys Wallis, Sharon Winter, Paula White, Kara Williamson, Johanne Winwood, Aileen Yorke, Stephanie Young,

A portion of the proceeds of the book will go to the restoration of St Margaret's Church, Thimbleby, and to Combat Stress, the Veteran's mental health charity.

ELIZABETH LOVICK (editor, author, historian) was taught to knit by her Cornish grandmother when very young and kept herself in clothes through school by knitting arans for friends! She lives and works on the small Orkney island of Flotta where she spins and knits, researches and writes. She is the author of 'The Magic of Shetland Lace Knitting'.

PAULINE LOVEN is a period costumier with 30 years experience in researching and reproducing period clothing and ten years of experience in design and making of costumes for film. A published historian and illustrator, Pauline lives near Lincoln and is married with three children and one grandson.

JUDITH BRODNICKI (graphic designer, knitter) has more than 25 years of experience in print production and graphic design. Her patterns are published on Knitty, Ravelry, and Knit Picks web sites. She lives in Omaha, Nebraska, with her husband, 2 dogs and 2 cats.

ELLY DOYLE (technical editor, knitter) moved to Orkney a year ago after living in the Faroe Islands. She is a self-confessed 'numbers person' and enjoys the detail of technical editing. As a designer she specialises in colourwork accessories; as a dyer she specialises in the fibre of the local North Ronaldsay sheep.

CPSIA information can be obtained at www.ICGtesting.com
Printed in the USA
BVOW10s0005051115

425637BV00002B/4/P